LORD DURHAM'S
REPORT
ON THE AFFAIRS OF
BRITISH NORTH AMERICA

VOLUME I

LORD DURHAM'S
REPORT
ON THE AFFAIRS OF
BRITISH NORTH AMERICA

EDITED

WITH AN INTRODUCTION

BY

SIR CHARLES LUCAS

THREE VOLUMES
VOLUME I

[1912]

AUGUSTUS M. KELLEY · PUBLISHERS

NEW YORK 1970

First Edition 1912
(Oxford: At The Clarendon Press, 1912)

Reprinted 1970 by
AUGUSTUS M. KELLEY · PUBLISHERS
REPRINTS OF ECONOMIC CLASSICS
New York New York 10001

By Arrangement With OXFORD UNIVERSITY PRESS

. . . .

I S B N 0 678 00647 4
L C N 73 117388

. . . .

PRINTED IN THE UNITED STATES OF AMERICA
by SENTRY PRESS, NEW YORK, N. Y. 10019

LORD DURHAM'S REPORT
ON THE AFFAIRS OF
BRITISH NORTH AMERICA

EDITED

WITH AN INTRODUCTION

BY

SIR C. P. LUCAS, K.C.B., K.C.M.G.

IN THREE VOLUMES

VOLUME I: INTRODUCTION

OXFORD

AT THE CLARENDON PRESS

1912

PREFACE

THE Sketch of Lord Durham's Mission by Charles Buller is published—as far as I am aware for the first time—by the kind permission of Mr. A. G. Doughty, C.M.G., Dominion Archivist at Ottawa, to whom it was given by the present Earl of Durham.

My thanks are due to him; and among many friends in England and Canada who have given me help, I must specially mention Professor Egerton, and Mr. A. B. Keith of the Colonial Office, author of *Responsible Government in the Dominions*. I have also to thank Mr. Henry Lambert, C.B., of the Colonial Office, Mr. C. Atchley, C.M.G., I.S.O., Librarian of the Colonial Office, and Mr. H. P. Biggar, of the Dominion Archives Department.

Any views expressed in the Introduction or the Notes are my own alone.

C. P. LUCAS.

March 1912

ERRATUM

P. 97, l. 12. *for* 1838 *read* 1837

CONTENTS OF VOLUME I

CHAPTER I

	PAGE
LORD DURHAM	1

CHAPTER II

THE ACCESSION OF QUEEN VICTORIA . . . 10

CHAPTER III

ORIGIN AND DEVELOPMENT OF THE POLITICAL DIFFICULTIES IN THE CANADAS 24

CHAPTER IV

LORD DURHAM'S COMMISSION AND INSTRUCTIONS . 106

CHAPTER V

THE REPORT: ITS SCOPE, CHARACTER, AND SUBSTANCE

The Scope of the Report	114
The Character of the Report	116
The Substance of the Report	123
Reunion of the two Canadas	124
Responsible Government	137
Public Lands	152
Emigration	188
Means of Communication	198
Municipalities and Local Government . . .	210

vi CONTENTS

THE REPORT: ITS SCOPE, CHARACTER, AND SUBSTANCE
(*Continued*)—

Administration of Justice	223
Education	232
General Union of British North America	247
References to the United States	257
Colonial Office and Colonial Administration	266

CHAPTER VI

RETROSPECT, FORECAST, AND SEQUEL 276

CHAPTER VII

THE REPORT AND THE EMPIRE 303

APPENDIX

LORD DURHAM'S REPORT AS BEARING ON THE QUESTION OF HOME RULE FOR IRELAND 318

INDEX 325

CHAPTER I

LORD DURHAM

JOHN GEORGE LAMBTON, first Earl of Durham, was born in 1792. He died in 1840 at the age of 48. He was born a year after an Act had been passed by the Imperial Parliament dividing the Province of Quebec, as it then was, into the two provinces of Upper and Lower Canada, and granting to either province representative institutions without responsible government. In the year in which he died another Imperial Act was passed, in consequence of his own recommendations, reuniting the two provinces with a view to granting to the single colony wider powers of self-government.

He was the son-in-law of Lord Grey, the Prime Minister who carried the great Reform Bill. He was the father-in-law of Lord Elgin, who, as Governor-General of Canada, made responsible government in that colony a reality. He was the grandfather of the Secretary of State for the Colonies, who gave responsible government to the Transvaal and the Orange River Colony. His life was comparatively short: he never held high administrative office in England : he was a colonial governor for only five months : and he gave to the world a state paper on colonial matters which will live to all time.

He was educated at Eton, and, after two years in the Army, he was in 1813 elected to the House of Commons on the Whig or Liberal side as member for the county of Durham. In 1828 he was made a peer. In 1830 he was included in Lord Grey's Cabinet, being given the sinecure office of Lord Privy Seal, and he was a prominent member of the Committee of Ministers who framed the Reform Bill. In 1833 he left the Government and was made an Earl. For about two years, from 1835–7, he was Ambassador to Russia. In January 1838 he accepted the appointment of Governor-General of the British North American provinces. He left England on the 24th of April 1838; he reached Quebec on the 27th of May. On the 29th of May he landed and was sworn into office. He left again for England on the 1st of November following. On the 30th of November he landed at Plymouth. His Report is dated the 31st of January 1839; and on the 28th of July 1840 he died.

Lord Durham was an aristocrat in temper and habits, lordly and imperious, fond of pomp and circumstance. He was a pronounced Radical in his political creed. But he was poles asunder from the Radicals of the Manchester School, and was more allied to such men as Sir William Molesworth than to Richard Cobden. He seems to have been a man of high character, transparent honesty, great courage and promptness, and of outspoken convictions, but masterful and arrogant, with a self-will intensified by want of health, and by having come into his kingdom in early boyhood. He was a good man to serve, but a difficult man for a colleague, a man impatient of contradiction and restraint, one who made enemies and risked losing friends.

His life has been fully told in Mr. Stuart Reid's two interesting volumes, and no reference will now be made to any of its incidents in or out of Canada. Nor will words be wasted upon the much-debated question whether or not he wrote the Report which bears his signature. No one would suppose that he drafted every line of the document himself. On the other hand, to maintain that Lord Durham, of all men in the world, allowed somebody else to dictate what he was to recommend is ridiculous. When dispatches or state papers are published bearing the signature of one minister or another, it is not to be supposed that they have in all cases been written, word by word, from beginning to end, by the man who signs them. Yet every such document is presumed to embody his instructions, to have been under his eye, and corrected by his hand, and, bearing his signature, is credited to him for good or ill. Whether Lord Durham's own pen actually wrote much or little of the Report, in form and substance it is his and his alone, able as were the members of his staff.

For he seems to have had the high quality of choosing competent advisers and assistants, and the courage or indiscretion of selecting them without regard to public opinion. The principal member of his staff was Charles Buller, pupil and friend of Carlyle, and satirist of the Colonial Office, who was widely credited with being the real author of the Report, and whose brilliant promise was cut short by early death in 1848. Next in importance was Gibbon Wakefield, whose personal antecedents gave occasion for cavilling at his being attached to

Lord Durham's Mission, but whose living and stimulating interest in colonial questions was beyond dispute. Durham's private secretary was Edward Ellice the younger, son of ' Bear ' Ellice, who had been the whip in Lord Grey's Ministry, and to whose merits in the capacity of a Canadian seignior the Report pays the graceful and kindly tribute of an old friend.

The Report was published before all the supplementary reports which form its appendices had been received. A list of these appendices is given in vol. iii, and the following documents have been reprinted in the hope that they will be of use and interest to students of colonial, more especially of Canadian history. From Appendix A, papers 1, 2, 5, 6, and 9, being Mr. Hanson's Report on the excessive appropriation of public land under the name of Clergy Reserves ; a special report by Charles Buller on militia claims to grants of land ; a letter from Mr. William Young on the State of Nova Scotia ; a letter from the Roman Catholic Bishop Macdonell ; and an address from the Constitutional Association of Montreal. From Appendix B, Charles Buller's Report on Public Lands and Emigration with the Royal Commission under which Lord Durham appointed him to make the Report, but without the Minutes of Evidence. Appendix C, including the Reports of the Commissioners of Inquiry into the Municipal Institutions of Lower Canada, but excluding both the Appendix to those reports and also the Report from the Anglican Bishop of Montreal on the state of the Church within his diocese. From Appendix D, the

Report of the Commissioner of Inquiry into the state of Education in Lower Canada, without the Returns, and an extract from the Report on the Jesuits' Estates. It has also been thought well to reprint three dispatches, dated 20th January 1838, 3rd April 1838, and 21st April 1838, which embody Lord Glenelg's instructions to Lord Durham; Lord Durham's dispatch of 9th August 1838, in which he foreshadowed the terms of his Report; Lord John Russell's dispatch of 14th October 1839 on the subject of Responsible Government; and lastly, to add Charles Buller's sketch of Lord Durham's Mission.

The Report, clear and powerful, speaks for itself, but some notes have been appended to it, and in this Introduction it is proposed to try to answer the following questions. (1) What were the conditions prevailing in the United Kingdom and in the British Empire generally at the time of Lord Durham's Mission? (2) What was the position in the two Canadas at the time, and what circumstances had led up to it? (3) What were the terms of Lord Durham's Commission, and what were his instructions? (4) What was in summary the scope, the character, and the substance of his Report? (5) How far, according to the lights of the present day, did he read the past correctly? How far did he correctly forecast the future in Canada, and how far were his recommendations adopted? (6) How far are the principles laid down in his report of universal application?

Before, however, dealing with these specific questions it is necessary to say a word of general caution. The popular view of Lord Durham and his mission is that an abnormal crisis having arisen in a British colony, or a group of British colonies, which crisis was due in the main to ignorance and want of intelligence on the part of the rulers both in the colony and at home, the hour came and the man who discovered once for all the true principles of colonial administration. This view needs to be corrected. The crisis in Canada was only in part abnormal, though it had attained to undue proportions. Discontent is the common accompaniment of growth. Given a young man or a young community, with increasingly large capacities, and full of life and vigour, then desire for greater freedom and a wider field of vitality, and restlessness until the desire has been satisfied, is healthy, natural, and in no sense abnormal. Given again a community, in which to the desire for a greater measure of self-government is superadded the further element of friction caused by rival races, in different stages of development, living side by side in the same country, and it is obvious that the restlessness will be intensified. The conditions in the Canadas which Lord Durham set out to remedy were, therefore, not altogether abnormal. They were to some extent the necessary outcome of the time and place.

Nor did Lord Durham achieve some wholly new and wonderful discovery when he recommended the reunion of the two provinces, and the grant of self-government to Canada. The reunion of the Canadas had been talked of almost from the date when they were divided from each other; while as far back as 1822 a reunion bill had, on the instance of Ellice the elder, been introduced into the House of Commons by the Tory Government of the day, and, but for the opposition of a handful of Radical members led by Sir James Mackintosh, might have been passed into law. Self-government for the colonies again, in one form or another, was not first conceived by Lord Durham. His merit consisted in the fact that, though he had not been born and bred in the colonies, probably because he had not been born and bred in the colonies, but had been a leader of the Reform movement in England, he advocated self-government for the colonies in the form in which it existed in the United Kingdom. It consisted in the force and clearness with which he pointed out existing evils, and the remedies which must be applied; the statesmanship with which, not content with generalities, he prescribed definite and immediate action; and the courage and insight, amounting to genius, with which he gave to the world the doctrine of responsible government, not as a prelude to the creation of separate peoples, but as the cornerstone upon which a single and undivided British Empire should be reared to abiding strength.

One other comment is necessary. Lord Durham was only five months in North America, and of that time only eleven days were spent in Upper Canada,[1] the whole of the rest of the time being

[1] The Report of the Select Committee of the House of Assembly of Upper Canada, made in April 1839, which severely criticized Lord Durham and his Report, stated that 'His lordship's personal observation was confined to his passing up the River St. Lawrence, and crossing Lake Ontario, in a steamboat occupied exclusively by his family and suite, a four days' sojourn at the Falls of Niagara, and a twenty-four

devoted to the Lower Province. Moreover, during these five months, he had not only to attend to all the everyday business of administration, but to deal with the most pressing and vitally important questions, carrying on his own shoulders at a time of crisis the whole load of responsibility. He was not, like other commissioners, sent to make an inquiry, while all the ordinary machinery of government was steadily working from day to day irrespective of the commissioner and without disturbing the course of the inquiry. Nor was he sent out with command of railways, telegraphs, and all the swift and sure means of communication which science has since perfected or devised. The field of his inquiry was very wide, the population was very scattered, the problems were as varied as they were numerous, means of communication were most inadequate. That such results should have been achieved in so short a time, when that short time had been overfilled with harassing questions of administration, is evidence to monumental industry and striking ability on the part of Lord Durham and his assistants. But, at the same time, it is clear that, under these conditions, it was humanly impossible for the Report to have embodied the fullest first-hand knowledge on every point of detail, or to have been written with all the judgement and reflection which a longer residence in North America might have brought. Possibly in the latter case the view of the forest

hours' visit to the Lieutenant-Governor at Toronto' (Parliamentary Paper, No. 289, June 1839, Copies or Extracts of Correspondence relative to the Affairs of Canada, p. 22).

might have been obscured by the trees, and the picture of the whole might have been no more accurate and less vivid than that which is presented in the Report ; but, none the less, on the one hand it is only fair to Lord Durham to bear in mind the disadvantages under which the Report was written, and on the other it would be wrong to ignore the very strong exception taken to the statements and inferences which it contained, in and on behalf of Upper Canada.

CHAPTER II

THE ACCESSION OF QUEEN VICTORIA

QUEEN VICTORIA came to the throne on the 20th of June 1837. Lord Durham, therefore, started on his mission towards the end of the first year of her reign. It is noteworthy how the beginning of the great Queen's reign coincided with various measures or movements which tended to recast and regenerate the British Empire. In 1833, Sir James Stephen, then legal adviser and three years later permanent head of the Colonial Office, between a Saturday morning and the middle of the day on the following Monday, drafted the Imperial Act for the Abolition of Slavery. Passed into law in that year, it provided that, from the 1st of August 1834, slavery should be abolished throughout the British dominions; but the emancipated negroes were to continue to labour under a system of apprenticeship until the 1st of August 1838 in the case of non-praedial apprentices, and the 1st of August 1840 in the case of praedial apprentices, the term of apprenticeship being in some cases shortened by local legislation. The last remnants of legalized slavery were therefore being blotted out in the British Empire when the young girl of eighteen became Queen; and when sixty-three years later she died in fullness of age and of honour, she was mourned in the lands which

CHAP. II ACCESSION OF QUEEN VICTORIA 11

slavery had once blighted, as the giver of freedom to the negro race. Great as an act of humanity and justice to a class of British subjects, the Emancipation Act is also interesting to students of colonial history as an instance of the mother country enforcing its will on colonies, some of which had from the earliest times enjoyed no small measure of self-government. An island like Barbados was never a Crown Colony in the ordinary sense. It had from the first been to a large extent a self-governing community, though the self-government was limited to the white oligarchy; and to this day it retains its elected Assembly and the power of the purse. Thus we have the noteworthy coincidence of the birth of responsible government in British North America with the most pronounced enforcement of the will of the mother country in the British West Indies; though the latter had enjoyed representative institutions in times when Canada, so far as it was colonized, was under a French despotism, with no semblance even of municipal liberties, while what was afterwards Upper Canada was in the main a wilderness.

Somewhat later in time than the anti-slavery movement, but roughly coincident with the accession of Queen Victoria, was another fruitful philanthropic effort, which resulted in the gradual abolition of the system of transportation. Archbishop Whately and others had been active in pointing out the evils and abuses to which this system gave rise, and in 1837 a select committee was appointed by the House of Commons 'to inquire into the system of transportation, its efficacy as a punishment, its influence on the moral state of Society in the penal colonies, and how far it is susceptible of improvement'. It was a strong committee. Sir William Molesworth was the Chairman, and among the members were Charles Buller, Sir George Grey, Lord Howick, afterwards Lord Grey, Lord John Russell, and Sir Robert Peel. The report was made in August 1838 : it condemned the existing system : and the first of its recommendations was 'that transportation to New South Wales, and to the settled districts of Van Diemen's Land, should be discontinued as soon as practicable'. In 1840 transportation to New South Wales was suspended. This was the beginning of the end of a system which died hard, for some convicts were sent to Western Australia up to 1867, Western Australia being, it should be noted, the only colony in Australia which at that date had not received responsible government. The system died hard, for it was not, like slavery, evil in its essence ; it was evil only in the conditions under which it was enforced or which gathered round it.

The Act of Parliament which abolished slavery throughout the British dominions affected mainly the colonies of Great Britain in the western hemisphere, the West Indies, which were her oldest colonies, and which were in fact, as they had been in name, plantations. The anti-transportation movement principally affected the British colonies in the south, the youngest colonies of Great Britain, those in Australia which had been originally founded as penal settlements. Slavery

CHAP. II ACCESSION OF QUEEN VICTORIA

was abolished by the will of the mother country imposed upon the slave-owning colonies; transportation was eventually abolished in obedience to the will of the colonies imposed upon the mother country. In the West Indies, where slavery prevailed, and where in past times the white oligarchies were in great measure self-governing communities, there is now but the *remanet* of representative institutions. The area where the transportation system was most fully applied is, at the present day, the scene of colonial self-government in its fullest expression.

The Cape, on the way between East and West, on the way between North and South, was touched alike by the abolition of slavery and by the movement against transportation. One of the dramatic incidents in the later stages of the anti-transportation campaign, and one of the most emphatic pronouncements of colonial rights in advance of colonial self-government, was the refusal of the Cape colonists, in September 1849, to allow the *Neptune* to land her freight of ticket-of-leave men in Simons Bay. Earlier in the history of the Cape, the inadequacy of the compensation paid to the slave-owners had embittered colonial feeling against the British Government; there followed the reversal of Sir Benjamin D'Urban's policy by Lord Glenelg; and when Queen Victoria came to the throne, the Great Boer trek was taking place, which coloured the whole subsequent history of South Africa.

Returning to Australasia, the colony of South Australia dates from 1836, the year before the

Queen's accession. The date usually given to the founding of Melbourne is 1837. In 1837 the New Zealand Association was formed. In 1838–9 it was followed by the New Zealand Land Company. In 1839 this company forced the hands of the Government by sending out the ship *Tory* to New Zealand, with Gibbon Wakefield's brother on board, and the forerunners of a larger band of settlers ; and early in 1840 New Zealand became formally and finally a British possession. The settlement of South Australia, and the acquisition of New Zealand, were the outcome of the colonization movement with which Gibbon Wakefield's name is for ever associated, and the chairman of the New Zealand Company was Lord Durham. This movement was at its flood-tide when Queen Victoria came to the throne.

But while thinkers and statesmen and philanthropists were at work, more potent in their effects upon the world at large, and upon the British Empire in particular, were the inventions and discoveries of men of science. When Queen Victoria began her reign, the forces of steam were in their cradle, and the forces of electricity were being brought to birth. The first railway upon which the locomotive was used, the line from Stockton to Darlington, was opened in 1825, the line from Manchester to Liverpool in 1830. In his Report (ii. 212–13), Lord Durham wrote, ' there is but one railroad in all British America, and that, running between the St. Lawrence and Lake Champlain, is only fifteen miles long.' That line was the only railroad in the British Empire outside

CHAP. II ACCESSION OF QUEEN VICTORIA 15

the United Kingdom at the date of the Queen's accession. In his Essay on the Government of Dependencies, which was published in 1841, Sir George Cornewall-Lewis speaks of the possibility of countervailing the difficulties in administration due to distance by 'the goodness of the roads and bridges, and an advanced state of the art of navigation, affording the means of rapid locomotion both by land and sea ',[1] but he makes no specific reference in this passage to railways, steamers, or telegraphs; and in one note only in his book does he refer in unfamiliar terms to 'the invention of steam railways', as about to reduce 'to sober truth' the passage in which the poet Claudian depicted the unity and the facility of intercourse which peace and good roads had given to the Roman Empire.[2] Almost the greatest merit of Lord Durham's Report is the writer's obvious appreciation of what the future, aided by science, might have in store for British North America; and had Lord Durham lived to see the 8th of November 1885, when railway connexion was completed from Montreal to Vancouver, he would have been hardly older then than one of the chief pioneers of the Canadian Pacific Railway, the present High Commissioner for Canada, is now.

'The success of the great experiment of steam navigation across the Atlantic,' says Lord Durham in his Report (ii. 316-17), 'opens a prospect of a speedy communication with Europe, which will materially affect the future state of all these provinces.' On the wall at the entrance to the

[1] p. 178 (1891 ed.).   [2] pp. 128-9 note.

Parliamentary Library at Ottawa there is an inscription 'in honour of the men by whose enterprise, courage, and skill, the *Royal William*, the first vessel to cross the Atlantic by steam power, was wholly constructed in Canada and navigated to England in 1833'. This ship was built at Quebec under the cliffs of Cape Diamond, and launched in April 1831. On the 18th of August 1833 she started from Pictou in Nova Scotia and steamed across the Atlantic, reaching Gravesend on the 12th of September, twenty-five days after leaving Pictou.[1] Regular steam communication, however, between England and America did not begin till 1838, the year in which Lord Durham went to Canada. The Peninsular Company, formed in 1837, received its charter as the Peninsular and Oriental Company in 1840; and on the 4th of July 1840 the *Britannia*, a steamer belonging to a citizen of Halifax in Nova Scotia, of the name of Cunard, started from Liverpool for Halifax and Boston, being the first regular steamer of the great Cunard line.

In 1837, Cooke and Wheatstone took out a patent for an electric telegraph, and in 1840 Wheatstone is said to have drawn plans for a submarine telegraph from Dover to Calais; but it was not until 1858 that a submarine cable was laid between the United Kingdom and America, and the connexion was not finally and successfully made until 1866. It may be summed up that when Queen Victoria's reign began, and when Lord Durham went out to

[1] The brass tablet was erected in 1894, and a full account of the *Royal William* is given in the Report of the Secretary of State of Canada for 1894, published in 1895.

CHAP. II   ACCESSION OF QUEEN VICTORIA   17

Canada, science was about to recast the meaning of space and time ; but it was as yet the dawn only, and not the full brightness of day. Lord Melbourne, who succeeded Lord Grey as the leader or nominal leader of the Whig party, was Queen Victoria's first Prime Minister, and it was during his tenure of office that Lord Durham's mission took place. The battle of Waterloo had ended an age of war. Before 1815, for England and for the world generally, war had for a long series of years been the rule and peace the exception. The people had grown up not merely familiar with the conditions of life in time of war, but so accustomed to war that peace must have seemed a novelty. It had been a fight for national existence. England, though spared the horror of war on her own shores, had paid a heavy price for victory, but she had survived and she had won. When peace came again, the English, by a perfectly wholesome instinct, still kept in power the men who had led them in war times and with whom the Duke of Wellington was associated, and they kept out of power the Whigs who had been or seemed to have been the less patriotic of the two parties. This went on until peace had become the rule and not the exception, and until, if ever there was going to be a transfer of power from one party to another, it was absolutely inevitable that it should take place. Then in 1830 the Whigs, who had especially espoused or professed to espouse the cause of Parliamentary Reform, came into power, and with a short break held office for rather more than ten years.

They passed the great Reform Act of 1832, the Acts for the abolition of slavery, for the reform of the Poor Law, for the reform of municipal corporations, and other valuable legislation. It stands to their lasting credit that they thoroughly repaired the parliamentary machinery of England, gave some measure of representation to the great cities, and made the House of Commons an exponent of popular wishes and popular movements to an extent which had never been the case before. It stands to their credit, too, that, having improved the machinery, they used it for a short time in an undeniably beneficial manner. On the other hand, their enthusiasm for democratic measures, and the enthusiasm of the people for them, cooled somewhat rapidly; and at the beginning of Queen Victoria's reign the Whig ministers were not much more than caretakers, the leaders of the Ins as opposed to the Outs, not entrusted with any great mission or standing for any great principle.

The reasons for this result are not far to seek. The inevitable outcome of passing the Reform Act and having a reformed Parliament was disunion, more or less pronounced, more or less rapid, both in the Government and in the country. The door had been unlocked, obstructions had been removed, people were moving on, and they moved at different rates of speed and in different directions. The individual ministers, or some of them, may well have become tired and half-hearted, and there was probably, as is always the case, a large section of the public disappointed because extension of the franchise did not at once bring the millennium.

Moreover there was, after all, no great gulf fixed between the Whigs and the Tories. On the one hand the Whig Government was not wholly composed of traditional Whigs, and on the other the Tories, whom they succeeded, had had a strong leaven of Liberalism among them. Melbourne had served under Canning and the Duke of Wellington. Stanley, nominally a Whig, had served under Canning. Palmerston, Goderich, Lord Glenelg, among others, had been in the so-called Tory ranks. In those ranks, Canning had been the very antipodes of a benighted Tory; Huskisson had gone further than any responsible minister in the direction of Free Trade; while, even when the Duke of Wellington, the very embodiment of Toryism, was Prime Minister, the Test and Corporation Acts had, on Lord John Russell's initiative, been repealed, and Catholic emancipation had been carried. Canning and Huskisson were dead, but Peel survived; and Peel, the country knew well, was no more of a reactionary than Melbourne and his friends. Thus at the beginning of Queen Victoria's reign there was a somewhat colourless Government in power, representing a spent force, no better and no worse than an ordinary party Government in ordinary times of peace. War as a normal condition of English life had passed more or less into oblivion, and there were a large number of movements at work, political, social, and industrial, and a considerable number of individual men, like Lord Durham himself, not hide-bound by party ties, but independent of and prepared, if their principles called for such a course, to be antagonistic to the Government. In 1838 the Anti-Corn Law Association was formed, which developed in the following year into the Anti-Corn Law League. Free Trade had not been a plank in the Whig platform, and there was no love lost between the official Whigs and Richard Cobden. 1838-9 was the date of the Chartist movement, and those who sympathized with he Chartists made small account of the Whigs as represented by Lord Melbourne's Government.

In that Government, when Lord Durham went out to Canada, the Colonial Secretary was Charles Grant, Lord Glenelg. Sir Henry Taylor, who served under him at the Colonial Office, wrote of him as ' high-minded, accomplished, and occasionally eloquent, but habitually and incurably sluggish and somnolent; . . . amiable and excellent as he was, a more incompetent man could not have been found to fill an office requiring activity and a ready judgement.' [1] A much more favourable estimate of him was given by Taylor's friend and colleague, Sir James Stephen, who, during Lord Glenelg's tenure of office was promoted to be permanent Under-Secretary of State for the Colonies. When Lord Glenelg resigned, Stephen wrote:

' Lord Glenelg's resignation is, as you may well suppose, a sad subject with me. He is the tenth Secretary of State under whom I have served, and from the most certain knowledge, I can declare that of the whole of that long list he is the most laborious, the most conscientious, and the most enlightened minister of the public. . . . His

[1] *Autobiography of Sir Henry Taylor* 1885, vol. i, pp. 147-8.

CHAP. II ACCESSION OF QUEEN VICTORIA 21

real and only unfitness for public life arises from the strange incompatibility of his temper and principles with the tempers and with the rules of action to which we erect shrines in Downing Street.'[1]

There can be no doubt that Lord Glenelg was a man of very high principles. He was actuated by the purest motives of justice and philanthropy, when he ordered withdrawal from the native territory which Sir Benjamin D'Urban had annexed to the Cape Colony; but the result of his action in that case was most disastrous, and in general by common consent he was a weak and incompetent Secretary of State for the Colonies. In 1838 Sir William Molesworth moved a vote of censure on him in the House of Commons, charging him by implication with want of diligence, forethought, judgement, activity and firmness, and early in the following year he was made to resign.

Stephen, who described himself in the letter quoted above as Lord Glenelg's 'intimate personal friend', and who, as permanent Under-Secretary of State, was his principal adviser at the Colonial Office, was anything but a weak man. He was strong enough to be exposed to attacks from which permanent officials are usually exempt, and he was supposed to be the embodiment of all the vices of the Colonial Office when Charles Buller denounced it and talked about 'Mr. Mother Country'.

'I am scarcely twenty-four hours off Sir William Molesworth's impeachment,' Stephen wrote in 1838, 'in which I hear from Charles Buller, a great friend of Sir William's, that I am to have a con-

[1] *The First Sir James Stephen*, pp. 56-7, Letter of February 12, 1839.

spicuous share. I am, it seems, at your service, a rapacious, grasping, ambitious Tory. On two unequal crutches propped he came, Glenelg's on this, on that Sir G. Grey's name ; and it appears that by the aid of these crutches I have hobbled into a dominion wider than ever Nero possessed, which I exercise like another Domitian.'[1]

If some took Stephen to be a rapacious Tory, the eccentric Governor of Upper Canada, Sir Francis Bond Head, abused him as a rank republican. From his predominance at the Colonial Office he was christened Mr. Over-Secretary Stephen, and he seems to have been regarded by men of the school of Molesworth and Buller as the type of a rigid and unsympathetic official. He had been brought up in the evangelical atmosphere of the Clapham sect, and with their virtues and their philanthropy may well have inherited also some narrowness, but his private letters show no want of kindly feeling or of human sympathy.

'It fell to his lot,' wrote his son, Sir FitzJames Stephen in 1860, ' to assist in two of the most remarkable transactions even of this century. The first was the abolition of slavery, the second was the establishment of responsible government in Canada. . . . The principles which he always advocated ultimately obtained complete recognition, but he was constantly obliged to take part in measures which he regretted, and of which he disapproved.'[2]

It must be remembered that, when the United States were severed from the British Empire, little

---

[1] *The First Sir James Stephen*, p. 53. Sir G. Grey was then the Parliamentary Under-Secretary at the Colonial Office, and represented it in the House of Commons. [2] pp. 51-2.

CHAP. II ACCESSION OF QUEEN VICTORIA

trace of colonial self-government was left within the Empire except in the West Indian Legislatures. The tendency of the time was, as in the case of the abolition of slavery, to override these Legislatures, not to extend their powers; and in 1839, the very year in which Lord Durham's Report appeared, Lord Melbourne's Government brought in a Bill for temporarily suspending the constitution of Jamaica, which led to the resignation of the Ministry. Outside the West Indies, Canada had been given representative institutions by the Act of 1791, but the Colonial Office had necessarily none of the experience of dealings with self-governing communities which it has at the present day. It may be summed up therefore that, when Lord Durham went out to Canada, the Colonial Office with which he had to deal was in the main what would now be called a Crown Colony Office, presided over by an exceptionally weak Secretary of State and an exceptionally strong permanent Under-Secretary. Such conditions would give a notable opportunity for reflections and comments on bureaucracy; and inasmuch as the evils of bureaucracy were a favourite theme with Charles Buller, perhaps his hand may specially be traced in the very able passages of the Report (ii. 101–6) which refer to this subject, and one of the side notes to which is ' Evils of committing details of government to Colonial Department '

CHAPTER III

ORIGIN AND DEVELOPMENT OF THE POLITICAL DIFFICULTIES IN THE CANADAS

IN 1837, the year of the Queen's Accession and the year before Lord Durham went to Canada, the discontent and unrest which had long prevailed alike in Lower and in Upper Canada, culminated in open rebellion in either province. In order to make clear how the trouble arose, it is necessary to give an outline of the previous condition of the two provinces.

Between French and English colonization in North America, and between French and English colonists, there was a great gulf fixed. Race, religion, language, customs, prejudices divided them, but the division did not end here. French colonization was born of the State, it was reared by the State, it was controlled by the State. Its essence was feudalism, imported from the old world to the new, which was not, however, as in the old world, a growth but the creation of the Crown. In New France the authority of the Crown and of the Church was absolute. 'The institutions of France,' wrote Lord Durham (ii. 27–8), 'during the period of the colonization of Canada, were, perhaps, more than those of any other European nation, calculated to repress the intelligence and freedom of the great mass of the people. These institutions followed the Canadian colonist across the Atlantic. The same central, ill-organized, unimproving and repressive despotism extended over him. Not merely was he allowed no voice in the government of his province, or the choice of his rulers, but he was not even permitted to associate with his neighbours for the regulation of those municipal affairs, which the central authority neglected under the pretext of managing.' Lord Durham regarded the political and social system of Canada under French rule from an English point of view, and he emphasized that view as an advanced Liberal. It is true that there was no liberty, as Englishmen understood it, in New France, no vestige of popular representation in political or even in municipal matters; but the system was not without its merits. It was not ill organized. In its inception it was well and skilfully organized. The object was to reproduce in the new home the conditions which the colonists had known in the old, to create a New France in America. New France was created, and it would be difficult to find a parallel in history for a handiwork so artificial, which was at the same time so strong and lasting. Two features in French Canada call for special notice. The first is that it tended to be a land of extremes, or at any rate a land of strong contrasts. Within the settled area life was lived rigidly according to rule, on fixed lines in fixed places. Outside the settled area French quickness of mind and body found unlimited scope: the *voyageurs* and the *coureurs de bois* went far and wide and knew no law. The second characteristic to be noticed is that Canada in old days was better framed for war than for peace. It had a natural stronghold in Quebec, to which there is no parallel in North America ; it had a race of men in the *coureurs de bois* specially adapted for border forays ; while the system, at once feudal and centralized, under which the ordinary community lived, was a most effective organization for war purposes. The English in America were many, the French were one ; and, as the days of New France were more often days of war than days of peace, Canada reaped the benefit of unquestioned authority, unquestioning obedience, and a whole population trained for service to the King.

Canadian colonization was the product of the State, and the State was the Crown. The British colonies, which were the neighbours and rivals of Canada, were largely the product of antagonism to the State. The typical New Englanders were men or the descendants of men who had gone out to America to live their lives as they wished, and not as the King or the Home Government wished. They were cradled in freedom, political and religious, and self-government in one form or another was of the essence of their being. They did perforce a good deal of warring, in a spasmodic and slipshod fashion, but their real business was to grow and multiply, to settle in their own way and on their own lines. There were backwoodsmen and hunters among them, but there were no such extremes in the English colonies as were to be found in Canada. There were no habitants or seigniories on the one hand, and on the other no definite class of Indianized Europeans like the *coureurs de bois*. The English colonists were all citizens, more often than not grudging and selfish citizens, but in all cases keenly conscious of their rights if not of their responsibilities.

The conquest of Canada and the Peace of Paris made the French Canadians, who had in the past been most loyal subjects of the French King, subjects of the British King, and fellow subjects with these wholly dissimilar British colonists, who had no instinct or tradition of heart-whole obedience, and a few of whom, bad specimens of their kind, found their way into Canada. A most difficult position was created for the British Government. That Government wished to treat the new subjects, the French Canadians, with the fullest consideration, to respect their religion and their customs. At the same time the British ministers wished to extend to the French Canadians within reason British laws and institutions, because those laws and institutions embodied, so it was assumed, better conditions of life than the Canadians had hitherto known, and because it was desired to convert the Canadians gradually into British citizens. Further it was desired, as far as possible, while conciliating the French Canadians, not to run counter to the wishes and prejudices of the neighbouring British colonies, and also as far as possible to meet the wishes of the very small but very noisy British minority in Canada, and to make Canada an attractive field for British settlement. The result was, and could only be, a measure or measures of compromise.

Canada, as a British possession, began with military rule, and it throve under military rule. The Canadians had been accustomed to it or to something very like it. They had been trained on military lines. Their loyalty and obedience had been to persons; to the King, to the priest, to the seignior, not to a State. They had obeyed rules and customs made from above, not laws made by themselves. They had been brought up under authority and had inherited discipline. Military men, therefore, who had known discipline themselves, and who were by reason of their calling essentially the King's men, who, moreover, had in fighting learnt to appreciate the bravery and the stubbornness of the French Canadians, sympathized with them more and understood them better than did civilians, and far better than well-meaning ministers at a distance or the ill-disposed British minority on the spot.

When civil government was established by the Royal Proclamation of 1763, soldier governors were continued. James Murray, the first Governor, and his successor Carleton, were in full sympathy with the Canadians, and Carleton urged the importance of interfering as little as possible with Canadian laws and customs, and of employing the Canadian seigniors in the King's service, thereby giving them the personal link which they had known under the old régime. The absence of some such recognition left the Canadian *noblesse* half-hearted in their new allegiance. The introduction of English laws and of English legal procedure led to confusion and to general uneasiness. The

POLITICAL DIFFICULTIES

habitants found the bonds of discipline relaxed, and began to unlearn obedience. The British minority clamoured for a General Assembly, on the model of the Assemblies of the adjoining provinces, the grant of which had been foreshadowed by the Proclamation of 1763, and they made the ignorant French peasantry familiar with the claptrap phrases of colonial democracy. Under these conditions, after the most anxious inquiry and guided to a great extent by Carleton's advice, the Home Government passed the Quebec Act of 1774.

The Quebec Act gave great offence to the old colonies, already on the eve of revolt, mainly because it included within the Province of Quebec the western lands which those colonies looked upon as their own sphere of future settlement and colonization; nor did it satisfy the British minority, inasmuch as it made no provision for an elected Assembly. By the Canadians, on the other hand, it was regarded at the time with great satisfaction, for it safeguarded their religion and gave them their old laws in civil matters. The Act created a Legislative Council, but not on an elective basis; and it withheld from the Council powers of taxation except in the form of purely local rates. Another Imperial Act was passed at the same time, the Quebec Revenue Act, which repealed various taxes levied under the French Government, and imposed instead certain duties on spirits and molasses as well as certain licences, the proceeds of which were applied to meeting the expenses of the civil government and of the administration of justice.

The passing of the Quebec Act was followed almost immediately by the War of American Independence. In this war the Canadians as a whole were neutral; they were a lately-conquered people, they had no great reason to love their conquerors, and they were invited and urged to rise for freedom and for imaginary privileges which they did not understand. On the other hand, they had liked their soldier governors; they, or some of them, had recognized the fair and kindly dealing embodied in the Quebec Act; if they had no great love for the English from over the seas, they had less love for the English in their immediate neighbourhood; and the sentiment for a King had not wholly died out. The better classes tended to take the King's side. Of the peasantry not a few joined the Americans; but the large majority waited on events.

The outcome of the war was that Quebec was well defended and well kept; that Canada remained a province of the British Empire with far greater relative importance attached to it than when it had been overshadowed by the adjacent colonies, now no longer British possessions; and that the Loyalist immigration from the United States led to the creation of two new British provinces in North America, New Brunswick, which was the mainland of Nova Scotia, and Upper Canada, which was the hinterland of Quebec. The Loyalists brought with them intense animosity to the newly-formed Republic of the United States, intense loyalty to the British Crown, but none the less the traditions and the instincts of colonial self-government. Their coming into the old Province of Quebec produced a new set of conditions. The British population of Canada was now no longer an insignificant minority, but a strong and substantial number of tried and approved citizens, whose political training had been wholly different from that of the French Canadians. They were mainly settled in a part of the province which the French had not colonized; and this fact made it possible, if it was thought desirable, to divide the province, and give to either half a separate legislature and administration. This course was taken, again after the most careful attention to all the facts and features of the case; and, by the Imperial Act of 1791, the Province of Quebec was divided into the two provinces of Upper and Lower Canada, either province being given a constitution consisting of a nominated Legislative Council and an elected Assembly, but neither province being given full control either of their revenues or of their executive officers. By thus dividing the old Province of Quebec it was hoped that friction would be avoided, and that French Canada, being side by side with a British province, and enjoying the same institutions, would gradually become assimilated to it without jealousy or ill-will. William Pitt's words, when introducing the bill into the House of Commons, were as follows: 'This division, it was hoped, would put an end to the competition between the old French inhabitants and the new settlers from Britain, or British colonies, which had occasioned the disputes and uncertainty respecting law, and other disputes of less importance, by which the province had been so long distracted.'[1]

At almost any time in Canadian history between 1783 and 1867, when British North America was federated into a dominion, the arguments for having one Canada or two Canadas (exclusive of the Maritime Provinces) left little to choose between them. There were obvious advantages and obvious disadvantages in either alternative. The division into two provinces led to the following among other difficulties. As is pointed out in Lord Durham's Report, it tended to widen the gulf between French and English by marking out one part of Canada for the French and the other for the English. At the same time it did not effect the object which the framers of the 1791 Act contemplated, of preventing conflict between the two races by giving them separate spheres of influence; for in the French province there came into being an English district, the townships as opposed to the seigniories, the settlers in which, for many years, were not represented in the Quebec Legislature and keenly resented French domination.

The division of the provinces again necessarily involved divided executive authority in an area over which it was clearly desirable that there should be one supreme head. Nominally there was a Governor-General of the two Canadas, and the Governor of Upper Canada only bore the title of Lieutenant-Governor: but for all practical pur-

[1] *Parliamentary Register* 1791, vol. xxviii, p. 514, Debate of March 4 1791.

poses the Governor-General soon became Governor of Lower Canada only, and the substitution of two Governors for one militated against uniformity of policy and tended to weaken the executive power in the face of growing democracy. Once more, the division of the two provinces, as the dividing line was drawn, created a purely inland colony, whose outlet to the sea was either through the sister colony or through a foreign country. The result of this was to make Upper Canada, as far as customs duties were concerned, dependent upon Lower Canada, and thereby to create a perpetual dispute between the two provinces. The Imperial Canada Trade Act of 1822 was an attempt to remove this cause of friction.

It may be summed up that from 1791 onward until Lord Durham's time there were, exclusive of what are now the Maritime Provinces of the Dominion, two Canadas, one mainly French, the other mainly English, each province enjoying representative institutions without responsible government, and the Legislatures consisting in either case of a nominated Legislative Council and an elected Assembly. There were thus obvious and abundant opportunities for friction; between the Governors, as occurred at the outset between Lord Dorchester and Simcoe; between the provinces, for the reason already given; between the races and religions, wherever French and English were brought into close contact; between the two houses of the Legislature—a species of political friction which is common everywhere; between the executive power on the one hand as represented by the Crown and the officers of the Crown, especially the Governor, and on the other the Legislature, or rather the elected branch of the Legislature, the main ground of dispute being control of the public purse. On the whole it may fairly be said that the history of Canada from 1791 to the time of Lord Durham's mission is, with the exception of one interlude, the war of 1812, a record of friction of this last-named kind, coloured by race feeling and by the special conditions of the respective provinces.

When the two Canadas received representative institutions, the French Canadians were thereby given a machinery which was familiar to Englishmen, but which had never previously been handled by Frenchmen in America. The French population consisted of an intensely conservative gentry and a wholly uneducated peasantry, both dominated by a Church, the essence of which was absolutism. As far as the French Canadians had any guidance in handling their new tools, it came from the British minority in Quebec and Montreal; but not many years passed before the French began to better their instruction. With the early years of the nineteenth century Nationalist views gained ground, a French Canadian press came into existence, and, while French and English more or less combined against an administration which was out of touch with the people, and various officers of which, sent out from home, were notoriously unfit for their posts, the line of race cleavage became more and more distinct, and the struggle for popular control of the finances was embittered by being fought with French acuteness and French impatience of compromise. Meanwhile Upper Canada, though as a whole intensely loyal to the British Crown, was leavened to some extent by American immigration. It has been stated that, during the earlier years of British rule in Canada, military men proved themselves to be sympathetic Governors of the French Canadians. As time went on, and the Canadians grew towards political manhood, the soldier, unless he was an exceptional man, was less likely than had previously been the case to be in harmony with conditions which were becoming increasingly democratic. In 1807, after a long interregnum, Sir James Craig came out as Governor-General, a soldier of tried worth, but with a soldier's views of discipline, which were not softened by ill health. He came into collision with the elected chamber of the Legislature in Lower Canada, had resort to repeated dissolutions, and put down with a high hand the Nationalist paper *Le Canadien*, which persistently vilified the Government. In a long dispatch to the Secretary of State, written in May 1810, in which he reviewed existing conditions in Lower Canada, Craig represented French and English in the province as bitterly opposed to each other. 'The line of distinction between us,' he wrote, 'is completely drawn; friendship, cordiality are not to be found, even common intercourse scarcely exists.' But, though the sentiment of French Canadian nationality was gathering force year by year, the struggle at this time was not so much a race conflict as a squabble between the Executive and the Legislature, one of the Governor's leading opponents, whom he relieved of the office of Solicitor-General, being James Stuart, who was the son of a United Empire Loyalist, and who in after years was appointed by Lord Durham to be Chief Justice of Canada. It was during the governorship of Sir James Craig, in the year 1810, that the Quebec House of Assembly, in view of the prosperity of the province, offered to take upon themselves for the time being the whole charge of the civil administration. This offer, which came to nothing at the time, was much quoted at a later date. It meant that the elected representatives realized that power is in the hands of those who pay, and that so long as the Imperial Government, either by direct subsidies, or from territorial revenues, or from taxes levied under permanent Acts, paid a large proportion of the cost of the civil government of Canada, so long would the power be in the hands of the Governor and his officers as being the servants of the Imperial Government, and not in the hands of the Assembly which represented the people of Canada. Sir James Craig left Canada in 1811. His successor, Sir George Prevost, was a man of very different stamp. Prevost set himself to conciliate the French Canadians, and in that respect did good service to the Empire during the war of 1812, though in the actual operations of the war he did not distinguish himself. Quebec was little troubled by the war, and the Assembly which sat there continued to a large extent its vendetta against the existing system, impeaching the Chief Justice of

Lower Canada on the ridiculous charge of having conspired against the civil liberties of the people. The war, however, had beyond question a wholesome effect in softening, under the influence of common danger, the jealousies and the animosities of race. French and English stood shoulder to shoulder to repel invasion, and some sense of unity came into Canada, effective at the time in reducing friction, salutary in after years as a memory of common patriotism. The brunt of the war fell upon Upper Canada, with the result that in this province, for the time being, all constitutional wrangles were swallowed up in a fight for national existence, and that the loyalty of the Loyalists to the British connexion was intensified. It may be said in brief that the war of 1812 did not affect the continuity of history in the Lower Province, whereas in the Upper Province it made a complete break and supplied a new starting-point.

The war ended, and the old difficulties revived. In Lower Canada the judges were still harried by the Legislature. In Upper Canada the loyalty of those who had fought and suffered was tried by delays in settling arrears of pay and in giving grants of land, while the development of the province was retarded by restrictions on American immigration, which at the time were neither unreasonable nor unnecessary, as well as by the amount of land which was locked up in Crown and Clergy reserves. In 1816 Sir John Sherbrooke was appointed Governor-in-Chief of the two Canadas, and once more proved that a good soldier may be also a tactful and diplomatic administrator.

Unfortunately his term of office was shortened by ill health, and only lasted for two years. Handling the political situation in Lower Canada with much skill, Sherbrooke brought to an end the quarrel with the judges. He detached support from Stuart, still a pronounced opponent of the Government, with the result that the latter for the time being retired into private life, and he worked in harmony with the Speaker of the Assembly, the future leader of rebellion in Lower Canada—Louis Papineau. He then took stock of the finances of the provinces, which during the war had fallen into some confusion, and he warned the Secretary of State of the fact, which previously does not appear to have been fully appreciated at the Colonial Office, that the civil administration could not be carried on independently of the votes of the elected Assembly. It was on this point that the whole future conflict turned. Had the revenues which were at the disposal of the Crown been sufficient to meet the cost of the administration, the opposition of the Assembly to the Government would have had little practical effect, and there would have been no adequate lever for the grant of responsible government; but, inasmuch as those revenues did not cover the annual charges of government, and the taxpayers of the United Kingdom could not be asked to make good the deficit, the executive power in Canada was so far at the mercy of the elected Assembly.

The result of Sherbrooke's correspondence on this subject with Lord Bathurst, the Secretary of State, was that in the session of 1818 the Governor-

General laid the estimates of the year before the Assembly, showing clearly what was the total estimated expenditure, what proportion of the total was covered by revenue at the disposal of the Crown, and how much the Legislature was asked to provide. He reminded the Assembly of the offer made by the elected representatives in 1810 to take upon themselves the whole cost of the civil administration, and after considerable debate the Assembly voted the sum whereby the total expenditure of the year exceeded the revenue at the disposal of the Crown.

This result was largely due to personal respect for Sherbrooke, and the Assembly was not minded to make permanent provision for the expenses of the civil administration in the form of a Civil List, as the Home Government desired. Sherbrooke's successor, the Duke of Richmond, had therefore, in the following year, to face the same difficulty, and to face it without Sherbrooke's tact and influence. The estimates which he laid before the Assembly unfortunately showed a large increase on the expenditure side, and the Assembly took upon themselves to recast the budget, scrutinizing all the separate items, including the charges against the Crown revenues, and reducing or omitting salaries at will. In their reckless procedure they arrogated to themselves control of the finances to an extent which would not be paralleled at the present day either in the British House of Commons or in any colonial Parliament. The Bill which they sent up to the Legislative Council was promptly and rightly thrown out by that body, and a crisis then began which years afterwards ended in armed rebellion, in the suspension of the constitution in Lower Canada, and in Lord Durham's mission.

The revenues at the disposal of the Crown in Lower Canada were twofold. There were in the first place certain rents and dues which had been paid to the French King and which had passed to his successor in title. They were known as the casual and territorial revenues of the Crown. 'They are enjoyed by the Crown,' Lord Aylmer informed the Assembly in 1831, ' by virtue of the Royal Prerogative, and are neither more nor less than the proceeds of landed property, which legally and constitutionally belongs to the Sovereign on the throne.' [1] In the second place, there were the proceeds of certain taxes imposed by law, mainly the customs and licence duties received under the Imperial Quebec Revenue Act of 1774. These latter receipts, more especially, the Quebec Assembly designed to secure under their own control; on the other hand they were the *quid pro quo*, by which the Imperial Government might hope to effect its object of obtaining a more or less permanent Civil List.

In asking for a Civil List for the life of the King, the Imperial Government were only proposing that the practice which prevailed at the time in England should be followed in Canada. Prior to the accession of King William the Fourth, the term Civil List purported to mean the provision made out of the hereditary revenues of the Crown,

[1] *Canada Crown Revenues*: Return to an Address of the House of Commons, July 1831, p. 3.

POLITICAL DIFFICULTIES

supplemented by the proceeds of certain taxes, which were placed at the disposal of the reigning sovereign to cover the ordinary civil expenses of the State (other than debt charges), including the expenses of the Court and the Royal Household. The recalcitrant Assembly in Lower Canada contended that the conditions of the province differed from those of England and would not allow of more than annual votes: they also contended that the Civil List as proposed for Canada was more extensive than the Civil List of the United Kingdom. Their contentions were ill founded: they were the contentions of a body of men who were mainly French in race and in cast of mind; and who, being French, and having tasted the beginnings of political freedom, were intolerant of compromise. They wanted not merely the powers which the British House of Commons enjoyed, but more also. On the other hand, Lord Bathurst was insistent that the Assembly should have no authority to dispose of public money without the concurrence of the Upper Chamber, the Legislative Council, thereby restricting the powers of the Assembly as compared with those of the House of Commons. There was thus a great gulf fixed between the democrats and demagogues of Lower Canada on the one hand, and the conservative Imperial Government on the other, but there was still, at any rate, the semblance of loyalty to the Crown; for, when King George the Third died, Louis Papineau took occasion to deliver an eloquent eulogy on the blessings which Canada owed to British rule.

The Duke of Richmond was a Tory of the old school. He formulated for the confidential consideration of the Secretary of State proposals which were probably illegal, and were certainly impracticable, whereby sufficient revenue should be secured to the Crown to make the Government of Lower Canada independent of the Legislature. His death under tragic circumstances, after he had only held office for one year, prevented any constitutional experiments such as he suggested from being tried. An able and high-minded Governor succeeded him, the Earl of Dalhousie. He took up his duties in June 1820, and did not finally leave Canada until September 1828. During the term of his government the quarrel between the Executive and the Legislature became more and more embittered, and tended more and more to follow the lines of race. Unreasoning and unreasonable, the French Canadian majority in the Quebec House of Assembly stand condemned by their persistent hostility to a ruler so courteous and so public-spirited as was Lord Dalhousie. It must be borne in mind that the democratic movement in Canada was coincident with and parallel to the democratic movement in the United Kingdom. England was gradually moving towards the great Reform Bill, while Papineau and his colleagues were refusing supplies and making speeches in Canada; but there was no slow broadening out in French Canada; and there was greater haste and bitterness in fighting for the fullness of liberty, in that the existing instalment of freedom had not been earned by long years of training and of steady growth.

POLITICAL DIFFICULTIES

Lord Dalhousie's instructions were to aim at securing 'the permanent assignment of a fixed annual revenue to meet the charge of such a Civil List as the Province requires for its proper administration'.[1] This was precisely what the Quebec Assembly was determined not to concede. In their crusade against the Government the legislators of Lower Canada had been able to point to sinecures, to abuses in salaries and pensions, which they contended should be abolished, before the people were asked to make good an expenditure which included such items. The abuses existed and were notorious, but they were not peculiar to Canada: they were rife in England also; and such Governors as Sherbrooke and Dalhousie objected to them as much as did Papineau and his friends. Their existence, however, gave material for agitation to the popular party, and so did the defalcation of the Receiver-General of Canada, an Imperial officer, which came to light in 1823. When Dalhousie first met the Legislature in December 1820, he set out clearly the average and recurrent cost of the civil administration of Lower Canada, and invited the Assembly to make permanent and adequate provision for it. The Assembly refused to give more than a vote for one year, and in doing so they introduced new items of expenditure and assumed control of the Crown revenues. Their Bill went up to the Legislative Council, who threw it out and coupled the rejection with strongly worded resolutions, the result of the quarrel between the two Houses being that the

[1] Dispatch of Lord Bathurst, September 11, 1820.

Governor was left without any legal authority to meet the expenditure of the year. In December 1821 the Legislature met again, and it was made clearer than before that the Assembly were only asked to make permanent provision for permanent expenditure, casual contingencies being left to be covered by annual votes. This time the direct issue was raised by a motion in the House that permanent provision should be made for the support of the civil administration of the province during the life of the King. The motion was lost by a majority of six to one; the Assembly then embodied their grievances and views in an address to the King, refused to vote the necessary supplies for the coming year, and refused also or threatened to refuse to renew certain expiring Revenue Acts, so as entirely to cripple the Executive for want of funds.

At the same time, and by the same action, they were crippling Upper Canada, which was entitled to a share of the customs duties under the Acts in question; and already the Upper Province, unable to obtain a satisfactory adjustment of its financial relations with Lower Canada, had asked for the intervention of the Imperial Government. The result was that in June 1822 the Under-Secretary for the Colonies, Wilmot, afterwards Wilmot Horton, introduced a Bill into the House of Commons, 'to make more effectual provision for the government of the Provinces of Lower and Upper Canada, and to regulate the trade thereof.' The Bill provided for reunion of the provinces; it was strongly supported on the Liberal side of the House by

'Bear' Ellice, with whom it had in fact originated; but it was opposed by Mackintosh and some other Radical members, not so much on its merits as on the ground that the peoples and legislatures of the two provinces had not been given an opportunity of expressing their views. In consequence of this opposition, as the session was drawing to a close, the Government contented themselves with legislating on the subject of the financial relations between the two provinces, leaving the wider question of reunion to stand over for another session. Thus the Canada Trade Act was passed on the 5th of August 1822, and by its terms the Quebec Legislature was restricted from varying the customs duties levied at the ports of Lower Canada to the detriment of the Upper Province. Under existing conditions the Act was both necessary and salutary, but it was avowedly only an instalment, and the matter as a whole was badly handled. The British Government made the mistake so common in the colonial history of Great Britain, of putting their hand to the plough and looking back. They went forward, and stopped half-way. They proposed a large constitutional change, and, having given their scheme to the public, they did not carry the change through. At the same time they went far enough to override by Imperial legislation the representative Assembly of Lower Canada and to restrain their taxing powers. In short, there was interference from home with a colonial legislature, enough to irritate, but not enough to cure more than a part of the evil which it was sought to remedy. In speaking on the Reunion Bill Ellice warned the House of Commons that 'the only consequence of delay would be the excitement of feelings of animosity between the English and French inhabitants in the meantime, and that the House ultimately would find it absolutely necessary to pass the Bill',[1] and years afterwards Lord Durham wrote in his Report (ii. 47):

'It is said that the appeals to the national pride and animosities of the French became more direct and general on the occasion of the abortive attempt to reunite Upper and Lower Canada in 1822, which the leaders of the Assembly viewed or represented as a blow aimed at the institutions of their province. The anger of the English was excited by the denunciations of themselves which, subsequently to this period, they were in the habit of hearing.'

It had been intended by the Home Government to take up again the Reunion Bill, as soon as the people of Canada had had time to express their views upon it; but the reception of the Bill in the two provinces was on the whole so unfavourable that no more was heard of it in the House of Commons. In Upper Canada opinion was divided, but such leading men as Dr. Strachan and Beverley Robinson were opposed to it. In Lower Canada the French Canadians were heart-whole in their opposition. They regarded the Bill, or professed to regard it, as an attempt to 'anglify'—to denationalize French Canada. The English in the province were divided; only in the Eastern Townships, unrepresented in the Quebec Legislature and chafing against French indifference to their

[1] *Hansard* for 1822, vol. vii, p. 1709

interests, was there strong and solid backing of the Bill. The opponents of the measure at Montreal and Quebec sent Papineau and John Neilson, the latter being a Scotchman and a journalist, as their spokesmen to England : while Stuart, no longer in line with the French, took the lead of the party who favoured reunion.

Papineau's absence, and appreciation of the fact that the Canada Trade Act had been passed and that a Reunion Bill was pending, made the Quebec Legislature, which met again in January 1823, more amenable than before. The estimates, as presented to the Assembly, were divided into two schedules, one of which contained the general or permanent establishments, the cost of which was covered by the Crown revenues ; the other contained what were termed local establishments, for which the Assembly was asked to provide. The necessary supplies were voted, other useful work was done, and Lord Dalhousie closed the session with compliments and thanks.

Soon after its close the announcement was made that the Imperial Government would not proceed with the Reunion Bill. Papineau came back to Quebec and to the Legislature ; and, when the Assembly met again towards the end of November 1823, for the last session of an expiring Parliament, the irreconcilables had it their own way. Papineau distinguished himself by personalities against the Governor ; and when the estimates were brought in, arranged in two schedules as before, he and his followers assumed control of the whole finances and of all the establishments, and reduced the salaries, including the Governor's, by 25 per cent. The Bill which embodied these proceedings was at once thrown out by the Legislative Council. In this session, which lasted till the 9th of March 1824, the majority of the Quebec Legislature found occasion to flout the wishes and injure the interests of the people of Upper Canada, as well as to cripple the administration and check the progress of their own province; and when Lord Dalhousie closed the session, he pointed out the grave mischief which had resulted from the unwarranted and unconstitutional claim of the one branch of the Legislature 'to appropriate the whole revenue of the province according to its pleasure', and the withholding of supplies in order to enforce the claim. 'This subject,' he continued, 'has occupied every session from the first to the last, and is now transmitted to those which shall follow. It has caused incalculable mischief to the province; and now leaves it to struggle under difficulties, while every inhabitant of it must see that the encouraging aid of the Legislature is alone wanting to arouse powerful exertions and draw forth those resources which, without that aid, must, in a great measure, be dormant and useless within its reach.'

On the 6th of June, 1824, Lord Dalhousie sailed for England on leave of absence, and the Lieutenant-Governor, Sir Francis Burton, took over the administration. Burton's case was one of those which had given the Quebec Assembly substantial ground for complaint. His commission as Lieutenant-Governor was dated November 1808, but he did not go out to Canada till 1822, after his absence had called forth remonstrances from the Legislature. Notwithstanding, he seems to have attained considerable popularity among the French Canadians, possibly because the opponents of the Government hoped thereby to emphasize their antipathy to Lord Dalhousie. A general election was held in July and August; and in the following January the new Legislature met, Papineau being again chosen as Speaker, and an opportunity being found by the Government in the course of the session to secure their former opponent, James Stuart, for the post of Attorney-General. The Lieutenant-Governor brought in the estimates in a different form from that which had been adopted by Lord Dalhousie. He abandoned the two schedules, and with them the distinction which had been drawn between the charges against permanent funds and those for which local votes were required. The estimates which he presented treated the whole expenditure as one, and he asked the Assembly to vote a sum sufficient to cover the excess of the total expenditure over the revenue provided by law. The Assembly went through the whole estimates, including the permanent establishments, and, after making large reductions, voted the sum which they considered to be adequate for one year. They had now, so they thought and hoped, made good their claim to control the disposal of all revenues, permanent as well as temporary, and to give supply only from year to year. So they held, and Lord Bathurst interpreted what had taken place in much the same sense, for, in a dispatch dated the 4th of June 1825, he severely censured Sir Francis Burton. Burton, it afterwards appeared, had acted with imperfect knowledge of previous instructions, and was consequently exculpated. The instructions to the Governor-General, said Lord Bathurst, in the dispatch referred to, had imposed upon him

'the necessity of refusing all arrangements that went in any degree to compromise the integrity of the revenue known by the name of the permanent revenue ; and it appears to me, on a careful examination of the measures which have been adopted, that they are at variance with those specified and positive instructions. The Executive Government had sent in an estimate in which no distinction was made between the expenditure chargeable upon the permanent revenue of the Crown and that which remained to be provided for out of the revenues raised under colonial Acts. In other words, had the whole revenue been raised under colonial Acts, there would have been no difference in the manner of sending in the estimates. . . . Instead of the King's permanent revenue having certain fixed charges placed upon it, of which the Assembly were made cognisant, the revenue was pledged together with the colonial revenue, as the ways and means of providing for the expenses of the year. . . . The consequence of this arrangement is, that the permanent revenue will not be applied for the payment of such expenses as His Majesty may deem fit, but on the contrary, for the payment of whatever expenses the colonial Legislature may think necessary.' [1]

This misunderstanding about the estimates made Lord Dalhousie's position more difficult than ever.

[1] This dispatch will be found printed at pp. 93-4 of vol. iii of Christie's *History of Lower Canada*.

CHAP. III POLITICAL DIFFICULTIES 51

He returned from England in September 1825: the Legislature met again in January 1826, and in February he laid before them the estimates, divided into two parts, as they had been before Sir Francis Burton tried his hand at compromise. The Secretary of State's criticism of Burton was communicated to the Assembly later in the session, but the only result, as far as the Assembly were concerned, was an Appropriation Bill in the same form as that to which Lord Bathurst had taken exception, and a claim, formulated at once in Resolutions of the House and in an Address to the King, 'that to the Legislature alone appertains the right of distributing all monies levied in the colonies.' Lord Dalhousie, on the other hand, in proroguing the Legislature, intimated very courteously that he must continue to adopt the form of estimates 'showing to you one branch of the revenue for your information, and the other branch for your appropriation '.[1]

In the next session, however, which opened in January 1827, Lord Dalhousie did make a change in the form in which he presented the estimates to the Assembly, for he laid before them an estimate of that portion only of the year's expenditure which would not be a charge against permanent revenues, thus removing the latter from the purview of the elected representatives. The latter retorted by practically refusing supply, and they added to the difficulties of the Government by refusing to renew the militia laws, and thereby recalling into existence two old ordinances on the subject, which the

[1] Christie, vol. iii, pp. 106-7.

Governor-General found himself bound to enforce, and in enforcing which he encountered disloyalty and intrigue.

In July 1827 he dissolved the Parliament: a general election left matters much as they were: the new Legislature met in November: Papineau was again chosen as Speaker: in view of his virulent opposition to the Government and personal insults to the head of the Government, Lord Dalhousie refused to confirm the choice: and, as the majority of the Assembly upheld their champion, the Legislature was prorogued before any business had been transacted. Petitions and counter-petitions were now drawn up, and delegates were sent to England in the Spring of 1828. Shortly after their departure, Lord Dalhousie learnt that he had been appointed to be commander-in-chief of the forces in India, and in September 1828 he finally left Canada, having, in an impossible position and amid every form of malignant misrepresentation, held the reins of government with dignity, impartiality, and a single eye to the welfare of the Canadian people.

In England there had been changes. In April 1827 Lord Liverpool resigned, and Lord Bathurst left the Colonial Office, having presided over it for a longer time than any Secretary of State before or since. For three and a half months in Canning's administration Lord Goderich was Colonial Secretary. In July 1827 he wrote a dispatch offering to hand over the revenues of the Crown to the Assembly in exchange for a Civil List of £36,000 per annum, but, as the Assembly never met for business,

POLITICAL DIFFICULTIES

the dispatch could not be communicated to them, and if it had been laid before the House, the offer would have been at once refused. Huskisson succeeded Goderich, again only for a few months from the middle of August 1827 till the end of May 1828, and, while he was Secretary of State, he moved in the House of Commons, on the 2nd of May 1828, that a select committee should be appointed to inquire into the state of the Civil Government of Canada, as established by the Act of 1791.

When the Duke of Richmond came out to govern Canada in 1818, his son-in-law, Sir Peregrine Maitland, came with him to take up the appointment of Lieutenant-Governor of Upper Canada. Maitland had served with much distinction in the Peninsula, and had commanded the First Brigade of Guards at Waterloo. In later years he was Governor of the Cape. He took up his appointment in Upper Canada in the midst of an agitation against the Government, which had been excited by Robert Gourlay, a well-meaning but crackbrained Scotchman, who attributed the stagnation of the province to the obstructive character of the Government, and who was taken too seriously—being tried and imprisoned by a course of procedure which was harsh and impolitic as well as of doubtful legality. In March 1822 Sir John Sherbrooke, now living in retirement, who had been consulted by Lord Bathurst as to the advisability of reuniting the two provinces, wrote that ' I could not avoid remarking when I was in Upper Canada, that in many instances a stronger bias prevailed in favour of the American than of the British form of government.'[1] Already, before Maitland's arrival, there had been in Upper Canada friction between the two Houses, and a protest had been made by the elected Assembly against the Executive Council being composed of men who were members of the Upper House. Maitland introduced into the Upper Province a similar classification of the finances to that which was made in Lower Canada, marking off the King's revenues from those which depended on the votes of the Assembly, and he took his advisers from a circle of able and patriotic though not democratic men, such as Beverley Robinson and Dr. Strachan, who were subsequently grouped under the name of the 'Family Compact'. Thus there grew up year by year antagonism between a more or less despotic Government, and the general community, the most loyal part of which, the United Empire Loyalists, had yet brought into their new homes the traditions of self-government, while the least loyal were leavened by American Republicanism. It is true that the feeling was not all dangerous, and the administration was not all reactionary. A law passed in 1820 for 'increasing the representation of the Commons of this province in the House of Assembly' was a wise and liberal measure of electoral reform, and the resentment of the people of Upper Canada against the French Canadian majority in the Quebec Assembly for crippling their customs revenue, which led to an appeal to the Imperial Government and to the passing of

See *Canadian Constitutional Development* (Egerton and Grant), p. 125.

CHAP. III POLITICAL DIFFICULTIES 55

the Canada Trade Act, diluted to some extent their discontent with their own administration. Yet it was under Maitland's régime that the men came to the front who were afterwards prominent in constitutional agitation or in open rebellion, among others Marshall Spring Bidwell, son of an American immigrant, Barnabas Bidwell, who was elected to the Assembly in 1825, and subsequently became Speaker, Dr. Rolph, and William Lyon Mackenzie, the last of whom started in 1824 an anti-Government paper, the *Colonial Advocate*, and in after years played much the same part in Upper Canada that Papineau played in the Lower Province. In 1828 Sir Peregrine Maitland was succeeded as Lieutenant-Governor of Upper Canada by Sir John Colborne, another veteran soldier of the Napoleonic wars, who had commanded the far-famed 52nd regiment at Waterloo.

The Select Committee of the House of Commons which, at Huskisson's instance, had been appointed to inquire into the state of the Civil Government of Canada, reported in July 1828. By this time Huskisson had left the Duke of Wellington's administration, and his place as Secretary of State for War and the Colonies had been taken by Sir George Murray. The report, though a short one, covered much ground, and was not wanting in sympathy with the complaints which had come from Canada. On the vital question in Lower Canada, the control of the public revenues, its terms were as follows :

'Although, from the opinion given by the Law Officers of the Crown, your Committee must conclude that the legal right of appropriating the revenues arising from the Act of 1774 is vested in the Crown, they are prepared to say that the real interests of the provinces would be best promoted by placing the receipt and expenditure of the whole public revenue under the superintendence and control of the House of Assembly.'

The Committee advised that the Governor, the members of the Executive Council, and the judges should be rendered

'independent of the annual votes of the House of Assembly for their respective salaries . . . and if the officers above enumerated are placed on the footing recommended, they are of the opinion that all the revenues of the province (except the territorial and hereditary revenues) should be placed under the control and direction of the Legislative Assembly.'

It was suggested that in both the Canadas a more independent character should be given to the Upper Houses, the Legislative Councils, and 'that the majority of their members should not consist of persons holding offices at the pleasure of the Crown', but the Committee were not prepared under existing circumstances to recommend the union of the two provinces. Various other subjects, including land tenure in Lower Canada, the disposal of the estates which had belonged to the Jesuits, and the Clergy reserves in Upper Canada, were dealt with in the report, and a kind of postscript advised 'strict and instant inquiry' into the allegations which had been made against Lord Dalhousie's administration, and which had been brought up at a late stage of the proceedings.

The Committee had only sat for between two and three months, and their work had been hurried. Their reference to the charges against Lord Dalhousie was unfair to the latter in creating a presumption that the charges were true, and the recommendations made in the report were, in the main, too general to give much guidance towards a detailed and practical solution of the difficulties. Meanwhile Sir James Kempt, reputed to have been a personal friend of Huskisson's, had succeeded Lord Dalhousie, but as Administrator only, not as Governor-General. He was another veteran soldier, had been Quartermaster-General of the Forces in Canada when Sir James Craig was Governor, and had followed Lord Dalhousie as Lieutenant-Governor of Nova Scotia. As Administrator of Canada, he did little more than mark time for two years, when in October 1830 he was succeeded by Lord Aylmer. Kempt's opening speech to the Legislature had been prescribed for him by Sir George Murray, who also addressed to him a dispatch for communication to the Legislature dealing with some of the matters which had come under the purview of the Select Committee. The Secretary of State laid down that, while the Imperial Statutes on the subject continued in existence, the revenues raised under their provisions could not be handed over to the control of the Provincial Legislature, but that after the salaries of the Governor and of the judges had been met from this source, the balance of the funds would not be appropriated until the Assembly had had an opportunity of advising as to the best method in which it could be applied to the public service. The dispatch went on to say that a scheme was in contemplation 'for the permanent settlement of the financial concerns of Lower Canada'. This scheme was embodied in a Bill introduced into the House of Commons in 1829 by Sir George Murray, but not passed into law, whereby it was intended to hand over to the Canadian Assemblies the proceeds arising from the Imperial Act of 1774 in return for a Civil List. Murray's dispatch produced no effect, and the Quebec Assembly still arrogated control of the whole public revenues. The session of 1828-9 in Lower Canada, however, resulted in one important new electoral law, whereby the Eastern Townships were given eight representatives in the Assembly; and in 1830 another grievance of the Townships was temporarily remedied by the establishment in these districts of Land Registry Offices.

Lord Aylmer, a soldier like his predecessors in the Government of Canada, held office, for a few months as Administrator and subsequently as Governor-General, from October 1830 to August 1835. Meanwhile the Reform Ministry came into power in England, and Lord Goderich, afterwards Earl of Ripon, went to the Colonial Office. Both Secretary of State and Governor-General were bent on a policy of conciliation, and by the Secretary of State's instructions Lord Aylmer, in February 1831, offered to the Assembly to hand over to their control all the Crown revenues, other than the casual and territorial revenues, in return for a Civil List for the life of the King. The amount to be handed over was estimated at £38,000 per annum, the casual and territorial revenues at over £7,000 per annum, and the cost of the Civil List at £19,500, which included the salaries of the Governor, the Civil Secretary, the judges, and the law officers. The offer fared no better than previous offers of the kind; the Assembly persisted in their opposition and in their claims; they refused to grant a Civil List, and embodied a statement of their grievances in a petition to the King. The Home Government meanwhile continued its efforts at conciliation. A dispatch, written in February 1831, while Lord Aylmer was sounding the Assembly, intimated that in the event of permanent provision being made for the payment of the judicial salaries, the judges should in future hold office during good behaviour and not at the Royal pleasure, thereby securing their independence both of the Royal authority and of the control of the popular branch of the Legislature. The dispatch at the same time laid down that no judge would in future be nominated as a member either of the Executive or of the Legislative Council, with the single exception of the Chief Justice of Quebec, who would remain a member of the Legislative Council of the Lower Province, in order to advise on permanent legislation, while at the same time abstaining from party politics. In a later dispatch, dated the 7th of July, Lord Goderich answered in detail the complaints which had been embodied in the petition to the King, and gave every indication of meeting to the utmost within reason the wishes of the Assembly. Yet another dispatch, written in November of the same year, dealt with the disposal of Crown lands, and laid down that for free grants open sale in the public market ought to be substituted. Nor did the Imperial Government content itself with friendly dispatches from the Secretary of State and instructions to the Governor to move along the path of constitutional reform. Before the session of 1831 ended in England, a law was passed in September whereby the revenues which the Crown had controlled under the Quebec Revenue Act of 1774 were handed over unconditionally to the Legislatures of the two Canadian Provinces. These were revenues which had hitherto been offered in return for a Civil List, and they were now ceded in the hope that the Legislatures would repay confidence with confidence, and having freely received would freely give. In the case of Upper Canada the confidence was not misplaced, for the Legislature voted a Civil List, but the Quebec Assembly took what was given and made no return. The act was a grave mistake. It deprived the Imperial Government of a lever, which had hitherto been in its hands, for bringing the French Canadian Assembly at Quebec into line with the House of Commons in England, and it left hardly any funds in Canada at the absolute disposal of the Crown other than the casual and territorial revenues. The Duke of Wellington protested against the Bill in the House of Lords, but the protest was unheeded, and, armed with greater powers, the Quebec Assembly became more unmanageable than ever.

The Secretary of State invited from that Assembly, in return for the concessions which had been

POLITICAL DIFFICULTIES

made, a law securing the independence of the judges and providing permanently for their salaries, and also a small Civil List to cover the salaries of the Governor and four of the principal officers. In the session of the Quebec Legislature of 1831-2 a Bill was passed nominally securing the independence of the judges, but leaving their salaries dependent upon annual votes and claiming the right of the Assembly to control the casual and territorial revenues ; while a Civil List amounting only to £5,900 was rejected. The Imperial Government disallowed the Judicial Bill, and intimated that no further application would be made to the Assembly for a Civil List, but that the Civil List charges (other than the salaries of the judges) would be met from the funds which still remained at the disposal of the Crown. Meanwhile an election riot at Montreal in 1832, which resulted in two or three deaths from the firing of the soldiers, embittered political feeling ; the dismissal from office of the able Attorney-General Stuart, who had been specially obnoxious to and virulently assailed by the Assembly, gave to that body an added sense of power and increased their aggressiveness ; the incorporation of the British American Land Company, which was formed to develop the lands in the Eastern Townships, and which came into existence about the year 1833, was resented by the French Canadians as an attempt to anglicize the province ; and year by year added to the intensity of race feeling and to the impossibility of compromise on constitutional lines.

Early in 1833 Lord Goderich was succeeded as

Secretary of State for the Colonies by Mr. Stanley, afterwards Earl of Derby. In June 1834 Stanley was succeeded by Spring Rice. During Sir Robert Peel's short administration in 1834–5 Lord Aberdeen was Secretary of State, and when Lord Melbourne returned to power in 1835, Lord Glenelg went to the Colonial Office. The contumacy of the Quebec Assembly culminated in February 1834 in a kind of Petition of Rights embodied in ninety-two resolutions, which, among other points, demanded an elective Legislative Council, held up the United States as a model for Canada, and called for the impeachment of the Governor-General. In the House of Commons the French Canadians had now found a spokesman violent enough for their purpose in John Arthur Roebuck, member for Bath, who in April 1834 moved for the appointment of a Committee ' to inquire into the means of remedying the evils which exist in the form of government now existing in Upper and Lower Canada '. Stanley met his attack by moving for a Select Committee to inquire into and report how far the recommendations of the Committee of 1828 had been carried out, and to inquire into the other grievances set forward by the Assembly of Lower Canada, the scope of the Committee being confined to the Lower Province. This Committee, which included all the members of the earlier 1828 Committee who still had seats in the House of Commons, reported at the beginning of July, but its report was confined to a few lines stating that the Home Government had shown the greatest anxiety to carry out the recommendations made by the Committee of 1828, that the efforts had been in part successful, but in part had failed owing to the differences between the two Houses of the Legislature, and between the Assembly and the Imperial Government, and that the committee thought it unadvisable to express any opinion on the points at issue, or to lay the evidence which they had taken before the House, being persuaded 'that the practical measures for the future administration of Lower Canada may best be left to the mature consideration of the Government responsible for their adoption and execution'. This report left matters where they were: possibly the members of the Committee were unwilling to exhibit divergent views, or they were minded to keep the House of Commons outside the controversy between the Imperial Government and the Quebec Assembly.

In Lower Canada matters went from bad to worse. A new general election, held in the autumn of 1834, resulted in further strengthening Papineau's following, and the British element in Lower Canada, now thoroughly alarmed, formed constitutional associations at Quebec and Montreal. The withholding of supplies had meant withholding of the salaries of the public officials, and to relieve the position, the Secretary of State, Spring Rice, authorized in September 1834 an advance of £31,000 from the military chest. This action of the Home Government was made a fresh grievance on the part of the French Canadian majority, when the new Parliament met in 1835, for they regarded it, to quote their own words, as 'destroying the wholesome and constitutional influence which the people ought to have through their representatives over every branch of the Executive Government'. The Legislature met on the 21st of February 1835, and was prorogued on the 18th of March, as the Assembly declined to transact any further business. In April, Lord Aylmer published a dispatch from Lord Aberdeen in which it was stated that the Government—Sir Robert Peel's Ministry—had decided to send out a Royal Commissioner to Lower Canada. It had been at first intended to send Manners Sutton, Viscount Canterbury, who had been Speaker of the House of Commons, and when he declined, the second Lord Amherst was offered and accepted the appointment; but the change of Ministry, which took place before he could leave England, resulted in different arrangements for the mission and a different personnel. It is not quite clear what were contemplated by Sir Robert Peel and Lord Aberdeen to have been the relations between Lord Amherst, had he gone out, and Lord Aylmer; but apparently Lord Amherst was, like Lord Durham at a later date, designated both as High Commissioner for the special purpose of investigating the grievances of which the Quebec Assembly had so abundantly complained, and also as Governor, so that Lord Aylmer would have been superseded for the time being, but not necessarily recalled. When Lord Melbourne returned to office and Lord Glenelg became Colonial Secretary, Lord Aylmer was told, though in flattering terms, that his administration must be considered to be terminated, and it was decided to send out three Royal Com-

POLITICAL DIFFICULTIES

missioners, the Chairman of the Commission being also appointed Governor-in-Chief of the two Canadas and of the other British North American provinces, with the exception of Newfoundland. The man selected for the post was an Irish peer, the Earl of Gosford, who was the first civilian Governor of Canada since it became a British possession, and his colleagues as Commissioners were Sir George Gipps, afterwards Governor of New South Wales, and Sir Charles Grey, a retired Indian judge. Gipps was an exponent of Whig views, as they were then understood. Grey was an exponent of Tory principles, and as such was credited with being a nominee of King William the Fourth. The Secretary to the Commission was T. F. Elliot, a member of the Colonial Office, afterwards Assistant Under-Secretary of State for the Colonies. The Commissioners reached Quebec on the 23rd of August 1835, and on the 17th of September Lord Aylmer left for England, regarded by the British population of Canada as sacrificed to the clamour of a disloyal majority.

What were in rough outline the main demands of the majority at this date, and what was the tenor of Lord Glenelg's instructions to the Commissioners? The Quebec Assembly had many grievances real or alleged, but the points on which they specially laid stress were the following. In the first place, they demanded unconditional control of all the public revenues of every kind. In the second place, they demanded an elective Legislative Council. In the third place, they attacked the composition of the Executive Council. In the fourth place, they complained of the way in which the patronage of the Crown had been exercised in the matter of appointments. Fifthly, they demanded the repeal of the Imperial statutes dealing with the tenure of land in Lower Canada; and sixthly, in connexion with the disposal of waste lands, they demanded that the charter given to the British American Land Company should be cancelled. They had not hitherto in so many words demanded that the Executive Council should be responsible to the Legislature, but the essence of their demands was to obtain full control of all the Executive offices by securing entire command of all the means of paying them; and their hostility to the British American Land Company was dictated not only by seeing in it an agency for increasing the proportion of the British population of the province, but also by appreciating that the payments made by the Company to the Crown added to the revenues which were withheld from the elected Assembly.

Lord Glenelg's instructions were embodied in terms indicating the utmost desire of the Home Government to meet, as far as possible, the wishes of the Assembly; but he laid down, as necessary preliminaries to handing over all the remaining Crown revenues to popular control, that provision should be made for securing the independence of the judges, that an adequate Civil List should be granted, that the management of the waste lands of the province, as opposed to the receipts from those lands, should remain with the Crown, and that existing pensions of retired public officers should be continued. He authorized inquiry into the constitution of the Legislative Council, but pointed out, without in so many words vetoing the proposal, that the introduction of the elective principle in connexion with that Council would be a constitutional change of the gravest and most vital kind. He instructed the Commissioners to consider any amendment which would increase the efficiency of the Executive Council; to investigate the tenures of land in the province, including the seigniorial rights claimed by the Sulpicians in and around Montreal; and to advise whether or not any further charters should be granted by the Crown, such as had been given to the British American Land Company. He also directed attention to the state of education in Lower Canada, and to the possibility of so adjusting the financial relations between the two Canadian provinces as to admit of the repeal of the Canada Trade Act.

Cotemporaneously with the instructions to the Commissioners, Lord Glenelg addressed a dispatch to Lord Gosford, not as Chief Commissioner but as Governor, in which he dealt with such complaints of the Assembly as needed no investigation, but could be dealt with at once by the executive authority of the Governor. Prominent among these was the alleged abuse of patronage, as to which the Secretary of State reiterated and enlarged previous instructions. It is worth while to quote Lord Glenelg's own words on this subject, as the allegation that French Canadians had been unduly excluded ' not only from the larger number, but from all the more lucrative and honourable of the public employments in their native country', was, if true, the most reasonable and substantial of the grievances. Adopting 'in their fullest extent' instructions, which he said had been given by Lord Goderich, to exercise 'the utmost impartiality in the distribution of public offices in Lower Canada, without reference to national or political distinctions, or to any consideration, except that of superior capacity and fitness for the trust', Lord Glenelg went on, somewhat inconsistently, to suggest that modified preference might be given to French Canadians.

'Your Lordship will remember that between persons of equal or not very dissimilar pretensions, it may be fit that the choice should be made in such a manner as in some degree to satisfy the claims which the French inhabitants may reasonably urge to be placed in the enjoyment of an equal share of the Royal favour. There are occasions also on which the increased satisfaction of the public at large with an appointment, might amply atone for some inferiority in the qualifications of the persons selected.'[1]

He then laid down that the patronage of the Governor in making appointments should be subject to the approval of the Secretary of State, and that the general rule should be, as it had been, to appoint residents in Lower Canada. In other points of detail, which need not be specified, Lord Glenelg enjoined on the outgoing Governor consonance with the wishes of the Assembly. Assuredly, never was the Home Government more anxious to work in harmony with public feeling in a colony

[1] See House of Commons Paper, No. 113, March 1836, pp. 47-8.

than was the British Government in its relations to Lower Canada in the year 1835.

Lord Gosford called the Quebec Legislature together on the 27th of October 1835. In his opening speech he gave, as desired by Lord Glenelg, the substance of his own instructions and of those to the Royal Commissioners; and intimating that one object of the coming inquiry was to hand over, on such conditions as should be carefully matured, the whole of the revenues of Lower Canada to the control of the elected representatives, he invited the Assembly to make good the arrears of salary due to the public officers and to continue to provide for their pay while the inquiry was taking its course. The Session dragged on until, in February 1836, the Assembly learnt from a letter written to Papineau, Speaker of the Assembly of the Lower Province, by Marshall Bidwell, Speaker of the Assembly of Upper Canada, that Sir Francis Bond Head, the new Lieutenant-Governor of Upper Canada, had communicated to the Legislature of that Province verbatim extracts of the Instructions to the Commissioners. These were alleged to be at variance with the substance of the instructions as contained in Lord Gosford's opening speech, and, following Papineau's lead, the Assembly voted supplies for six months only and drew up a fresh address of grievances to the King. The Supply Bill was thrown out by the Legislative Council as not being in accordance with what the Government had requested, and for a fourth year in succession Lower Canada was left without legal supplies to carry on the public service. The

Legislature was prorogued on the 21st of March 1836. Before the prorogation took place, Papineau had written to Bidwell a violent letter, attacking the Home Government, and inviting the co-operation of the Assembly of Upper Canada in the struggle in which Lower Canada was engaged. Meanwhile Lord Gosford and the other two Commissioners continued an inquiry which was already doomed to failure. They were not at one, and their reports were accompanied by qualifying minutes and counter minutes by Sir Charles Grey and Sir George Gipps. The first report, dated the 30th of January 1836, dealt with the proposed Civil List and the conditions upon which the Crown revenues should be ceded to the Assembly, the recommendations being made on the assumption that they would not be carried into effect until the Legislature had made good the outstanding arrears of salary to the public servants. A second report, dated the 12th of March, dealt with the position which had arisen owing to the Assembly having shelved the question of these arrears until their demands should have been complied with, and noted that those demands now included making the Executive Council responsible to the Legislature. The Commissioners came to the conclusion that, under the circumstances, the best course to adopt was to repeal the Imperial Act of 1831 by which the taxes levied under the Quebec Revenue Act of 1774 had been handed over to the Provincial Legislature. A third report at the beginning of May dealt with reform of the Executive Council, again negativing the responsibility of that Council to the Legislature. A fourth report in June contradicted statements made with regard to the Commission by Mr. Roebuck in a pamphlet distributed to members of the House of Commons. A fifth report in October dealt with the seigniorial rights of the Seminary of St. Sulpice at Montreal; and a sixth report in November, a general report, dealt with the Legislative Council, tenures of land, and other matters indicated in the instructions. Sir Charles Grey left for England shortly afterwards, Sir George Gipps and Mr. Elliot followed in the spring of 1837, and Lord Gosford was left to face alone what had long been an impossible position.

The Commissioners, in recommending the repeal of the Act of 1831, and the resumption by the Imperial Government of control of the revenues which had been handed over to the Assembly, had not taken sufficient account of the effect which such a strong measure might have produced on public opinion in the other British North American provinces. There was discontent in Upper Canada and New Brunswick, and there was danger lest they should make common cause with Lower Canada. This danger was present to Lord Glenelg and his colleagues. Accordingly they rejected the proposal, and in a dispatch of the 7th of June, which answered the last Address from the Quebec Assembly to the King, Lord Glenelg directed Lord Gosford to lay the whole of the Instructions to the Commissioners before the Assembly, in order to clear away the misapprehension which was supposed to have arisen, and again to invite payment of the arrears of salaries and provision of adequate supplies. Lord Gosford did as he was instructed. He summoned the Legislature on the 22nd of September 1836, laid before them copies of the Instructions, and communicated Lord Glenelg's dispatch as an answer to the address from the Assembly to the King. The only result was that the Assembly still refused to comply with the Secretary of State's wishes, still persisted in their demands, especially in that for an elected Legislative Council, that they referred to existing conditions as a 'system of metropolitan ascendancy and colonial degradation', and that the Legislature was prorogued on the 4th of October without having transacted any business or passed any laws.

It was now time for the Imperial Parliament to interfere, and the ministry was encouraged in taking action by the fact that public feeling in Upper Canada and in New Brunswick had undergone a change, which seemed to indicate that the attitude of the Assembly at Quebec would no longer find much support in those provinces. The Session opened in England on the 31st of January 1837; the King's Speech directed the special attention of Parliament to the state of affairs in Lower Canada; the Reports of the Commissioners were laid before both Houses; and on the 6th of March Lord John Russell moved ten Resolutions in the House of Commons. The Resolutions provided for making good the outstanding arrears of pay, by empowering the Governor-General to apply to that purpose the revenues in the hands of the Receiver-General of the province; they negatived

POLITICAL DIFFICULTIES

the demand for an elective Legislative Council, for the introduction of the principle of responsibility to the Legislature into the Executive Council, and for the cancellation of the charter of the British American Land Company; they promised repeal of the tenures Acts, as soon as a law adequate for the purpose should have been passed by the provincial Legislature; they proposed to hand over to the Legislature the net proceeds of the remaining Crown revenues, as soon as a Civil List should have been voted covering the judicial expenditure and the salaries of the principal civil officers; and they authorized the Legislatures of the two Canadian provinces to make provision for adjusting the trade disputes between the two provinces. The Resolutions did not pass without debate. In addition to Roebuck, various members, such as Hume, O'Connell, and Sir William Molesworth, keenly opposed the Government; while in Canada, so cool and experienced a judge of local conditions as Sir John Colborne, who was at the time at Quebec in command of the troops, wrote of the eighth Resolution, whereby provincial funds were to be appropriated to the payment of arrears: 'The eighth resolution, of seizing money which does not belong to us, must produce further coercion on the part of Ministers.'[1] By the middle of May, however, all the Resolutions had been carried through both Houses of Parliament, and steps were taken to bring in a Bill to give to them the force of law.

On the 22nd of May Lord Glenelg wrote to Lord

[1] Letter dated Quebec, June 5, 1837 (*Life of Lord Seaton*, 1903, p. 277).

Gosford, directing him to call the Legislature together again, and once more to invite the Assembly to make good the arrears and to vote supplies, so as to render it unnecessary to have recourse to the powers which the Imperial Parliament was about to embody in the form of a law. Shortly afterwards the King died, and, unwilling that the reign of Queen Victoria should open with a measure of coercion, the Government, at the beginning of July, obtained a vote of credit to meet the immediate requirements of the administration in Lower Canada and remitted legislation to a new Parliament. When Lord John Russell's Resolutions became known in Lower Canada, they caused much excitement: indignation meetings were held by the partisans of the Assembly, Dr. Wolfred Nelson, who lived on the Richelieu river, taking a prominent part in the agitation, and Papineau being extolled as the Canadian counterpart of O'Connell. Lord Gosford, in accordance with his instructions, called together the Quebec Legislature on the 18th of August, but the Assembly replied to his opening speech by a protest against the Royal Commissioners and the Home Government, and by demanding that the Resolutions passed by the two Houses of Parliament should be rescinded. The Governor, therefore, on the 26th of August, prorogued the Legislature, and with the prorogation, as events proved, came the end of the Constitution which had been framed for Lower Canada under the Act of 1791.

It is now time to give an outline of what had been taking place in the other provinces of British

POLITICAL DIFFICULTIES

North America. Sir John Colborne became Lieutenant-Governor of Upper Canada in November 1828. The Report of the Select Committee of the House of Commons upon the Civil Government of Canada, which had been made in the previous July, together with the evidence which had been taken by the Committee, pointed to the conclusion that the two main grievances in this province were the want of independence in the Legislative Council, which was little more than a mouthpiece of the Government, or rather of the dominant bureaucracy, and the favoured position given to the Church of England, especially in the matter of the Clergy Reserves. Colborne was a man of kindly sympathies and no narrow views. He was keenly interested in education, and was the founder of the Upper Canada College. But he was surrounded by the men who formed the so-called 'Family Compact', and whose influence, used against the more democratic section of the community, was strong because it was largely the outcome of real ability and high character. Shortly before his arrival a general election had taken place, and the newly-elected Assembly contained a progressive majority. Marshall Bidwell was the Speaker, William Lyon Mackenzie was one of the members, and in the course of the year 1829 Robert Baldwin was elected to fill a seat which had been vacated by the appointment of the Attorney-General, Beverley Robinson, to be Chief Justice of Upper Canada. Robinson's successor, as Attorney-General, Boulton by name, was a man of far inferior type; domineering and aggressive, he provoked, instead of conciliating, opposition to the Government. The death of King George IV, in June 1830, necessitated a new election, and this time the partisans of the Government secured a substantial majority in the Assembly. The Imperial Act of 1831, which handed over to the Legislature the proceeds of the taxes levied under the Quebec Revenue Act of 1774, was met by the grant of a Civil List to the amount of £6,500 per annum, and thus one great element of friction with the Imperial Government was eliminated. But the Government party in the Assembly had a most unwise leader in Boulton, and on the other side Mackenzie made himself impossible. The violence with which the latter in speech and writing attacked his political opponents was met by proceedings which were equally indefensible. He was repeatedly expelled from the Assembly, and repeatedly re-elected. He carried his grievances to England and found a champion in Joseph Hume, while the obvious unfairness and unwisdom of the treatment to which he had been subjected led to his chief opponent, Boulton, being dismissed from the appointment of Attorney-General by the Secretary of State.

In 1834 the town of York was incorporated as the city of Toronto, and Mackenzie became the first mayor. Towards the end of the year there was a general election for the provincial Parliament, and the Reform party once more gained the upper hand in the Assembly. Mackenzie had somewhat lost in popular estimation by publishing a letter from Joseph Hume, in which the latter had

CHAP. III   POLITICAL DIFFICULTIES   77

expressed himself to the effect that a crisis was coming in Canada ' which will terminate in independence and freedom from the baneful domination of the mother country ', and he gravitated away from the more moderate reformers and towards making common cause with Papineau in the Lower Province. Still he was the mouthpiece of the Reform party in the new Parliament of Upper Canada, and it was upon his motion that a select committee on grievances was appointed, of which he was chairman, and ' by which ', to quote Lord Glenelg's words, ' a report was made impugning the administration of affairs in every department of the public service, and calling for remedial measures of such magnitude and variety as apparently to embrace every conceivable topic of complaint.' [1] This Report, made in April 1835, and widely distributed in England, specified the almost unlimited patronage of the Crown and the abuse of that patronage as the chief sources of colonial discontent, and it demanded responsible government and an elected Legislative Council. Lord Glenelg dealt with it at length in December 1835 in his instructions to Colborne's successor, Sir Francis Bond Head; and in the dispatch which embodied these instructions, he enclosed extracts from his previous instructions to Lord Gosford and his colleagues, the publication of which by Sir Francis Head caused, as already told, a ferment in the Quebec Assembly.

When the grievances report was made public,

[1] See Lord Glenelg's Instructions to Sir F. Bond Head, December 5, 1835, House of Commons Paper, No. 113, March 1836, p. 55.

Colborne had been for more than six years Lieutenant-Governor of Upper Canada. To the Whig Government in England, anxious to conciliate public feeling in the Canadas, it seemed advisable to make a change, and Colborne himself realized that he was out of harmony with his employers. While Lord Glenelg wrote to recall him, he in turn wrote resigning his appointment, and in the middle of winter, on the 23rd of January 1836, a week after the Parliamentary Session in Upper Canada had been opened, his successor, Sir Francis Bond Head, arrived at Toronto, no intimation of his coming having been received in Upper Canada until he had already reached New York. Head was sworn in on the 25th of January, and on the following day Colborne left for Montreal on his way to England. He stayed at Montreal till the middle of May, then went to New York to embark for home, and while at New York was offered by Lord Glenelg the appointment of Commander-in-Chief of the Forces in both Canadas. He accepted it and went back to Montreal.

One of Colborne's last acts, as Lieutenant-Governor of Upper Canada, was to call into operation the sections of the Constitutional Act of 1791, which authorized the Governor or Lieutenant-Governor in either of the Canadas, with the advice of the Executive Council, to constitute and endow Church of England rectories. He signed documents which endowed with lands forty-four rectories, and in doing so he stirred up the dangerous Clergy Reserves question, aroused the wrath of the Scotch Church, the Wesleyans, and others, and was accused of hurriedly perpetrating a job for the Church of England before he was superseded, though, as a matter of fact, he was only taking the last step in carrying out views which had been expressed by Lord Goderich when Secretary of State in 1832. He gave offence, too, in Lower Canada by a reference to the dissensions in that province which he made when opening the Parliamentary Session at Toronto on the 14th of January 1836, just before Head's arrival. It seemed, therefore, as though an estimable but somewhat reactionary Governor was being replaced by a man of broader outlook and more enlightened views. The sequel was to prove that the new-comer was dangerous and flighty in the extreme, and that when a crisis came Colborne was the man to meet it.

Sir Francis Bond Head had been a soldier, a traveller, a writer, and a Poor Law Commissioner, before he was appointed Lieutenant-Governor of Upper Canada, but he had had no previous experience of colonial administration. His two years' career as Lieutenant-Governor was that of a self-willed though well-meaning eccentric, not amenable either to an Assembly or to a Secretary of State. He began by publishing his instructions *in extenso*, instead of communicating their substance to the House of Assembly. In order to bring new blood into the Executive Council, he induced Robert Baldwin and Rolph, leaders of Reform, to take seats upon it, together with the Receiver-General of the province; but Baldwin's views of what an Executive Councillor should be did not square with those of the Lieutenant-Governor, who had no intention of giving to the Council any real power or responsibility, and the result was that in three weeks' time the whole Council resigned. Head then procured a new Council, came into collision with the Assembly, dissolved the Legislature, and, managing to present the issue to the people as being in effect whether or not Upper Canada should remain a loyal province of the British Crown, he secured at the general election of June 1836 an overwhelming majority of supporters in the New Assembly. Bidwell, Mackenzie, Lount, among others, lost their seats, and, resenting the Government influence which had been used against them, the more violent members of the Reform party turned their minds towards revolution. The new Parliament met in November 1836, and sat till the following March, passing among many other measures a much criticized law that the Legislature should not be dissolved upon the sovereign's death, which was, in other words, an Act for prolonging its own existence. It met again in June 1837 for a short and special session, to deal with a financial crisis caused by commercial depression in the United States; and the next session, the last which Sir Francis Head opened, began at the end of December 1837, after the close of the abortive rising in Upper Canada, and lasted till the 6th of March 1838. In 1836 Head had dismissed from office a district judge of the name of Ridout, on the alleged ground that he had been an opponent and critic of the Government. In the following year he passed over Bidwell for a judgeship in the Court of Queen's Bench. Lord Glenelg, on learning Ridout's side of the case, directed that he should

POLITICAL DIFFICULTIES

be reinstated; and he also gave instructions that Bidwell should be offered the next vacant judgeship. Head point blank refused either to reinstate Ridout or to offer a judgeship to Bidwell, and in September 1837 tendered his own resignation. Lord Glenelg accepted the resignation in a dispatch written towards the end of November and received in January 1838, Mackenzie's rising having taken place in the meantime; on the 23rd of March the new Lieutenant-Governor, Sir George Arthur, arrived at Toronto; and Head returned to England to continue unavailing protests against men and events, obstinate and wrongheaded, but none the less the spokesman in exaggerated fashion of the sentiments held by the Conservative section of the community of Upper Canada.

The causes which produced friction and led to constitutional changes in Lower and Upper Canada, were at work also in the Maritime Provinces. Nova Scotia was the first of the present Canadian provinces to be given representative institutions, for its House of Assembly dates from 1758, and in later days perhaps the most cogent of all the Canadian advocates of responsible government was the Nova Scotian, Joseph Howe, who first entered the House of Assembly in that Province in 1836. Both in Nova Scotia and in New Brunswick, which, as the result of Loyalist immigration from the United States, had been created a separate province in 1784, the same persons constituted both the Executive Council and the Upper House of the Legislature, viz. the Legislative Council. At the end of 1830, Lord Goderich, then Secretary of State for the

Colonies, who was dealing with the Report on the Government of Canada made by the House of Commons Committee of 1828, wrote to the Lieutenant-Governors of Nova Scotia and New Brunswick, suggesting the desirability of giving a more independent character to the Councils by introducing a larger number of unofficial members and excluding the puisne judges; and in May 1832 he wrote to Sir Archibald Campbell, Lieutenant-Governor of New Brunswick, proposing that the Executive and Legislative Councils should no longer consist of the same members; that the Executive Council should be small in number, 'including one or two influential members of each branch of the Legislature;'[1] that the number of the Legislative Council should be increased, and that its members should cease to be necessarily members of the Executive or Privy Council.

Sir Archibald Campbell agreed that 'the inconsistency of the same members forming the Privy and Legislative Councils as a body, is an anomaly that never ought to have existed, and the sooner that it is abolished the better'. Accordingly, by Royal Commission to the Governor-General dated the 20th of November 1832, New Brunswick was endowed with two distinct and separate Councils, one Executive and one Legislative. Between three and four years later, in 1836, two delegates from the New Brunswick House of Assembly came to London to support an Address to the King from that body, one of them being the reform leader,

[1] See the House of Commons Paper, Nova Scotia, &c., No. 579, August, 1839, pp. 49–50.

Lemuel Wilmot. New Brunswick asked for no more than Lord Glenelg had already embodied in his instructions to Lord Gosford and Sir Francis Head; there was no demand for an Executive Council responsible to the people, nor for an elected Legislative Council, though improvements were suggested in the composition of either Council. The control of all the Crown revenues in return for a Civil List, and different management of the Crown lands, were asked for and readily conceded; the terms of a Civil List Bill to be passed by the provincial Legislature were amicably settled; and the delegates went back, gratefully acknowledging the liberal and enlightened policy of the Imperial Government and the personal attention which Lord Glenelg had given to their representations. There was a slight hitch later on, because the new policy was distasteful to Sir Archibald Campbell, and either on principle or through misunderstanding he resigned in 1837, instead of passing the Civil List Bill; but his successor, Sir John Harvey, as tactful a Governor as he had shown himself to be a good fighter in the war of 1812, speedily carried into effect the reforms which had been contemplated, and paved the way for responsible government, which came into being about ten years later.

Nova Scotia was more conservative than New Brunswick. It was closely in touch with England, the port of Halifax being open all the year round; and soldiers and sailors, active or retired, formed a strong element in the community. Accordingly, while in New Brunswick the Executive was, in 1832, separated from the Legislative Council, the two continued in Nova Scotia to be identical down to the year 1837. In that year the Assembly forwarded an Address to the King, claiming control of the casual and territorial revenues, and asking His Majesty 'to grant us an elective Legislative Council; or to separate the Executive from the Legislative Council, providing for a just representation of all the great interests of the province in both; and by the introduction into the former of some members of the popular branch, and otherwise securing responsibility to the Commons, confer upon the people of this province what they value above all other possessions, the blessings of the British Constitution'.[1] Lord Glenelg made similar concessions in the case of the constitution of Nova Scotia, as had been made in regard to the other North American provinces, but it is noteworthy that he expressed great doubt as to the advisability of separating the Executive from the Legislative Council. 'The separation of this body into two distinct chambers,' he wrote in April 1837, 'the one Legislative and the other Executive, is an experiment which was first tried in the Canadas by the Act of 1791, and repeated in New Brunswick in the year 1832. So far as I have been able to judge, the result of this innovation has not been such as to exclude very serious doubts respecting its real usefulness.'[2] In reference to the suggestion that the Executive officers should be under popular control, he wrote that 'Her Majesty's Govern-

---

[1] House of Commons Paper, as above, p. 17.
[2] Ibid., pp. 11, 12. The third quotation, from a dispatch of July 6, 1837, is not included in the extracts given in this Blue Book.

ment must oppose a respectful but, at the same time, a firm declaration that it is inconsistent with a due advertence to the essential distinctions between a metropolitan and a colonial Government, and is therefore inadmissible.'

The separation of the Executive from the Legislative Council was formally completed by means of the Commission which appointed Lord Durham to be Governor of Nova Scotia, and which was dated the 6th of February 1838; and in his Report Lord Durham described the political condition of Nova Scotia as one in which, though there were various questions at issue, there was no strong antagonism between the Government and the people. Nova Scotia had, as a rule, been fortunate in her Lieutenant-Governors. More than one had, like Lord Dalhousie, gone on to be Governor-General of Canada. Sir Peregrine Maitland, who had been transferred from Upper Canada to Nova Scotia in 1828, had been mainly an absentee; but his successor in 1834, Sir Colin Campbell, a soldier of high repute, at the time when Lord Durham wrote, commanded public confidence and esteem, though a little later he was found too conservative for Joseph Howe and the partisans of responsible government.

In March 1834 the House of Assembly of Prince Edward Island asked that that colony might be placed upon an equal footing with the sister province of New Brunswick, by being given a Legislative Council distinct from the Executive Council, but the request was refused by the Secretary of State, Spring Rice. In May 1837 Lord Glenelg invited Sir Charles Fitzroy, who was then going out to Prince Edward Island as Lieutenant-Governor, to look into the composition of the Legislative Council; and in March 1838 Fitzroy enclosed an Address from the House of Assembly, again asking that the Executive and Legislative Councils might be separated from each other, in accordance with the change which had taken place in Nova Scotia. Fitzroy supported the proposal and suggested an Executive Council of nine members, three of whom should be selected from the House of Assembly. Lord Glenelg then sanctioned the separation of the Councils. In Prince Edward Island, however, as will be gathered from Lord Durham's Report, the chief causes of complaint were connected more with the land than with the constitution, for in this island the evils arising out of absentee ownership were most acutely felt.

The conditions of Newfoundland had always been wholly dissimilar to those of the mainland provinces of British North America, and its story had run in a different channel, but in Newfoundland, too, constitutional difficulties had arisen, and accordingly it was included within the scope of Lord Durham's Commission. By the year 1832 the system had broken down, 'the fundamental principle of which was to prevent the Colonization of the island, and to render this kingdom the domicile of all persons engaged in the Newfoundland fisheries',[1] and in that year the island was given a representative Assembly, created not by Act of Parliament but by the King's Commission

---

[1] Lord Goderich to Governor Sir T. Cochrane, July 27, 1832 (House of Commons Paper, as above, p. 82).

to the Governor and by the Royal Instructions. There was also a Council which was in effect, though not in name, at once a Legislative Council and an Executive Council. Foreseeing the likelihood of friction between the Council and the Assembly, Lord Goderich, the Secretary of State who called the constitution into existence, suggested that an arrangement might be made and embodied in a local Act, 'which should consolidate the Council and the Assembly into a single House, in which the representatives of the people would be met by the official servants of the Crown.'[1] The proposal met with general disapprobation in the colony, and was not carried into effect; and almost immediately the two houses came to loggerheads, the Council being the aggressor by throwing out a revenue Bill. This was in the first session of the new Legislature in the spring of 1833, and matters were not improved when later in the same year Boulton, who had proved so cantankerous as Attorney-General of Upper Canada, was consoled for losing that appointment by being made Chief Justice of Newfoundland. In that capacity he presided over the Council and arrogated to himself the title of Speaker, until his pretensions and those which he made on behalf of the Council were, in October 1834, somewhat summarily disallowed by Spring Rice, then Secretary of State. The disputes between the two Houses went on. In 1837 an Appropriation Bill was thrown out by the Council, whose action was in February 1838 disapproved by Lord Glenelg. Religious animosity had been

[1] House of Commons Paper, as above, p. 85.

added to the political squabble, the Irish Roman Catholics being specially bitter against Boulton, who was relieved of his office in 1838. Matters came to such a pass that, under an Imperial act of 1842, the existing Legislature was ended, and replaced by a single chamber, as had been suggested by Lord Goderich. Another Imperial act of 1847 restored the old constitution; and, finally, in 1855 responsible government came into being.

It has been seen that the Quebec Legislature was prorogued by Lord Gosford on the 26th of August 1837. The news of the death of King William IV and of the accession of Queen Victoria had reached Canada at the end of July, but had not affected the political situation or softened party feeling. Montreal was Papineau's birthplace and home, and he was one of the parliamentary representatives of the city. Accordingly, both in 1837 and later, in 1838, disloyalty was more aggressive and more pronounced in the district of Montreal than lower down the river. In the town itself there was a strong element of loyal citizens, but on the other side of the St. Lawrence, in the counties along the line of the Richelieu river, the proximity of the American frontier gave encouragement to disaffection; and behind the island of Montreal, in the county of the Two Mountains on the north bank of the Ottawa river, sedition and lawlessness were rife.

The rising, such as it was, was mainly a French Canadian movement, though it was a nondescript kind of disturbance. The Roman Catholic Church, with rare exceptions, exercised its authority on the side of law and order, and there were many French Canadian loyalists, magistrates, and others; while on the other hand, among the leaders of the so-called 'Patriots', British names were as prominent as French. There were the brothers Nelson, for instance, and Thomas Storrow Brown, and no paper attacked the Government with greater violence than the English *Vindicator*, edited at Montreal by Dr. O'Callaghan. But, naturally, the followers of Papineau were in the main French Canadians, whereas the overwhelming majority of the British, including the Irish, population were staunch and determined for the Government. The would-be rebellion had no chance. The towns were on the whole not revolutionary, and the seditious districts had neighbours to hold them in check. The Glengarry Highlanders, in Upper Canada, but on the border line of the two provinces, Roman Catholics of traditional and long-tried loyalty, publicly announced their intention to uphold the Government, and the English-speaking Eastern Townships were strongly opposed to Papineau and his friends. Most of all, though the Governor-in-Chief Lord Gosford was, it would seem, reputed to be somewhat weak and temporizing, the man in whose hands was the ultimate issue, the commander of the troops, was pre-eminently cool and strong. Sir John Colborne left nothing to chance, he prepared for the crisis and practically forestalled it. In the latter part of July he went up from Quebec to Sorel at the mouth of the Richelieu river, to be near the probable scene of disturbance; and on the 9th of November, after a riot had taken place in Montreal, he moved into that city. In July, at Lord Gosford's instance, a regiment was brought up from Halifax to Quebec; and at the end of October, with the cordial consent of Sir Francis Bond Head, the 24th regiment was brought down from Toronto to Montreal, where it arrived on the 13th of November. When the trouble came, the military forces, regulars supplemented by volunteers, were mainly concentrated at Montreal; but preparations had also been made at Quebec, and towards the end of the year more regiments came in overland from Nova Scotia and New Brunswick, recalling the winter marches of the war of 1812.

For the winter, when the navigation of the St. Lawrence was closed, was the dangerous time, and as the winter drew on, matters came to something like a climax. Dr. Wolfred Nelson was, as not a few men have been, in public a violent politician, in private a kindly humane man. Ten years previously, at a general election, he had opposed and defeated James Stuart, then Attorney-General, for the borough of Sorel or William Henry, his brother Robert Nelson being at the same election returned as Papineau's colleague for one of the wards of Montreal. He lived and practised his profession at St. Denis on the Richelieu river, and on the 23rd of October 1837 he presided at a public meeting at St. Charles near to his home, on which occasion Papineau was present, a cap of liberty was hoisted, and the representatives of the six confederated counties, as they styled themselves, being the counties bordering on the

Richelieu, passed a series of lengthy resolutions, the most practical of which was an invitation to the soldiers to desert their colours and emigrate to the United States. One of the resolutions expressed approval of the political organization in Montreal entitled the ' Fils de Liberté ', of whom Christie contemptuously remarks that they were ' chiefly idle boys, stripling Attornies, and merchants' clerks '.[1] On the 6th of November the Sons of Liberty, led by Storrow Brown, who was reputed to have been of American birth and who was at the time a dealer in hardware at Montreal, came into collision with the members of a loyalist association, known as the Doric club. In the end the Sons of Liberty fared badly, the office of the *Vindicator* was gutted and sacked, the Riot Act was read, and troops patrolled the streets. After this outbreak Colborne took up his quarters at Montreal. By this time a kind of reign of terror had come into being in the district of Montreal outside the city itself, and especially in the counties on the southern side of the St. Lawrence. Magistrates were intimidated and called upon to resign, and the lives and property of the loyalists were no longer safe. In consequence, on the 16th of November, warrants were issued for the arrest of the leaders of sedition, including Papineau himself, who, however, fled fom Montreal and joined Dr. Wolfred Nelson at St. Denis. A small party of soldiers was, on the evening of the 16th, sent to St. John's on the Richelieu, to arrest two French Canadians named Demaray and Davignon. The

---

[1] Christie, vol. iv, p. 395.

arrest was effected, but as the prisoners were being taken to Montreal, their guard was fired upon, and they were rescued. Colborne immediately sent more troops into the district. One body, under Colonel Wetherall, went straight across the river to the fort at Chambly; a second body, under Colonel Gore, was taken down the St. Lawrence, and landed at Sorel at the mouth of the Richelieu. Gore was to march up the Richelieu, and Wetherall down it, so as to disperse armed insurgents who were understood to have gathered at St. Denis under Dr. Wolfred Nelson and at St. Charles under Storrow Brown, St. Denis being about eighteen miles up the Richelieu from Sorel, and St. Charles six or seven miles further up the river. Gore started from Sorel with some 250 men on the night of the 22nd of November, and marching all night through sleet and rain did not reach St. Denis till nearly 10 o'clock on the following morning. Here he found Dr. Nelson and his followers prepared for defence, having converted a large stone house into a fort. He attacked with his tired troops, but was not strong enough to carry the position; and after some hours' fighting he was obliged to retreat, with the loss of six men killed and ten wounded and of the one field piece which he had taken with him. He did not reach Sorel again till the afternoon of the 24th. Wetherall, with a rather larger force than Gore's, left Chambly at precisely the same time to march on St. Charles and eventually join Gore. In the same bad weather he marched through the night of the 22nd and the forenoon of the 23rd, and eventually, being brought

POLITICAL DIFFICULTIES

to a stand by a broken bridge some few miles short of St. Charles, he encamped for the night, rested his troops, received reinforcements on the following day, the 24th, and did not move until the 25th. Some entrenchments had been thrown up at St. Charles, and they were defended by a considerable number of insurgents, of whom Storrow Brown had taken command. Wetherall summoned the people to disperse, and when they resisted he carried the position, after about an hour's fighting, not without loss, and effectually broke up all resistance, returning to Montreal on the 29th of November. This was practically the end of the rising in the Richelieu counties, although towards the end of the first week of December there was a brush near the American frontier, in which loyalist volunteers intercepted and dispersed a band of rebels who had taken refuge in and crossed over from Vermont. At the beginning of December Gore was sent again to Sorel and up the river to St. Denis and St. Charles. He met with no resistance, he recovered his wounded and his gun, and his troops burnt some houses at St. Denis. Dr. Wolfred Nelson had at once shown more courage and been more unfortunate than his fellows. When he heard of Wetherall's success at St. Charles, he attempted to escape across the frontier into the United States; but after much suffering from cold and privation in the woodlands of the loyalist Eastern Townships, he was taken prisoner on the 12th of December and sent in to Montreal, his kindly care of the wounded being remembered in his own misfortunes. A reward had been offered for his capture, and a still larger reward was offered for the capture of Papineau, but the latter made good his escape. He left Dr. Nelson's house at St. Denis on the morning of the day when Gore attacked it, and with O'Callaghan found his way to the United States, leaving to after years a controversy as to the motives for his flight at the moment of danger. Storrow Brown also reached American soil, and he, too, was criticized, though apparently without good reason, for not having been on the spot at St. Charles when the actual fighting took place.

After an interval of years insurgents became good citizens again, and memories were softened, but there were two bad murders in this rising in the Richelieu district which could not be smoothed over or forgotten. A young officer, Lieutenant Weir, trying to catch up Gore's column between Sorel and St. Denis on the night of the 22nd of November, took a wrong road, reached St. Denis in advance of Gore's troops, and fell into the insurgents' hands. When Gore attacked, Weir was placed bound in a wagon to be taken to St. Charles: he jumped out of the wagon, and was there and then shot and stabbed to death by those who were in charge. His body, badly mangled, was subsequently found in the Richelieu river, and was buried at Montreal on the 8th of December. In 1839, a man of the name of Jalbert, who had been in principal charge of the wagon, was tried for the murder, but the jury disagreed and he went unpunished. Even more cold-blooded was the murder of a stone-mason Chartrand, a French

Canadian of St. John's, who had enrolled himself as a loyalist volunteer. Coming home from a place five or six miles off on the afternoon of the 28th of November, he was intercepted by a party of ruffians, some of them with loaded guns. He was subjected to a mock trial, condemned as a spy, tied to a tree, and shot. Four men were tried for his murder in 1838, but were acquitted by a jury of their countrymen in face of the strongest evidence of their guilt. Two of them, however, one a ringleader, were inculpated in the second rising in the autumn of 1838, were tried by court martial and hung early in 1839.

Gore's repulse at St. Denis acted as a stimulus to armed disloyalty, and the disloyal county of the Two Mountains, to the north-west of Montreal, gave some trouble. The centre of the disturbance was the village of St. Eustache, and the leaders were a Swiss adventurer of the name of Girod, and a French Canadian, like Wolfred Nelson, a brave but headstrong doctor, of the name of Chénier. Like Nelson at St. Denis, Chénier at St. Eustache turned a building into a fort. This was a convent, of which he took forcible possession on the 1st of December. Sir John Colborne waited for nearly a fortnight until he was fully prepared to settle the matter, and then marched out of Montreal on the 13th of December with 2,000 men. On the 14th the troops took possession of St. Eustache, where Chénier and—it is said— about 250 others held church, convent, and other buildings, and fought with spirit. Chénier was killed, much of the village was burnt, and a considerable number of French Canadians were killed or taken prisoners. Girod had taken flight early in the proceedings, but a few days later, being hard pressed, shot himself. The troops went on to St. Benoit, another little centre of disaffection, fomented by one of the very few French Canadian priests who actively opposed the government. Here there was no resistance, but notwithstanding there was burning of houses; a third village was also visited, and on the 16th the troops returned to Montreal.

This was the end of the rising in Lower Canada. The contemporary insurrection in Upper Canada was even more fatuous and abortive. The danger in this province arose from two causes. One was purely temporary, and has already been mentioned, the fact that, when Sir John Colborne asked if any troops could be spared, Sir Francis Bond Head somewhat theatrically denuded Toronto of all the regulars, being well inclined, it would seem, to show to the world the loyalty of the citizens of Upper Canada, his own confidence in them and their confidence in him. The second source of danger was the ease with which raids could be organized from the American shores of the Niagara and Detroit rivers. For the rest, the community of Upper Canada was in the main thoroughly loyal, and race feeling did not complicate the situation. What Papineau was to Lower Canada Mackenzie was to the Upper Province, but with far more courage, even less discretion, and certainly less widespread influence. In both provinces the medical profession seems to have produced

POLITICAL DIFFICULTIES

leaders among the Patriots or Rebels, whichever name may be thought more appropriate. As against Wolfred Nelson and Chénier in Lower Canada, Drs. Rolph, Duncombe, and Morrison were prominent in Upper Canada. Among the reformers, Baldwin had no part or lot in the rising, nor had Bidwell, though the latter did not escape suspicion, which induced him, wrought upon, it was said, unfairly by Sir Francis Head, to exile himself for the rest of his life in the United States.

During the summer of 1838 Mackenzie had been agitating through the province. The extreme men showed a disposition to come into line with Papineau in Lower Canada, but there was little talk of resort to force, and only gradually, in the country districts, some kind of secret preparation was made for taking up arms. Eventually the plan was evolved of capturing Toronto and the Government, the night of the 7th of December being fixed for the attempt. It was long before Sir Francis Head would admit the possibility of any danger or take any steps towards meeting it, although a good soldier, Colonel Fitzgibbon, whose name had been a household word in the war of 1812, was urgent in his warnings. At length, at the beginning of December, it was determined to arrest Mackenzie and to call out some of the militia, with the result that the conspirators hastened their movements, and resolved to make their attempt on Toronto on the night of the 4th. But when plans are changed in conspiracies, differences of opinion arise, there is uncertainty and confusion, warning is given to the other side, and the scheme miscarries. The rebels picketed Toronto on the night of the 4th of December, but made no attack. A loyalist, Colonel Moodie, was intercepted and shot; an insurgent leader, Anderson, was shot; citizens were stopped and arrested by the rebels, but one or two broke through, and the alarm was most effectually given in the town. On the next morning, the 5th, after a reconnaissance, Fitzgibbon, with sound military instinct, wished at once to attack the insurgents in their position, but Head refused his consent and sent Baldwin and Rolph to parley with them, in happy ignorance that Rolph was in their inmost secrets. The conference came to nothing, and when night fell, Lount and Mackenzie led their misguided followers towards the city. They came across a small picket of twenty-seven men whom Fitzgibbon had sent out. The picket fired and then ran away, and so did the 700 insurgents. Militia and volunteers were now fast coming into Toronto, and by the following night, the night of the 6th, the Government had some 1,200 fighting men at its back. On the 7th, Fitzgibbon and Colonel MacNab attacked, and within half an hour the rebels were dispersed and the rising was at an end. MacNab and a force of 500 men went on into the London district, where Dr. Duncombe, of American birth, had been organizing rebellion, but it had all melted away, and Duncombe had fled to the United States. Mackenzie, too, made his way across the frontier, and so did Rolph. Among other prominent rebels, one, Van Egmont by name, who was reputed to have served under

Napoleon, died in prison; two, Lount and Matthews, were hanged.

In the United States Mackenzie tried to organize invasion of Canada, and frontier raids followed. Just above the Falls of Niagara, a small island in Canadian waters, Navy Island, was, at his instigation, occupied by a band of filibusters from Buffalo, who held it for a month from the middle of December 1837 to the middle of January 1838. A small Buffalo steamer, the *Caroline*, had been chartered to carry warlike stores and supplies to the island, and on the night of the 29th of December a party of Canadians rowed across the river to the American shore, cut out and burnt the vessel, and killed one man on the wharf. This incident caused strong resentment in the United States, although, from the Canadian point of view, it was no more than a justifiable reprisal, inasmuch as American soil had been openly made a basis for attack upon a friendly nation, and the raiders were almost entirely American citizens. Eventually, between three and four years later, Daniel Webster obtained from Sir Robert Peel a friendly explanation and what was held to be an adequate apology. The raid, or attempted raid, on the Niagara frontier was supplemented by similar attempts in the neighbourhood of Detroit in January and February 1838, in the course of which an Irish American adventurer of the name of Theller was taken prisoner. He was said to have been a doctor, like various other men who were prominent in these Canadian disturbances, and he obtained some notoriety by making a bold escape from his prison in the citadel of Quebec in October 1838.

Martial law was proclaimed in the district of Montreal on the 5th of December 1837, and the district remained under martial law until the following 27th of April, when, just a month before Lord Durham's arrival, Colborne, as acting Governor-General, dispensed with it in accordance with wishes expressed from home.

In September 1837 Lord Gosford had placed himself in the hands of the Home Government, intimating that personally he would be glad to resign, though he was ready to continue in office, if the ministers so desired. He had been pledged to a policy of conciliation, and it was rapidly becoming evident that other measures would be necessary, which might better be entrusted to other hands. On the 27th of November Lord Glenelg wrote to accept his resignation, and he wrote also to Sir John Colborne intimating that the administration of the government would devolve upon him. Lord Gosford's departure from Canada was delayed by an injury which he received from a fall, but he finally left Quebec on the 27th of February 1838, and on the same day Colborne assumed the government. In the latter part of March, as already told, Sir Francis Head was replaced in Upper Canada by Sir George Arthur, who had previously been Lieutenant-Governor of Van Diemen's Land, now Tasmania.

The first Parliament of Queen Victoria met in November 1837. Just before the adjournment for the Christmas holidays news reached England of the outbreak in Canada. 'The adjournment before the Christmas recess,' says the *Annual Register* for 1838,[1] 'took place almost contemporaneously with the arrival of the intelligence of the Canadian revolt, though not before some younger members of the Radical section had found an opportunity of expressing their exuberant joy at the fact and their confident predictions of its inevitable consequences.' This statement may have been somewhat of an exaggeration, but some of the utterances were deplorable. One of the most violent speeches was made by Sir William Molesworth, who was not alone in hoping that Canada would pass from under the British dominion. That ' that dominion should now be brought to a conclusion I for one most sincerely desire'. This was on the 22nd of December 1837, but Molesworth's normal view was a saner one, for on the following 6th of March, in attacking Lord Glenelg's administration of the colonies, while he still expressed a hope that the people of Lower Canada would become independent, if their constitution was not restored to them, he stated that he yielded to no member in the House of Commons ' in a desire to preserve and extend the colonial empire of England '.

The House met again on the 16th of January 1838, and Lord John Russell immediately introduced into the House of Commons a Bill which, after being much amended and recast, became law on the 10th of February, entitled ' An Act to make temporary provision for the government of Lower Canada '.[2] It suspended the constitution of 1791

[1] p. 2. [2] 1 Vic. c. ix.

in Lower Canada from the date when the Act should be proclaimed in the province until the 1st of November 1840; and it empowered the Crown to constitute a special Council, by authorizing the Governor to appoint councillors in accordance with instructions. The operation of the laws to be passed by the Council was limited to the 1st of November 1842, ' unless continued by competent authority', and the Council was precluded from passing any legislation which should impose new taxes or involve constitutional changes. All laws were to be proposed to the Council by the Governor, and the presence of five councillors at least was required for the passing of a law. When explaining the proposals of the Government, Lord John Russell intimated that the extensive powers conferred by the Act would be entrusted to Lord Durham. Lord Durham himself in the House of Lords gave expression to the reluctance with which he undertook the charge. As a matter of fact he had been invited by Lord Melbourne in the previous July to take the governor-generalship of Canada, but had declined. He was again approached after the news of the rebellion had been received, and it was only on the day before Parliament met in January 1838 that he finally consented to go out.

The new Act practically created a dictatorship, and was, therefore, strongly opposed by the Radicals in its passage through Parliament. It would have been even more hotly opposed but that Durham was conspicuous for his Radical sympathies. Roebuck, not then in Parliament, was heard against the Bill at the bar of either

House. In the House of Lords Brougham was specially bitter against the Government and its policy. But the policy prevailed. The Act was sent out to Canada with instructions to Colborne to call together a special Council in order to deal with immediate requirements, but to make it clear that Lord Durham on arrival would constitute his own Council. Colborne acted accordingly and nominated a Council consisting of 21 members, 11 of whom were French Canadians. The Council met on the 18th of April and was prorogued on the 5th of May. Lord Durham arrived at the end of May, and on the 28th of June nominated his own special Council consisting of five members only, unconnected with political life in Canada.

Was there any real justification for the armed rising in the two Canadian provinces ? The answer must be that there was not. There was ground for discontent, the discontent of communities growing and conscious of growth, and desirous with reason of more extended control of their own destinies, the discontent in Lower Canada of a French race largely officered by Englishmen, the discontent in Upper Canada of a democratic party stonewalled by official Conservatism. But the popular demands were, for the time and place, excessive and unreasonable, the grievances were clothed in exaggerated language, and the weakness and speedy collapse of the outbreak in either province testified to the absence of deep-seated and widespread resentment against grinding tyranny. It may be said that the rebellion was the product of three causes, first the war of American Independence, secondly, unwise speeches in England, thirdly, real, though not overwhelming grievances. The war of American Independence and its outcome coloured the whole of the subsequent colonial history of England; especially it affected the history of the British provinces which bordered on the United States. The popular view of the war, adopted and embellished by the Whigs, was that it was a signal and crowning illustration for all time of the triumph of liberty over oppression: and the terms used of it implied that the English had been guilty of the wildest excesses of tyranny. This led to similar exaggeration, whenever in after years there was friction between a colony and the motherland; and in the case of Canada speeches made by men like Roebuck or Hume, who were either paid advocates of the colonies or so constituted as to be incapable of imagining that the Home Government for the time being could be right, or speeches again made from the Irish point of view by O'Connell, contributed to a distorted vision of the actual facts. Lower Canada had not even the cause of complaint which the thirteen colonies had been able to put forward, that new taxes were being imposed from without upon the provincials by the Government at home. As far as the finances were concerned, it was a question not of taxation but of appropriation. In the words of the *Annual Register* for 1838,[1] 'Throughout the unfortunate differences which we are about to notice, no question ever existed with respect to

[1] p. 4.

the imposition of duties or the levying of money. The claims of either party were limited to the right of appropriating what must, at all events, be collected and what, if not disposed of, must accumulate from year to year in the public chest.' In refusing a Civil List, in return for the control of their finances, the democratic party in Canada were refusing what it would have been right and reasonable to grant, and the attacks made upon successive Governors-General were unworthy and contemptible. None the less, there were wrongs to be righted and causes of friction to be removed : the time had come in all the provinces of British North America to recognize that the peoples were now not children but adults, and the man had come, in Lord Durham, to show the better way.

CHAPTER IV

LORD DURHAM'S COMMISSION AND INSTRUCTIONS

WHEN Lord Durham's Report was laid before Parliament in 1839, it was prefaced by the Commission which is now reprinted, and which had already been given separately to Parliament on the 9th of July 1838. It was a Royal Commission under the Great Seal, appointing him to be 'High Commissioner and Governor-General of all Her Majesty's provinces on the continent of North America, and of the islands of Prince Edward and Newfoundland'. The Commission recites that he had already received five several Commissions appointing him to be Governor-in-Chief of the four provinces of Lower Canada, Upper Canada, Nova Scotia, and New Brunswick, and of Prince Edward Island. Similar powers had been given to his predecessors; but, as appears from Lord Glenelg's letter to Lord Durham of the 3rd of April 1838, only three Commissions had previously been issued for the five colonies, instead of one for each. The Commission then goes on to appoint him 'to be our High Commissioner for the adjustment of certain important questions depending in the said provinces of Lower and Upper Canada, respecting the form and future Government of the said provinces', and to authorize him as High Commissioner 'to enquire into and as far as may be possible to adjust all questions depending in the said provinces of Lower and Upper Canada, or either of them, respecting the form and administration of the Civil Government thereof respectively'. Then, 'with a view to the adjustment of such questions,' the Commission appoints him to be Governor-General of all the British North American provinces and islands, including Newfoundland, but the commission of the existing Governor of Newfoundland is specially safeguarded.

Finally the Commission empowers him to hold the offices of 'High Commissioner and Governor-General of our said provinces on the continent of North America, and of the said islands of Prince Edward and Newfoundland'.

This document gave Lord Durham a threefold authority. In the first place he was, like his predecessors, Governor-in-Chief of Lower Canada, Upper Canada, Nova Scotia, New Brunswick, and Prince Edward Island. His legal powers were those of Governor-in-Chief. He was not, nor had his predecessors been, Governor-in-Chief of Newfoundland, for in Newfoundland there was a Governor and not merely a Lieutenant-Governor. In the second place he was High Commissioner to do special work in two of the provinces. In the third place he was Governor-General of all the provinces and islands, including Newfoundland. The appointment of Governor-in-Chief applied to each province or island separately, excluding Newfoundland. The appointment of Governor-

General applied to them all collectively, including Newfoundland; but it is not quite easy to appreciate why the appointment of Governor-General of all the provinces and islands collectively was conferred upon him 'with a view to the adjustment' of the special questions in Lower and Upper Canada, in connexion with which he had been appointed High Commissioner, nor is it clear why he is styled High Commissioner as well as Governor-General of all the provinces and islands.[1] The meaning of the document can be interpreted from the first two paragraphs of Lord Durham's Report. It was, that certain grave troubles had come into existence in two Canadian provinces which required a very special man, clothed with very special authority, to deal with them: that the conditions in other parts of British North America were not dissimilar: that the chosen man should, therefore, in addition to possessing the ordinary powers of government which previous Governors-in-Chief had enjoyed, be given a High Commissionership intended primarily to apply to Lower and Upper Canada and only to special purposes in those two provinces, but to apply also, if required, in combination with a general authority as Governor-General, to the whole of British North America, even including Newfoundland. In short, the difficulties which had arisen in Lower and Upper Canada differed

---

[1] In the Commission to Charles Buller empowering him to inquire into public lands (see vol. iii, Appendix B), Lord Durham appears as Governor-General only, not as High Commissioner, and Newfoundland is wrongly given a Lieutenant-Governor instead of a Governor.

CHAP. IV   LORD DURHAM'S COMMISSION   109

rather in degree than in kind from those which had occurred or might occur elsewhere in British North America, and therefore all the provinces and islands were, so to speak, grouped under Lord Durham's authority as Governor-General, and to all he might, if necessary, apply whatever powers appertained to him as High Commissioner. Thus, in the first of the three letters or dispatches in which Lord Glenelg conveyed to him the instructions of the Government, the letter of the 20th of January, it is stated: 'Neither . . . is it the intention of Her Majesty's Government to exclude other subjects from your consideration, or to restrict you from entertaining other proposals, whether affecting the two Canadas only or all the British North American provinces, which you may be induced to think conducive to the permanent establishment of an improved system of Government in Her Majesty's North American possessions. Your Commission will be co-extensive with the whole of these possessions'; and in the letter of the 21st of April reference is made to the powers which were vested in him 'for the purpose of a general superintendence over all British North America'.

The formal Royal Instructions, which accompanied Lord Durham's five Commissions as Governor-in-chief, were much the same as had been given to his predecessors. In the case of Lower and Upper Canada, the old Instructions which had been handed on from Lord Dalhousie's time were continued, with the proviso that they should apply 'so far only as the same are not obsolete or have not been superseded by any such statute as aforesaid or as the same may not be found to be inapplicable to the present state of affairs in our said province'; and in the case of Lower Canada, a separate Instruction was added as to constituting the special Council authorized by the newly passed Act 'to make temporary provision for the Government of Lower Canada'. Over and above these formal Instructions, Lord Glenelg conveyed to him the views of the Melbourne Ministry in the three letters of the 20th of January, 3rd of April, and 21st of April 1838, which are reprinted in vol. iii, and of which a few words must be said.

It will be remembered that Parliament met on the 16th of January 1838. The Instructions contained in the letter of the 20th of January were therefore given almost immediately after Lord John Russell had introduced the Bill for suspending the constitution of Lower Canada, which eventually, on the 10th of February, became the Act 'to make temporary provision for the Government of Lower Canada', and they followed close upon Lord Durham's acceptance of the charge which had been offered to him. The Government were anxious to lose no time in embodying their policy in the form of Instructions, but the letter of the 20th of January was absurdly premature, seeing that the law with which the Instructions were coupled had yet to be passed. It will be seen that in this letter Lord Glenelg authorized Lord Durham somewhat elaborately, though leaving him a discretion in the matter, to call together an advisory committee of the two Canadas with an elective element in it, for the purpose of consulting

CHAP. IV   LORD DURHAM'S COMMISSION   111

the members on some or all of the outstanding questions, especially those which were common to the two provinces. A reference to this proposed committee had been embodied in the preamble to the Bill which was then before the House of Commons. The first draft of the Bill recited that, whereas under existing circumstances the House of Assembly in Lower Canada could not be called together without detriment to the public interests,

' and whereas it is nevertheless expedient that the said Province should be permanently governed on constitutional principles adapted to promote the interests of all classes of Her Majesty's subjects in the said Province : And whereas, in order to the preparation of such measures as it may be desirable to propose to Parliament for improving the constitution of the provinces of Lower Canada and Upper Canada, or either of them, and for regulating divers questions in which the said provinces are jointly interested, Her Majesty hath been pleased to authorize the Governor-General of Her Majesty's provinces in North America to summon a meeting, to be holden within the said provinces of Lower Canada and Upper Canada, consisting of the said Governor-General and of certain persons to be by Her Majesty or on Her Majesty's behalf for that purpose appointed, and also consisting of certain other persons representing the interests and opinions of Her Majesty's subjects inhabiting the said provinces, and whereas it is in the meantime necessary that temporary provision should be made for the Government of the said province of Lower Canada, Be it therefore enacted . . . '

The fact was that the Whig Ministry, being driven to a measure of coercion, tried to sweeten it, and to conciliate their Radical following, by introducing into the preamble of the Bill and into the Instructions to their Commissioner evidence of the Liberal and Constitutional principles on which they prided themselves. But they had to reckon with Sir Robert Peel, who would have none of this preamble, and pointed out with irresistible force that it was an attempt, by a side wind in the form of a preamble to an Act, to make Parliament responsible for the acts and the policy of the Executive Government. On the same grounds he refused to give any Parliamentary recognition to Lord Glenelg's Instructions to Lord Durham,[1] and he pointed out the palpable absurdity of giving instructions in January to a man who would not arrive in Canada till the end of May. The end of it was that, being given a lead from his own side, by 'Bear' Ellice and Charles Buller, Lord John Russell struck the preamble out of the Bill, and no more was heard of the elaborate instructions for calling together an advisory committee.

Lord Glenelg's letter of the 20th of January 1838 is a wordy document with high phrases and fine sentiments, evidently designed for the shop-window; but it will be noted that the letter refers specially to the complaint made against the Quebec Assembly that it was animated by an 'anti-commercial spirit of legislation', and that prominence is given to the relations between the two Canadian pro-

[1] An extract from Lord Glenelg's letter of instructions to Lord Durham of January 20, 1838, was laid before Parliament on January 23, 1838. The whole letter, together with the letters of April 3 and April 21, was included in the Parliamentary Paper of February 11, 1839.

vinces and the difficulties which had arisen in this connexion. Some kind of federal legislature is suggested which should supplement, but not take the place of, the separate legislatures of Lower and Upper Canada. The letter also adverts to the constitution of the Legislative Council in Lower Canada, and to the resolution of the House of Commons that the Council should be given a more popular character without being made elective.

The letter of the 3rd of April deals with Lord Durham's Commissions and with his relations, under their terms and under the Royal Instructions, to the Lieutenant-Governors. It may be inferred from it that Lord Durham was not expected to visit Newfoundland, as no reference is made to the possibility of his doing so.

The letter of the 21st of April is by way of completing a series of Instructions. It is again a wordy document with a number of copybook platitudes. It refers more especially to relations with the United States, and to the desire of the Whig Government that gentle treatment should, in other than exceptional cases, be meted out to those in Canada who were inculpated in the late rising. With this end in view, Lord Durham is given an unrestricted power of pardon. The letter concludes with an assurance of the full confidence of Her Majesty's Government and 'of their utmost support and assistance'.

On the whole, it would be somewhat difficult to find a more futile set of Instructions to a strong man setting out on a difficult mission, but they had the merit of leaving him a wide discretion.

CHAPTER V

THE REPORT
ITS SCOPE, CHARACTER, AND SUBSTANCE

THE SCOPE OF THE REPORT

LORD DURHAM having been appointed Governor-General of all the British North American Colonies, including Newfoundland, the nominal scope of his Report was the whole of British North America; and, in so far as the Report laid down general principles, or foreshadowed a union of all the provinces, it did to a greater or less extent include them all. But the primary object of his mission was to adjust outstanding and pressing questions in Lower and Upper Canada, 'respecting the form and future Government' of those two provinces; and it has been seen that, as a matter of fact, his stay in British North America hardly exceeded five months, all of which time he spent in Lower Canada with the exception of eleven days which he gave to the Upper Province. Nova Scotia, New Brunswick, Prince Edward Island, and Newfoundland, he never visited at all. He interviewed delegates from Nova Scotia, New Brunswick, and Prince Edward Island; and the Crown Lands Inquiry, which was entrusted to Charles Buller, included these three colonies as well as the two Canadas; but, except in connexion with Crown lands, only three pages of the Report in its original Blue Book form are devoted to 'the Eastern provinces and Newfoundland'; and, while the Commission which empowered Buller to inquire into Crown lands included Newfoundland, the actual inquiry and Buller's Report left out that island altogether. It was in fact a farce, as events turned out, to have brought Newfoundland at all into the Commission and into the Report, for Lord Durham says plainly (ii. 202):—'With respect to the colony of Newfoundland, I have been able to obtain no information whatever, except from sources open to the public at large'. The scope of the Report may then be fairly summed up by saying that it deals in detail with Lower and Upper Canada, and that it contains information, deductions and suggestions which were applicable in the first place to the Maritime Provinces of North America, and in the second place to other parts of the world, including Newfoundland, which had been colonized by British citizens—more applicable indeed to some other provinces of the Empire than to Newfoundland, for the conditions of Newfoundland were *sui generis* and wholly different from those of an ordinary British colony. The Report is, in short, mainly a special report upon the two Canadas, but partly also a general essay upon the best method of adjusting the relations between Great Britain and British colonies which are not merely dependencies, including a model scheme of colonization by means of the proper application of the public lands of the colonies.

The Character of the Report

Turning to the character of the Report, critics wishing to find fault might lay stress upon one or two instances of direct misstatement, and more numerous instances of obvious exaggeration; but the Report must fairly be considered as a whole, and its two main features, apart from the substance of the recommendations which it contains, are in the first place its plain speaking, and in the second place its breadth of view. The first of these two characteristics may be illustrated by reference to the marginal notes, which form a running analysis, unusual in a Blue Book, and suitable rather to a history or a general essay than to the report of a special commission. Here are three notes which follow one another on ii. 59, 60: 'The Canadians would revenge themselves on the English by any aid'; 'The English population will never tolerate the French pretensions to nationality'; 'They complain of being the sport of parties at home.' And here are three more on ii. 292-4: 'Hopeless inferiority of the French-Canadian race;' 'Economical obstacle to perpetuation of their nationality;' 'The French nationality is destitute of invigorating qualities.' Notes of this kind, and such strong language as will be found in the body of the Report, would never see the light in the report of a Royal Commission at the present day, though possibly some approach to it might now and again be found in separate dispatches. It is interesting to speculate how far this plain speaking was the outcome of the man,

CHAP. V THE CHARACTER OF THE REPORT

and how far of the time—a time before summaries of speeches and reports were telegraphed to the ends of the earth. Lord Durham was not accustomed to mince his words, nor did he greatly regard the feelings of others. His right-hand man, Charles Buller, had a trenchant pen, and both men were at once indifferent to political niceties, and minded to read their countrymen at home a lesson for all time on the subject of colonial administration. Hence the Report is full blooded, and, while nothing is set down in malice, nothing is extenuated. The writer is determined to paint a graphic picture of the truth, as it appeared to his eyes, and he has beyond question succeeded in his effort. But if Lord Durham and Buller had lived in our own day, it cannot be doubted that the Report would not have been so outspoken. Violent party speeches are as common as ever, but in the matter of reports, especially with regard to the dominions beyond the seas, the men of the present time weigh their words more carefully than was the case seventy years ago. It is well that it should be so. We could wish that our Parliamentary Papers were marked by the vigour, the clearness, the eloquence, the honesty which, over and above its supreme ability, are conspicuous in Lord Durham's Report, but we could and would dispense with criticisms and terms of expression which may be valuable for confidential purposes, but in public documents are calculated to give abiding offence to classes or to communities.

And Lord Durham's Report, great and remedial as it was, by form as well as by substance gave grave offence in both Canadas. As late as the 3rd of February, 1910, Sir Wilfrid Laurier referred to it in the Canadian House of Commons in the following terms.

It is a singular fact that the report of Lord Durham was received by the French Canadians of that day with pained surprise. The reason is known to those who have studied the history of that period. Friend of liberty as he was, broad as he was in his conceptions, far-visioned as events show him to have been, Lord Durham himself did not appreciate the effect of liberal institutions. Coming to Canada at a time when the very atmosphere was reeking with rebellion, he formed a hasty judgement upon the French population of that day, which he expressed in hasty and somewhat haughty language. He thought they could not be reconciled to British rule, and stated in his report that the conditions should be such in Canada that the two provinces should be united, so that French Canada should be ruled by the stern and relentless hand of an English-speaking majority. It is not to be wondered at that when the report was made known in Canada, it not only caused, as I have said, pained surprise, but produced a feeling of injustice and wrong.'[1]

Equal irritation was aroused in Upper Canada by the publication of the report, as will be seen by the Report of the Select Committee of the House of Assembly of the Upper Province, which was forwarded by Sir George Arthur to England in May 1839. Here is one passage referring to Lord Durham's comments on the methods of expenditure on public works in the province.

[1] Quoted from the Canadian *Hansard*.

'There is something so offensive and unbecoming in these passages of the report, as to induce the committee, from that and other internal evidence, to believe that that portion of it which relates to Upper Canada was not written by and never received the careful revision of his Lordship.'[1]

The House of Assembly and its committee no doubt represented mainly those whom Lord Durham considered to be the Tories of Upper Canada, and the passage in his Report which they so bitterly resented hardly called for so much resentment. Still the Report might have achieved its purpose without giving such dire offence. Its great breadth of view might have been more appreciated at the time, if the comments had been somewhat more carefully worded and a little less uncompromising.

This breadth of view might be illustrated by quotations on almost every point and on almost every page, but it will be enough to take one point only and to note the strong and healthy Imperialism, the confidence in the English race, the love of and pride in the British Empire, which is really the keynote of the Report, and which was wholly alien to the ordinary Whig doctrines and modes of thought at the time when Lord Durham went to Canada. He was an Imperialist in the best sense. He believed in *Libertas*, but he believed also in *Imperium*. He was not afraid of force, if used for what he conceived to be a good purpose. He was not inclined to make concessions, merely

[1] Parliamentary Paper containing copies or extracts of correspondence relating to the affairs of Canada, No. 289, June, 1839, p. 27.

because the majority asked for them, but only, if they were sound in principle and likely to conduce to future greatness. He did not consider that undoing, or at the most giving new machinery, was the one and only thing needful. The bent of his mind was constructive, and he would not be content without creating something greater than before. He was not inclined to let the colonies go hang. He believed in their potential value to England, and in a future for England and for them of strength and partnership. England was to give them freedom and security, but she was to have something in return. 'The country which has founded and maintained these Colonies at a vast expense of blood and treasure, may justly expect its compensation in turning their unappropriated resources to the account of its own redundant population; they are the rightful patrimony of the English people, the ample appanage which God and Nature have set aside in the New World for those whose lot has assigned them but insufficient portions in the Old' (ii. 13). The marginal note to this fine passage is 'Advantages derivable by the Mother country from these Colonies'; and even the inaccuracy which may be noted in it, that of treating French Canada as though it had been an original colony of Great Britain, bears witness to the same breadth of conception, which refused to look upon the province of Quebec merely as a conquered dependency, the home of an alien race, and persisted in regarding it as an integral part of the British Empire. Similarly Lord Durham's scheme for

THE CHARACTER OF THE REPORT

the disposal of the public lands in the British North American provinces was 'intended to promote the common advantage of the Colonies, and of the Mother country' (ii. 327); and in the same spirit Charles Buller, in his Report on Public Lands, laid stress on the fact that the subject was one of Imperial concern. ' Higher interests than those of the Colonies, the interests of the Empire of which they form a part, demand that Parliament should establish at once, and permanently, a well considered and uniform system. The waste lands of the Colonies are the property, not merely of the Colony, but of the Empire, and ought to be administered for Imperial, not merely for Colonial, purposes' (Appendix B, iii. 37).

This British patriotism and Imperial outlook, the seeking for what is or may become great and broad, and strong, runs through the whole report. The French Canadians should be merged in an English nationality because they would thereby become an integral part of a greater community, and have a goodlier heritage. ' It is to elevate them from that inferiority that I desire to give to the Canadians our English character' (ii. 292). The legislative union of all the British North American provinces, if it could be accomplished, ' would form a great and powerful people, possessing the means of securing good and responsible Government for itself, and which, under the protection of the British Empire, might in some measure counterbalance the preponderant and increasing influence of the United States on the American continent' (ii. 309). Responsible government should be given not only as a means to popular contentment, but also as making for strength, whereas 'there is every reason to believe that a professedly irresponsible Government would be the weakest that could be devised' (ii. 298). One reason given for the union of the two Canadas is that 'the full establishment of responsible Government can only be permanently secured by giving these Colonies an increased importance in the politics of the Empire' (ii. 304); and this permanence of self-government in a strong community is held to be necessary 'for the wellbeing of the Colonies, and the security of the Mother country' (ii. 285). Any danger to the Imperial connexion from making the colonies greater and stronger is scouted. 'I am, in truth, so far from believing that the increased power and weight that would be given to these Colonies by Union would endanger their connexion with the Empire, that I look to it as the only means of fostering such a national feeling throughout them as would effectually counterbalance whatever tendencies may now exist towards separation' (ii. 310). By enlarging the colonial unit, by widening the area and adding to the population, by endowing with responsibility, greater men would be produced, new and wider interests would be created; and the danger of absorption into the United States would be met 'by raising up for the North American colonist some nationality of his own, by elevating these small and unimportant communities into a society having some objects of a national importance' (ii. 311). The spirit which

CHAP. V THE CHARACTER OF THE REPORT 123

inspires the Report is indicated by the concluding words, in which Lord Durham records his ' earnest desire to perpetuate and strengthen the connexion between this Empire and the North American colonies, which would then form one of the brightest ornaments in your Majesty's Imperial Crown '.

In the debates in the House of Lords on the Reunion Bill, in the summer of 1840, Lord Melbourne took exception to the terms of the Report. 'There were unquestionably many things in that report which he did not praise, and which he did not think were prudent matters to be brought forward, and which he thought it would have been wiser to have omitted.'[1] This was when the committee stage was reached on the 7th of July. A week earlier, in the debate on the second reading, Brougham had declared himself in favour of giving up the North American colonies, and so had Lord Ashburton. Lord Durham was too outspoken for the Whig Prime Minister: he was a better and broader Englishman than Brougham.

THE SUBSTANCE OF THE REPORT

In dealing, as briefly as the subject permits, with the substance of Lord Durham's Report, it is proposed to notice in the first place the two main recommendations which it contains, viz. the reunion of the two Canadas, and the grant of responsible government: then to take the recommendations made under the following heads: public lands, emigration, improvement of means of communication, municipalities, administration

[1] *Hansard*, 1840, vol. lv, p. 515.

of justice, and education; and finally to consider the passages of the report which refer to a future general union of British North America, those in which reference is made to the United States, and those which embody Lord Durham's views on the Colonial Office, and on colonial administration generally.

Reunion of the two Canadas

Why did Lord Durham recommend that the two Canadas should be reunited, and what form of reunion did he recommend? He recommended that the two provinces should be reunited, first and foremost, because under existing conditions he considered reunion to be a necessary preliminary to the grant of responsible government; secondly, because he considered that reunion would result in a greater and a stronger whole, with more possibilities for the future, and that the interests of the inhabitants of both provinces, especially of the French Canadians, demanded reunion. The form of reunion which he recommended was union, not federation, and not political union only but a complete amalgamation of peoples, races, languages, and laws. He recommended, as far as it was humanly possible, absolute unity, easier to depict on paper than to carry out into fact.

It has been noted that the Report is not only a special report upon the best means of solving the difficulties which had actually arisen in the two Canadas, but also in part an essay upon colonial administration in general, upon the advantages to

CHAP. V REUNION OF THE TWO CANADAS 125

be derived from giving responsible government to British colonies, which are not merely foreign dependencies. In itself the principle of responsible government was of wide application. Wherever the majority of the population consisted of British citizens, or of Europeans who had been trained in British citizenship, and had enjoyed some measure of British institutions, there it was, in Lord Durham's view, prima facie, good, sound, and desirable that self-government within certain defined limits should be established. But though the principle was so far of general application, the application was necessarily subject to conditions of time and place; and Lord Durham was sent out primarily to deal with a particular time and a particular place. The particular time was the close of armed rebellion, and the particular place, or one of the two particular places, was a province which adjoined the American Republic, but in which the large majority of the inhabitants were of French descent. Thus Lord Durham set before himself, in regard to Canada, something like the problem which Aristotle propounded for solution in the *Politics*. He set himself to consider in the first place, what is the best constitution; and in the second place, what is the best constitution, given a particular set of conditions. He answered the second problem not so much by departing from his model constitution, as by proposing to alter the conditions so as to enable the model constitution to be brought into being. On the grant of self-government he had clearly made his mind up before he went out to Canada. After arrival in Canada, when brought face to face with existing facts, he did not modify his theory to suit the facts, but he set himself to modify the conditions in order to make the theory practicable.[1]

Thus, in regard to Lower and Upper Canada, the two main recommendations of the Report are inseparably connected together. He recommended that the two Canadas should be reunited, and that to the single province thus formed responsible government should be given. He commented most strongly upon the bad effects produced by the want of responsible government in Lower Canada, but he did not recommend that under existing conditions, Lower Canada, as it stood, should be endowed with responsible government. He became convinced, when on the spot, that the root cause of the evils in French Canada was not to be found in the constitution, though the defects of the constitution had aggravated the evils. He traced the mischief ultimately to race antipathy and race conflict; and, therefore, he considered it to be a necessary preliminary to the grant of responsible government to French Canada that in the legislature, to which the new and wider powers should be given, a British majority should be assured. 'The fatal feud of origin, which is the cause of the most extensive mischief, would be aggravated at the present moment by any change which should give the majority more power than

---

[1] From the *Life of Sir John Beverley Robinson*, pp. 243-4, it would seem that Lord Durham was opposed to the Union of the two Canadas during his whole stay in Canada. He tells us himself in the Report (ii. 304) that on his first arrival in Canada he was inclined to a general federation of the provinces of British North America.

they have hitherto possessed. A plan by which it is proposed to ensure the tranquil government of Lower Canada, must include in itself the means of putting an end to the agitation of national disputes in the legislature, by settling, at once and for ever, the national character of the province. I entertain no doubts as to the national character which must be given to Lower Canada ; it must be that of the British Empire ' (ii. 288).

The first part of the Report, which deals with Lower Canada, begins with Lord Durham's statement that he himself, and most men in England, had wholly misapprehended ' the parties at issue in Lower Canada ' ; that he had been sent out to heal a quarrel between the Executive and the popular branch of the Legislature, and found a deeper seated cause of strife. ' I expected,' he writes in often-quoted terms, ' to find a contest between a government and a people : I found two nations warring, in the bosom of a single state : I found a struggle, not of principles, but of races ' (ii. 16). Lord Durham probably somewhat exaggerated the strength of the race antipathy, but that it existed was undeniable, and it is somewhat difficult to understand why there should have been any misconception on the point. The controversies in Lower Canada for thirty years past had borne the impress of antagonism between the French and British races, growing in intensity as the years went on. As far back as 1810 Sir James Craig had borne the strongest witness to the strength of the race feeling in the province, and this feeling had been constantly in evidence ever since.

Papineau had denounced the abortive Reunion Bill of 1822 as an attempt to Anglify French Canada, and the records of subsequent committees and commissions abundantly testified to the division of races in Lower Canada. It was well known that the Seigniories were French Lower Canada, and the Townships, English Lower Canada; that the Legislative Council represented the British community, and the Assembly more especially the French; while the last enclosure in Appendix A to the Report is 'An Address from the Constitutional Association of Montreal to the inhabitants of British America', denouncing in the strongest terms the evil influence of French domination in Lower Canada, and calling for union of the provinces in order to secure a British majority. This address is dated January 1836, and was, therefore, issued more than two years before Lord Durham went to Canada. How then, it may be asked, can there have been any doubt whatever that the troubles in Lower Canada were mainly due to race?

The explanation seems to be in the first place that, as has been pointed out, individual men of British birth, such as the brothers Nelson, were prominent among the popular party to the end, and took a leading part in the rising in Lower Canada. Their prominence and leadership tended to obscure to onlookers the lines of race. In the second place, that Lord Durham, broad-minded as he was, had been a strong party man; that, before he went out to Canada and faced the facts, he had formed an *a priori* view of the situation,

CHAP. V REUNION OF THE TWO CANADAS 129

based on his party creed; that, as one of the authors of the great Reform Bill, he had, while in England, an intense belief in the efficacy of constitutional reform, and had not contemplated the possibility of conditions for which it would not be an adequate remedy. Such would no doubt have been the view of the Whig Government, and of the friends and advisers with whom he would have taken counsel. But he was man enough, after he reached Canada, to recognize that constitutional reform alone would not meet the case of the Lower Province, that the evil was more deeply seated and required a more drastic remedy. ' At the root of the disorders of Lower Canada,' he writes in the Report, ' lies the conflict of the two races, which compose its population; until this is settled, no good government is practicable' (ii. 72); and again, ' Though I have mentioned the conduct and constitution of the Colonial government as modifying the character of the struggle, I have not attributed to political causes a state of things which would, I believe, under any political institutions, have resulted from the very composition of society ' (ii. 63).

How far Lord Durham formed a correct estimate of the French Canadian problem will be discussed later. At present we are simply concerned with the substance of his Report. He recommended in the plainest and most uncompromising terms the gradual extinction of the French Canadian nationality, the Anglifying of Lower Canada. ' I repeat that the alteration of the character of the province ought to be immediately entered on, and firmly, though cautiously, followed up; that in any plan which may be adopted for the future management of Lower Canada, the first object ought to be that of making it an English province; and that, with this end in view, the ascendancy should never again be placed in any hands but those of an English population' (ii. 295, 296). This was the recommendation of the most advanced Liberal among the leading English politicians of the day, the man who was most heartwhole in the cause of democracy. At first sight it seems curiously at variance with Liberalism, especially as Liberalism has been interpreted in later days. But Lord Durham, as has been seen, had a strong Imperial strain in his character; and moreover, had he been challenged as sinning against Liberal principles, his Report contained ample materials for reply. For he had contended earlier in the Report with great force that the English minority in Lower Canada represented progress and reform, while the French majority stood for unenlightened Conservatism. He was fully determined to entrust the internal fortunes of Canada to the will of the majority of the population, and his thesis was that there was one way, and one only, to carry out this great Liberal measure with safety and with the prospect of permanence, and that was to ensure that the majority should be a British majority. He wanted to give, and he determined to give, responsible government. Willing the end, he also willed the means. ' It is only by the same means, by a popular government, in which an English majority shall permanently predominate, that

Lower Canada, if a remedy for its disorders be not too long delayed, can be tranquilly ruled. On these grounds, I believe that no permanent or efficient remedy can be devised for the disorders of Lower Canada, except a fusion of the government in that of one or more of the surrounding provinces ' (ii. 303).

Further, we have seen that it was not only as a necessary preliminary to the grant of responsible government that he recommended the union of the two provinces. He recommended it also on its merits, in order to make a greater and a worthier whole. The permanent interests of the French Canadians, like the permanent interests of the old French Colony of Louisiana, would be promoted by merging the more conservative race in the population which had the keeping of the future, instead of gratifying 'some idle and narrow notion of a petty and visionary nationality' (ii. 265); Upper Canada would gain by being given access to the sea; and the citizens of both provinces would gain by co-operation for common purposes, by calling into existence new and common interests, 'by raising up for the North American colonist some nationality of his own' (ii. 311). To achieve such a great end Lord Durham was not afraid to recommend drastic measures. It may well be that Buller had a large share in forming his views, and in enunciating them in such clear and forcible terms; and Buller, it will be borne in mind, was a pupil of Carlyle. There is a strong savour of Carlyle in the attitude which the Report adopts towards the French Canadian nationality. There is no Whiggism whatever in it, no trace of *laissez-faire*.

Lord Durham was a democrat after the type of Cromwell, and few state documents ever embodied so strong a policy as is contained in his Report. He had originally contemplated federation only, not union; and federation of all the provinces, not of the two Canadas merely. He came to the ultimate conclusion that union was preferable to federation, for the reason already given, that thereby the French Canadians would no longer retain their individuality and their isolation, and would be merged in an English nationality. He would have preferred that the union should from the first include all British North America, but, under the conditions of the moment, he thought it better to confine it to the two Canadas, which when united would be the nucleus for further union. He was combining what he considered to be ideally best with what the time and the place demanded, but never losing sight of the conception of a single self-governing British North America. The union of the two Canadas, it must be repeated, was to be no half union, no 'mere amalgamation of the Houses of Assembly of the two Provinces' (ii. 323), such as had been attempted in 1822, and was subsequently carried out; much less was it to be merely some shadowy 'joint legislative authority, which should preside over all questions of common interest to the two provinces, and which might be appealed to in extraordinary cases to arbitrate between contending parties in either', such as Lord Glenelg had tentatively suggested in his instructions.[1] All was to be one; the separate

[1] Dispatch of January 20, 1838.

laws and institutions, the separate language, everything, except the religion, which marked the French Canadian nationality, and which led Papineau and his followers to dream and talk of a Canadian nation, was to be gradually but completely submerged.

He laid great stress upon the evils produced by difference of language. ' The difference of language from the first kept them [the two races] asunder ' (ii. 38). ' The difference of language produces misconceptions yet more fatal even than those which it occasions with respect to opinions; it aggravates the national animosities, by representing all the events of the day in utterly different lights ' (ii. 40). Similar views had been held years before by Lord Dalhousie, who wrote that the use of two languages nourished prejudice and separation of feelings between the two classes of people. Lord Durham would not have summarily proscribed the French language in Lower Canada, but it was an integral part of his policy steadily to substitute English for French, until all the inhabitants of the province should be English speaking and English reading citizens of the Empire. ' A considerable time must, of course, elapse before the change of a language can spread over a whole people; and justice and policy alike require that, while the people continue to use the French language, their government should take no such means to force the English language upon them as would, in fact, deprive the great mass of the community of the protection of the laws. But I repeat that the alteration of the character of the province ought to be immediately entered on and firmly, though cautiously, followed up' (ii. 296). 'Until Canada is nationalized and Anglified,' wrote the Commissioner of Enquiry into the State of Education in Lower Canada, 'it is idle for England to be devising schemes for her improvement' (Appendix D, iii. 273). Obviously the substitution of the English language for the French was absolutely essential, if Lord Durham's policy was to be carried out.

In discussing the disadvantages arising to a Dependency from its dependence on the Dominant Country, Cornewall Lewis, in the *Government of Dependencies*,[1] comments upon the inexpediency of attempting to make a sudden change in the language of the dependent people, and quotes the case of the attempt made by Joseph II to impose the German language on Hungary. He also notes 'that the use of a common language is consistent with the existence of the strongest antipathies between different communities'. But Lord Durham did not advocate a sudden change; on the contrary, in the passage which has been just quoted, he expressly laid down that the process must be gradual, and he advocated change of language in order to raise a particular dependency from the status of dependence to that of self-government. This question of difference of language has through the years complicated the task of England in working out her Imperial system, but probably most thinking men would agree that, while community of language would be best if it were practicable, at any given time or place,

[1] 1891 ed., chap. ix, pp. 267-9, and note *N*

CHAP. V   REUNION OF THE TWO CANADAS   135

whether in Canada or in South Africa, the only policy which is practically possible, and which is consistent with British traditions and instincts, is to let the different languages run their course side by side.[1]

[1] See on this question of language Lord Cromer's *Ancient and Modern Imperialism* (1910) ; he refers to the question in South Africa on p. 103 ; his essay, however, deals not with the self-governing dominions of Great Britain but with her dependencies ; and with special reference to the coloured races, he gives his view (p. 107) that 'language is not, and never can be, as in the case of ancient Rome, an important factor in the execution of a policy of fusion. Indeed, in some ways, it rather tends to disruption, inasmuch as it furnishes the subject races with a very powerful arm against their alien rulers'.

On the other hand, Lord Morley in an address to the English Association on January 27, 1911, spoke of the spread of the English language in India as a 'unifying agent ' :

'I called English the most widespread of living tongues. Surely not the least stupendous fact in our British annals is the conquest of a boundless area of the habitable globe by our English language. There is no parallel. You have been told here, I see, that Arabic is or has been our rival. This is a proposition that needs far deeper limitations and qualifications than I can either set forth or examine. Arabic scholars assure me that though Arabic in Islamic lands for some three or four centuries became the medium for an active propagation of ideas, and though by the Koran it retains its hold in its own area, and keeps in its literary as distinct from its spoken form the stamp of thirteen centuries ago, yet there is no real analogy or comparison with the diffusion of English. Latin is a better analogy. Latin was universally spoken pretty early in Gaul, Britain, Spain, and somewhat later in the provinces on the Danube. In the East it spread more slowly, but by the Antonines and onwards the spread of Latin was pretty complete, even in Africa. Greek was common throughout the empire as the language of commerce in the fourth century. St. Augustine tells us that pains were taken that the Imperial state should impose not only its political yoke but its own tongue upon the conquered peoples, *per pacem societatis*. This is what, among other things, is slowly coming to pass in India. Though to-day only a handful, a million or so, of the population use our language, yet English must inevitably spread from being an official tongue to be a general unifying agent. An Englishman who adds to the glory of our language and letters will deserve Caesar's grand compliment to Cicero, declaring it a better claim to a laurel crown to

South Africa is the latest case in which this particular question has given trouble, and in reference to this and other points, it is interesting to read Lord Durham's Report in the light of what has taken place in South Africa. His views no doubt would have been modified, and might have been entirely reversed, in the light of later experience, and no two sets of conditions in history are wholly alike. It would not have been possible to rearrange South Africa so as to secure a British majority over the Dutch; and the native problem and many others differentiate the case of South Africa from that of Canada. Still it should be noted that, while Lord Durham's Report was after the South African war freely used to support the case of giving responsible government to the conquered territories in South Africa, the all-important fact was rather left out of sight that this advanced democrat, this father of the system of colonial self-government, in dealing with a province in which there had been only a contemptible rising and not a life and death struggle, in which the non-British majority had lived and thrived not under republican institutions but under British rule, laid down as a *sine quâ non* for giving responsible government that a British majority should be permanently assured.

have advanced the boundaries of Roman genius than the boundaries of Roman rule. Whether Julius was sincere or insincere, it is a noble truth for us as well as for old Rome.'—' Lord Morley's Address to the English Association ', *Times*, Jan. 28, 1911.

Responsible Government

To the two Canadas, made into one; to all the other British North American provinces, as they stood, and when in years to come they should be united to the already united Canadian province, Lord Durham recommended that responsible government should be given. What did he mean by responsible government? What objections were raised to it by British statesmen at the time? and what limits or conditions did Lord Durham assign to it?

On the 14th of May 1829 Mr. Stanley (afterwards Earl of Derby) presented to the House of Commons a petition which had been agreed to at a meeting held at Yorktown (Toronto), and signed by 2,110 inhabitants of Upper Canada. According to Stanley's speech in presenting the petition, it asked, among other points, for ' a local responsible ministry '. This is commonly held to be the first mention of the term responsible government, which subsequently became so familiar. In itself it is a somewhat vague phrase, and in some passages of his Report Lord Durham uses general terms in referring to it. Thus he says that the grant of responsible government would be ' a change which would amount simply to this, that the Crown would henceforth consult the wishes of the people in the choice of its servants ' (ii. 285); but in other passages he makes it perfectly clear that he considered the essence of responsible government to be that the executive officers should be subordinate to the Legislature. ' The wisdom of adopting the true principle of representative government, and facilitating the management of public affairs, by entrusting it to the persons who have the confidence of the representative body, has never been recognized in the government of the North American colonies. All the officers of government were independent of the Assembly' (ii. 77). By responsible government, then, he meant, and all in England and Canada who used the phrase and discussed it meant, constitutional government in the accepted English sense, as constitutional government had been known and practised in England for generations. He meant a political system in which the Executive is directly and immediately responsible to the Legislature, in which the ministers are members of the Legislature, chosen from the party which includes the majority of the elected representatives of the people. He meant a British system, and therefore he would entrust its working only to a British majority.

The Act of 1791 had given to either of the two Canadas representative institutions without responsible government. It had embodied, to use Lord Durham's somewhat exaggerated words, ' the combining of apparently popular institutions with an utter absence of all efficient control of the people over their rulers' (ii. 74). To Lord Durham, as a student of English history, as an heir of English traditions, as a foremost fighter in the democratic ranks, as England understood democracy, representative institutions without responsible government were a monstrosity, a contradiction in terms. ' It is difficult to understand how any English

CHAP. V   RESPONSIBLE GOVERNMENT   139

statesmen could have imagined that representative and irresponsible government could be successfully combined' (ii. 79). 'From the commencement, therefore, to the end of the disputes which mark the whole Parliamentary history of Lower Canada, I look on the conduct of the Assembly as a constant warfare with the Executive, for the purpose of obtaining the powers inherent in a representative body by the very nature of representative government' (ii. 83, 84).

Now it will be noted that in his Report Lord Durham continually contrasts the condition of the two Canadas with that of the United States, and attributes the greater prosperity, which was in evidence in the United States, in part to the fact that the citizens of the American republic lived 'under a perfectly free and eminently responsible government' (ii. 261).[1] Moreover, in one passage he lays down that 'this entire separation of the legislative and executive powers of a state is the natural error of Governments desirous of being free from the check of representative institutions' (ii. 79). He never seems to have realized, or at any rate he ignores, the vital difference between the British and the American constitutions, that in the former the Executive is, to use Professor Dicey's terms,[2]

[1] On the other hand, Lord Durham says (ii. 331), 'The warmest admirers, and the strongest opponents of republican institutions, admit or assert that the amazing prosperity of the United States is less owing to their form of government, than to the unlimited supply of fertile land.'

[2] *The Law of the Constitution*, sixth ed., 1902, Appendix, note 3, on the 'Distinction between a parliamentary executive and a non-parliamentary executive'. Professor Dicey points out (p. 432) that 'the strong point of a non-parliamentary executive is its comparative independence'   On this subject see Mr. Bryce's *American Common-*

parliamentary, and in the latter non-parliamentary, that the American constitution is an instance of the successful combination of representative and (in the English sense) irresponsible government ; while his statement, that the separation of the legislative and executive powers of a state is an error due to the desire to be free from the check of representative institutions, is amazing in face of the fact that this separation had been originally recommended by political thinkers, and carried into effect in America and in France, as a supposed security against arbitrary government, as an indispensable guarantee of a free constitution.[1]

In the United States the people elect the President ; but, during the President's term of office, the executive officers whom he appoints, though they belong to the party to which he belongs, and therefore are so far in harmony with the wishes of the majority of the electors, are, like the President himself, not members either of the Senate or of

---

wealth. He writes : ' There exists between England and the United States a difference which is full of interest. In England the legislative branch has become supreme, and it is considered by Englishmen a merit in their system that the practical executive of the country is directly responsible to the House of Commons. In the United States, however, not only in the national government, but in every one of the states, the exact opposite theory is proceeded upon—that the executive should be wholly independent of the legislative branch ' (1888 ed., vol. i, pp. 385-6).

[1] See on this point Cornewall Lewis's *Government of Dependencies*, Preliminary Inquiry, 1891 ed., p. 41, &c. Locke, Montesquieu, Paley, &c., supported this theory of the separation of the legislative and executive powers, and Cornewall Lewis says that it ' became in the last (the eighteenth) century a sort of political axiom which every one supposed himself to understand, and which no one thought of questioning '.

CHAP. V RESPONSIBLE GOVERNMENT 141

the House of Representatives, but are wholly independent of and in no sense responsible directly or indirectly to the Legislature. Thus Lord Durham, on the one hand, insisted upon the vital necessity of responsible government as Englishmen understood it, and, on the other, held up as a model a country in which the system of responsible government in the English sense did not and does not exist. He would no doubt have contended, if challenged on the point, that the two cases of Great Britain and the United States were and are entirely differentiated by the existence of the Crown in the one case and of the elected President in the other,[1] and it is very noteworthy what importance this advanced Liberal attached to 'the stable authority of an hereditary monarchy' (ii. 263); but it is a weakness in the Report that, with its constant references to the United States, it does not seem to appreciate that the political system existing in the country, which bordered on Canada and which had been colonized from Great Britain, was not an accurate illustration of his theory of responsible government as embodying the one vital principle of a Parliamentary Executive. Why did the author of the Report not appreciate the difference between the two cases? Because he

[1] This is clearly pointed out by Merivale in the Appendix, written in 1861, to No. XXII of his *Lectures on Colonisation and the Colonies*. Speaking of the American system of a non-parliamentary executive, he says, ' Not to speak of other objections to this system, it is clearly incompatible with colonial institutions under a Governor appointed by the Crown. His ministers would be ministers of the Crown, and antagonistic, or so considered, to the community and legislature. It might work if governors were elected by the people, as is the American President' (p. 650).

was intensely British, because he could not conceive of liberties for white men in lands under the British Crown without British Parliamentary government. The citizens were to be made British, if not British already ; their institutions were to be those, and those only, which he had known in Great Britain and helped so largely to develop.[1]

As he understood responsible government—government with a Parliamentary Executive—so other English statesmen of the time understood it. What were the objections which they took to it ? The objections all resolved themselves into the one main contention that men cannot serve two masters. How, it was argued, is it possible to have divided responsibility ? If the Executive is responsible to the Colonial Legislature, it cannot be responsible to the Imperial Parliament ; whereas it was assumed that, if a colony was to remain part of the British Empire, its administration must be responsible to the Imperial advisers of the Crown and to the Imperial Parliament. Thus Lord Glenelg contended, in his Instructions to Sir Francis Bond

[1] Lord Durham's son-in-law, Lord Elgin, thoroughly understood the difference between the British and American systems. Writing to Lord Grey from Canada on November 1, 1850, he says : ' The faithful carrying out of the principles of constitutional government is a departure from the American model, not an approximation to it. . . . The fact is that the American system is our old colonial system with, in certain cases, the principle of popular election substituted for that of nomination by the Crown. Mr. Fillmore stands to his Congress very much in the same relation in which I stood to my Assembly in Jamaica. There is the same absence of effective responsibility in the conduct of legislation, the same want of concurrent action between the parts of the political machine '.—*Canadian Constitutional Development* (Egerton and Grant), p. 327.

CHAP. V   RESPONSIBLE GOVERNMENT   143

Head, dated the 5th of December 1835,[1] that the existing system in Upper Canada, if properly worked, was already responsible government, only the responsibility lay to the Home authorities.

' Experience would seem to prove that the administration of public affairs in Canada is by no means exempt from the control of a practical responsibility. To His Majesty and to Parliament the Governor of Upper Canada is at all times most fully responsib'e for his official acts. . . . This responsibility to His Majesty and to Parliament is second to none which can be imposed on a public man, and it is one which it is in the power of the House of Assembly at any time, by address or petition, to bring into active operation.'

It has been seen that in March 1837 the House of Commons passed a series of resolutions, one of which was in the following terms : ' That while it is expedient to improve the composition of the Executive Council in Lower Canada, it is unadvisable to subject it to the responsibility demanded by the House of Assembly of that province.' Speaking in support of this resolution, Lord John Russell said that the Assembly demanded that ' the executive council should be a responsible council similar to the cabinet in this country ', and his comment was :

' I hold this proposition to be entirely incompatible with the relations between the mother country and the Colony. . . . That part of the constitution which requires that the ministers of the Crown shall be responsible to Parliament and

---

[1] See House of Commons Paper, No. 113, March 2, 1836, p. 64.

shall be removable if they do not obtain the confidence of Parliament, is a condition which exists in an Imperial legislature and in an Imperial legislature only. It is a condition which cannot be carried into effect in a colony—it is a condition which can only exist in one place, namely the seat of the Empire.'

He used similar terms in the debates of the following January, when the constitution of Lower Canada was being suspended and Lord Durham was being sent out; and, after Lord Durham's Report had been received, laid before Parliament, and fully considered, he reiterated the same views to the new Governor-General of Canada, Poulett Thomson, in his dispatch of the 14th of October 1839, which will be found in the Appendix. It will be seen on reference to that dispatch that Lord John Russell apparently did not appreciate the full force and intent of Lord Durham's recommendations. He gives an unqualified negative to the grant of responsible government, treating the question as decided by the resolutions against it which had been passed in Parliament; but he adds that ' while I thus see insuperable objections to the adoption of the principle, as it has been stated, I see little or none to the practical views of colonial government recommended by Lord Durham, as I understand them '. The demand had been for a Parliamentary Executive on the model of the British constitution, for the conversion of the Executive Council into a Cabinet. To this Lord John Russell answers. The prerogative of the Crown in England is never exercised without advice. The Governor is the representative of the Crown and receives his orders from the Crown.

'Can the Colonial Council be the advisers of the Crown of England ? Evidently not, for the Crown has other advisers, for the same functions, and with superior authority. It may happen, therefore, that the Governor receives at one and the same time instructions from the Queen, and advice from his Executive Council, totally at variance with each other. If he is to obey his instructions from England, the parallel of constitutional responsibility entirely fails; if, on the other hand, he is to follow the advice of his council, he is no longer a subordinate officer, but an independent sovereign.'

Lord John Russell then goes on to point out that the force of these objections had been felt in regard to questions of other than internal concern, drawing the distinction which had been drawn in Lord Durham's report and to which further reference will be made; but he maintains that, even in regard to the purely domestic matters of a colony, the principle of responsible government is inadmissible. He held, and others held with him, that a colony must either be a dependency or an independent state. Cornewall Lewis, writing in 1841, took the same view.

'If the government of the dominant country substantially govern the dependency, the representative body cannot substantially govern it; and conversely, if the dependency be substantially governed by the representative body, it cannot be substantially governed by the Government of the dominant country. A self-governing dependency (supposing the dependency not to be virtually independent) is a contradiction in terms.' [1]

Many years later, in 1870, we find similar views still put forward by a Colonial Governor of great ability and long experience. Sir Philip Wodehouse, Governor of the Cape Colony, contending against the proposal to give responsible government to that colony, and opposing it largely on the ground of the existence of the native population, wrote:

'I have never regarded responsible government as applied to a colony, more properly speaking a dependency, as anything less than an absolute contradiction in terms. How can a ministry, responsible to its own constituencies, render obedience to the permanent power? The issue between them may be shirked or postponed, but it must come. Responsible government I have always held to be applicable only to communities fast advancing to fitness for absolute independence, and I think that the course of events in British North America, Australia, New Zealand, and Jamaica has, in different forms, gone very far to establish that view.' [2]

Occasion will be taken later to note how far these objections were valid, and what light subsequent history has thrown upon them. The contention in Lord Durham's Report was that a clear line could be drawn between matters of Imperial and matters of purely colonial concern, and that in regard to the second class of questions, those of purely colonial concern, the colony should no longer be

[1] *Government of Dependencies*, 1891 ed., chap. x, p. 289.
[2] Correspondence relating to the Affairs of the Cape of Good Hope, C. 459, 1871, p. 15.

a dependency ; that on the contrary, it should be given through national institutions the sense of national existence ; and that, in reference to these internal matters, the Governor, as the representative of the Crown, should act on the advice of a colonial cabinet, not on the advice given to the Crown by ministers in England. He states his case so clearly that it is difficult to understand how Lord John Russell could have felt any doubt about his meaning, except for the fact that the Report, in order to emphasize the opinions of the writer, is apt to exaggerate the contention of those who held the contrary view. Thus, in the following passage, Lord Durham represents those who were opposed to responsible government as maintaining that 'the administration of a colony should be carried on by persons nominated without any reference to the wishes of its people', a statement which is not only too wide but directly contrary to the tenor of Lord Glenelg's dispatches.

Otherwise the passage sums up precisely the meaning and intent of responsible government :

'I know that it has been urged, that the principles which are productive of harmony and good government in the mother country, are by no means applicable to a colonial dependency. It is said that it is necessary that the administration of a colony should be carried on by persons nominated without any reference to the wishes of its people ; that they have to carry into effect the policy, not of that people, but of the authorities at home ; and that a colony which should name all its own administrative functionaries would, in fact, cease to be dependent. I admit that the system which

I propose would, in fact, place the internal government of the colony in the hands of the colonists themselves; and that we should thus leave to them the execution of the laws, of which we have long entrusted the making solely to them' (ii. 280-1).

Thus, within certain limits or under certain restrictions, Lord Durham recommended that, given a majority of British citizens, Canada or any British colony under similar conditions to those of Canada, should be self-governing as England is self-governing, that is to say, that within those limits it should be subject to the Crown only, advised by the colonial ministers, who should be members of and responsible to the Colonial Legislature. What were these limits and restrictions? In the last pages of the Report Lord Durham sums up his recommendations, and we have an outline of the constitution which he proposed for Canada. The two provinces were to be reunited under one Legislature, and reconstituted as one province; the Bill to be introduced into the Imperial Parliament for reuniting the two provinces was to provide for the voluntary admission of the other North American provinces into the Union at a later date; a Parliamentary Commission was to be appointed to mark out electoral divisions and give representation as nearly as possible in proportion to population; the two provinces in this, as in other matters, were to be dealt with as one, and any plan for giving an equal number of representatives to Lower and to Upper Canada was to be discarded; the same Parliamentary Commission was to form a plan for constituting elective local bodies subordinate to the General Legislature, and the plan was to be embodied in an Imperial Act, so as to prevent the General Legislature from encroaching on the local bodies; 'a general Executive on an improved principle' was to be established, and with this recommendation is coupled a recommendation that a Supreme Court of Appeal should be established for all the British North American Colonies; this General Executive was to be such that 'the responsibility to the United legislature of all officers of the Government, except the Governor and his Secretary, should be secured by every means known to the British Constitution'; the constitution of the Legislative Council was to be revised by the Imperial Parliament, so as to enable it 'to act as an useful check on the popular branch of the legislature', without a repetition of the collisions between the two Houses which had occurred in past years; the entire administration of the public lands was to be left to the Imperial Government; all the other revenues of the Crown were to be given over to the Legislature in return for an adequate Civil List; the judges were to be placed in the same position, as regards tenure and salary, as in England; no money votes were to be proposed except with the consent of the Crown, i.e. by the responsible ministers. In a previous passage Lord Durham had specified that the only matters in which the mother country need retain control over the colony were, 'the constitution of the form of government, the regulation of foreign relations and of trade with the mother country, the other

British colonies, and foreign nations, and the disposal of the public lands ' (ii. 282).

The above being an outline of Lord Durham's proposals, the answer to the question, What limits or restrictions did he contemplate in respect to the grant of responsible government ?—is, first, that he drew a line between matters of imperial and matters of purely colonial concern ; and secondly, that in what he considered to be the purely colonial sphere, he made certain recommendations which would have the effect of restricting the powers of the elected branch of the Legislature. Under the first head he reserved to the control of the Imperial Government the constitution of the colony, its foreign relations, the whole of its external trade, and the whole of its public lands. It will be noted that he does not mention the control of the armed forces on land or sea. Presumably he would have included this most important matter under the head of foreign relations; but how far he would have left the militia laws, and the control of the militia in normal times, to the discretion of the Colonial Legislature, does not appear. By reserving to the Imperial Government the management of the public lands, he reserved control of no small proportion of the colonial revenues; and, turning to the second head, it will be noted that he insisted, as a matter of course, on also reserving a Civil List, and on securing in permanence the salaries of the judges. These reservations were directly contrary to the claims which had been so persistently advanced by the Assembly of Lower Canada. It is true that Lord Durham coupled them with the grant of responsible government, but the French-Canadian leaders had contended that, on its merits, a permanent Civil List was not suited to the circumstances of the Province of Quebec. In this respect, and in others, notably in the recommendation that money votes should only be initiated upon the authority of the Crown, we trace the intensely British cast of Lord Durham's mind. The new system in Canada was to be the British system; responsible government was to be given in internal matters, because England had responsible government; but all the British checks were to be applied. On the subject of the Legislative Council the Report is disappointing, and gives no guidance. Lord Durham tells us what the Council should not be; he condemns its existing composition, he dismisses the possibility of reconstituting it upon the lines of the House of Lords, and thereby departs from his British model, but he gives no hint as to how it should be recast, and contents himself with insisting that it should be an effective check upon the popular Legislature, again looking to the British system, and again controverting, to some extent at any rate, the French-Canadian views. Lastly, writing, we may assume, with the Municipal Corporations Act, which the Whig Government had carried in 1835, fresh in his mind,[1] Lord Durham lays the greatest stress upon the establishment of a good system of

---

[1] ' In 1835 the Municipal Corporations Act restored to the inhabitants of towns those rights of self-government, of which they had been deprived since the fourteenth century' (Green's *Short History of the English People*, Epilogue).

municipal institutions, as a check upon the General Legislature. The local bodies in Canada were to be subordinate to the General Legislature, but they were to take something from it, notably the opportunities which dabbling in purely local matters gave for jobbery and corruption. As colonial liberties were to be safeguarded against interference from home by the grant of responsible government, so local liberties were to be safeguarded by Imperial Statute and by the prerogative of the Crown against interference on the part of the Central Legislature. 'A general legislature, which manages the private business of every parish, in addition to the common business of the country, wields a power which no single body, however popular in its constitution, ought to have; a power which must be destructive of any constitutional balance' (ii. 287).[1]

Public Lands

Lord Durham's Report abounds in references to questions connected with lands and land tenure in British North America, seigniories, townships, clergy reserves, and the like; and twenty-one continuous pages of the Report in the original Blue Book form, out of one hundred and nineteen, are devoted to the. Disposal of Public Lands and Emigration. The best known of the Appendices

[1] On this subject, the value of municipal institutions as a corrective of the Central Legislature, see Merivale's *Lectures on Colonisation and Colonies*, Appendix of 1861, pp. 651-4. He points out how the colonial legislatures in Australia would not adopt the policy of creating local bodies 'partly because its adoption would have diminished the excessive power of the central legislature'. See also below, pp. 217-9.

is Charles Buller's Report upon the same question, which Buller tells us in his account of Lord Durham's mission was, as a matter of fact, really due to Gibbon Wakefield. Buller also supplied a short special Report upon militia claims to grants of land; his assistant, Mr. Hanson, made a special Report on the excessive appropriation of public lands under the name of clergy reserves; and among the Appendices which have not been reprinted are a long Report on the Jesuits' estates, made by Mr. Dunkin, secretary to the Commission of Enquiry into the State of Education in Lower Canada, another Report by Buller on the Commutation of the Sulpician feudal tenures, more especially in the island of Montreal, and a Report by Turton on the establishment of a Registry of Real Property in Lower Canada.

Corresponding to the space allotted to the consideration of land questions is the strength of the terms in which Lord Durham emphasizes the importance of the subject of public lands. 'The disposal of public lands in a new country has more influence on the prosperity of the people than any other branch of government' (ii. 242). 'In the North American colonies of England, as in the United States, the function of authority most full of good or evil consequences has been the disposal of public land' (ii. 206). Such a scheme as Buller outlined, and he adopted, for the disposal of public lands, was, in his opinion, 'more calculated than any other reform whatever to attach the people of British North America to Your Majesty's throne, and to cement and perpetuate an intimate connexion between the colonies and the mother country' (ii. 207–8). 'The warmest admirers, and the strongest opponents of republican institutions, admit or assert that the amazing prosperity of the United States is less owing to their form of government, than to the unlimited supply of fertile land, which maintains succeeding generations in an undiminishing affluence of fertile soil' (ii. 331).

Two points should be noted at the outset. The first is that the part of the Report which deals with the disposal of public lands is the one part which includes in fact, and not merely in name, the whole of British North America, with the exception of Newfoundland. The second point is that, when dealing with public lands and emigration, Lord Durham has in view the interests of the mother country as immediately and directly as those of the colonies. At the beginning of the Report he speaks of the lands and resources of British North America as 'the rightful patrimony of the English people, the ample appanage which God and nature have set aside in the New World for those whose lot has assigned them but insufficient portions in the Old' (ii. 13). At the end of the Report he sums up, 'I see no reason, therefore, for doubting that, by good government, and the adoption of a sound system of colonization, the British possessions in North America may thus be made the means of conferring on the suffering classes of the mother country many of the blessings which have hitherto been supposed to be peculiar to the social state of the New World' (ii. 331–2). Lord Durham had a scheme for, or a vision of, the true management of colonies, and their full and free development, but always in connexion with and in relation to the mother country. His scheme included on the one side constitutional reform, with subsidiary reforms appended. The basis of this was responsible government, and in proposing responsible government he was concerned to consider how much he could give to the colonies, so as to make the colonial legislatures national legislatures. The other side of the scheme looked rather towards the mother country, and in regard to the disposal of public lands he was concerned to hold for the mother country what he considered that the mother country had won. His conception was broad and generous. He looked out upon the Empire as a whole, and did not forget the interdependence of the interests of the different parts. He was imperially minded, whether he considered the colonies or whether he considered the mother country; and to his mind public lands and emigration formed a necessary complement to constitutional reform. In the matter of responsible government primarily he gave to the colonies, in the matter of public lands primarily he kept for the mother country.

It will be remembered that in emphasizing the importance of the subject of public lands, in dealing with it as a matter of prime interest to the mother country, and in the method of disposal of the lands which he put forward, he was the mouthpiece of Gibbon Wakefield's views. Wakefield had been with him in Canada, and the Report was written and published just at the time when the principles which Wakefield had laid down in regard to public lands and colonization found most general acceptance. In 1834 the South Australian Act had been passed, and at the end of 1836 that colony was founded, intended to be a model colony, planted upon the lines of the Wakefield system. In August of that same year, 1836, the Select Committee of the House of Commons upon the disposal of public lands in the British colonies issued their Report, embodying Wakefield's views; and although Canada, as Lord Durham reminds us, was not directly within the purview of that committee, there are abundant references in the evidence given by Wakefield himself, as well as by other witnesses, to the dealings with land in the British North American colonies. Both before he went to Canada and after his return, Lord Durham was in close touch with Wakefield in the schemes for the colonization of New Zealand. In short, he and Charles Buller alike were in this matter Wakefield's disciples; Wakefield must be credited with the special Report on the subject which bears Charles Buller's signature; and whoever actuàlly wrote the part of the main Report which relates to public lands and emigration, no one doubts that the inspiration came from Gibbon Wakefield.

The essence of the Wakefield system was, that all the public lands of a colony should be sold at a uniform substantial fixed price, and that the proceeds of the sales should be mainly devoted to sending out emigrants who, from the high price of the land, would not be able to become landholders in the first instance, but would supply the labour necessary for the development of the new country, while relieving the competition in the labour market at home. The system will be found fully discussed in Merivale's lectures on colonization and colonies,[1] and reference should be made to a speech made by Sir William Molesworth on the subject in the House of Commons on the 27th of June 1839, a few months after the publication of Lord Durham's and Buller's Reports.[2] Molesworth spoke in support of resolutions embodying Wakefield's principles. The resolutions set forth the advantages to the United Kingdom to be derived from 'the occupation and cultivation of waste lands in the British colonies by means of emigration'. They laid down that 'the prosperity of colonies, and the progress of colonization, mainly depend upon the manner in which a right of private property in the waste lands of the colony may be acquired', and that the most effectual method of disposing of the waste lands was 'the plan of sale at a fixed uniform and sufficient price, for ready money, without any condition or restriction, and the employment of the whole or a large fixed proportion of the purchase money' in providing passages for emigrants. They further laid down that 'it is essential that the permanence of the system shall be secured by the legislature, and that its administration should be entrusted to a distinct subordinate branch of the Colonial

[1] Among later accounts see chap. i in Book III of Professor Egerton's *Short History of British Colonial Policy*.

[2] See the *Selected Speeches of Sir William Molesworth*, edited by Professor Egerton, 1903. Speech on the Wakefield system of disposing of the colonial lands.

department, authorized to sell Colonial lands in this country', and to raise loans for emigration on the security of the land sales. Finally they cited the success which had attended the application of the system in the case of South Australia. Molesworth, in his speech, credited Wakefield with first enunciating in 1829 the principles set out in the resolutions, and developing them in 1833. He said that they had been partially adopted by the Colonial Office in 1832, and had been embodied in the South Australian Act; that in 1836 they were recognized by Lord Glenelg in a circular addressed to the West Indian colonies; that in the same year they were approved by the committee of the House of Commons, to which reference has already been made; and that they had been confirmed by the transportation committee which reported in 1838. 'They form,' he continued, 'no inconsiderable and by no means the least valuable portion of Lord Durham's report on Canada. My honourable friend the member for Liskeard (Charles Buller) has adopted them in his able report on the waste lands of the North American colonies. And lastly, within a few weeks, a company with a capital of £250,000, has been established on these very principles, to colonize New Zealand.'

Nowhere in the world, perhaps, have lands and land tenure figured so largely in political history as in British North America. A library of books might be written upon British North American land questions without exhausting the subject, and probably without elucidating the most confusing questions which present themselves to any one who studies the Blue Books and Reports.

There was in the first place the question of the dual system of land tenure in Lower Canada, the French and the English, the feudal tenure and that of free and common soccage. The competition and conflict between the two tenures had gone on ever since the date of the Royal Proclamation of 1763, long before the Constitution Act of 1791 had divided the Province of Quebec into the two Canadas; and in course of time, after the passing of that Act, its result had been to create in Lower Canada an English district, as opposed to the French regions of the seigniories. The seigniories lay along the St. Lawrence. 'Along the alluvial banks of the St. Lawrence and its tributaries, they [the French Canadians] have cleared two or three strips of land, cultivated them in the worst method of small farming, and established a series of continuous villages, which give the country of the seigniories the appearance of a never-ending street' (ii. 28–9). The townships lay away from the St. Lawrence on the borders of the United States. They formed the English part of Lower Canada. Thus the Assistant Commissioners of Municipal Enquiry reported that 'The bulk of the population of the townships is composed of old American loyalists and more recent settlers from the United States; the remainder are emigrants from Britain' (Appendix C, iii. 142); and earlier, in 1823, a petition from the townships to the House of Commons recited that 'The townships, or English Lower Canada, are peopled wholly by inhabitants of

British birth and descent, and American loyalists, amounting at present to about 40,000 souls, who have no other language than that of their British ancestors, who inhabit lands granted under the British tenure of free and common soccage, who have a Protestant clergy '.[1] Not the least interesting feature in the townships was the fact that they originated, as Buller and Lord Durham point out, in the practice of 'Leaders and Associates', whereby the land regulations were evaded and the lands which were granted by the Crown became accumulated in very few hands. The following is the evidence given on the subject before Buller's Commission by John Davidson, one of the Commissioners of Crown Lands in Lower Canada.

'After the passing of the Constitutional Act of 1791, lands were granted by patent to leaders of Townships and their associates. Under this system 1,200 acres were granted to the leader, and 1,200 acres to each of his associates, it being quite notorious that in many cases the whole, and in none less than 1,000 acres, were immediately reconveyed by each associate to the leader. . . . The whole was a plan devised for the purpose of eluding the instructions from the Home Government, under which no person could obtain a grant of more than 1,200 acres.'

Thus the land in the eastern townships was taken up, largely by Americans, on British tenure, and thus a distinctively English district grew up in the land of the French Canadians. But the

[1] Appendix to the Report of the Parliamentary Committee of 1828 on the Civil Government of Canada, p. 323.

English, with their predilection for the free and common soccage tenure, were not to be found only in the townships. They invaded also the seigniories. 'The wealthy capitalist,' Lord Durham tells us, 'invested his money in the purchase of seigniorial properties, and it is estimated that at the present moment full half of the more valuable seigniories are actually owned by English proprietors' (ii. 36). One of them was ' Bear ' Ellice, who became owner of the seigniory of Beauharnois, and it was at his instance that provisions were embodied in the Canada Trade Act of 1822 to facilitate the conversion of French into English land tenure. This was followed by the Canada Tenures Act of 1825, which was avowedly intended gradually to extinguish the French system. These enactments met with much hostility from the Nationalist party in the Quebec Assembly, who considered them to be part of a policy designed to denationalize French Canada, and contended that the effect of the Tenures Act was to convert the seignior into an English landlord, and to deprive the censitaire or habitant of the rights which he enjoyed under the old feudal tenure.

Again and again the French Canadian party renewed their protests, and in 1836 they went so far as actually to pass a Bill, which the Legislative Council rejected, repealing the two Imperial Acts, so far as they provided for commutation of French into English tenure. It seems strange that Lord Durham made no specific recommendations on the main subject in his Report; but Buller tells us that it had been fully intended to deal with the question; the extinction of the feudal tenures was a necessary part of the scheme for converting Lower Canada into a British province; and in reference to the Sulpician seigniory in the island of Montreal, Buller speaks of 'the pernicious influence of these feudal tenures, which in all parts of the province retard the extension of its commerce and the development of its natural resources', just as Lord Durham himself writes of 'ancient and barbarous laws' (ii. 265). The attitude which was taken up on the subject by the Imperial Government, and definitely stated in Lord Glenelg's Instructions to Lord Gosford in July, 1835,[1] was that the matter must eventually be settled by or at the instance of the local Legislature, and by the local Legislature of United Canada the question was finally determined, when, in the year 1854, they passed the Act 'for the abolition of feudal rights and duties in Lower Canada'.

The troubles arising out of conflicting systems of land tenure, one French and the other English, were confined to Lower Canada. The difficulties which were created by the system of clergy reserves were common to both the provinces, but were especially prominent in Upper Canada, where Lord Durham considered the clergy reserves to be 'the most mischievous practical cause of dissension' (ii. 179).

These reserves had been called into being by the Constitutional Act of 1791, certain sections of which provided that there should be a permanent

[1] Copy of Instructions given to the Earl of Gosford, &c., House of Commons, Paper, No. 113, March, 1836, p. 10.

appropriation of public lands in the two provinces for the endowment of a Protestant clergy. As regards the future it was enacted that, whenever grants of Crown land were made, an amount of land was to be reserved for the purpose of such endowment, as nearly equal in value as could be estimated to one-seventh of the lands which were granted for other purposes. The Act went on to authorize the creation of parsonages or rectories in each parish according to the establishment of the Church of England, and there ensued an interminable controversy, more especially in the Protestant province of Upper Canada, as to whether the scope of the Act was confined to the Church of England or included also other Protestant denominations. Apart from this fruitful element of dissension, the provisions in question operated as a bar to what would now be called closer settlement, for, whenever Crown land was alienated, a certain amount was locked up in clergy reserves, which remained undeveloped for want of the capital necessary to develop them. To meet this evil an Imperial Act was passed in 1827,[1] permitting the Government to sell a certain proportion of the reserves, the proceeds to be applied to the improvement of the unsold reserves or to the purposes for which the reserves were originally made. The action of Sir John Colborne in establishing a large number of Church of England rectories, to which Lord Durham refers (ii. 175), greatly increased the opposition to the system, although, as has been already pointed out,

[1] 7 & 8 Geo. IV. c. 62.

Colborne acted in accordance with the Secretary of State's views in 1832, and the course which he adopted was upheld in the courts of law. The system, in short, had given rise to abuses, as is shown in Mr. Hanson's Report on the excessive amount of land which had been appropriated for the purposes in question; it had caused much practical inconvenience; and it had proved to be out of place and out of time, for in Lower Canada the overwhelming number of the inhabitants were Roman Catholics, with a fully developed and time-honoured church organization, while Upper Canada was a new and sparsely settled country, in which the great majority of the colonists, though they were Protestants, were not members of the Church of England.

'The apparent right which time and custom give to the maintenance of an ancient and respected institution cannot exist in a recently settled country, in which everything is new; and the establishment of a dominant church there is a creation of exclusive privileges in favour of one out of many religious denominations, and that composing a small minority, at the expense not merely of the majority, but of many as large minorities' (ii. 178).

The prominence which the question of the clergy reserves attained in the politics of Upper Canada may be in part attributed to the strong character of Strachan, the leader (though a Scotchman) of the Church of England party in the province, and a foremost figure in the 'Family Compact'. Shortly after Lord Durham left Canada, Strachan was, towards the end of 1839, created the first Church of England Bishop of Toronto, and as he played a great part in the secular as well as in the Church politics of the time, so the system, of which he was the champion, became, apart from its merits or demerits, one of the burning questions in the political life of Upper Canada. Lord Durham was more specific in his recommendation on this subject than he was in regard to the seigniorial system.

' It is most important that this question should be settled, and so settled as to give satisfaction to the majority of the people of the two Canadas, whom it equally concerns. And I know of no mode of doing this but by repealing all provisions in Imperial Acts that relate to the application of the Clergy Reserves, and the funds arising from them, leaving the disposal of the funds to the local legislature, and acquiescing in whatever decision it may adopt ' (ii. 179).

As will be told later, this recommendation was eventually carried out, and in 1854 the Canadian Parliament passed an Act by which the clergy reserves were finally secularized.

It has been noticed that among the Appendices to Lord Durham's Report are Reports upon the Jesuits' estates, and upon the desired commutation of the feudal tenures enjoyed by the Seminary of St. Sulpice. At the time of the cession of Canada to Great Britain, the Jesuits owned various seigniories and other valuable landed property in Lower Canada. After the passing of the Quebec Act in 1774, the new Royal Instructions given to

Governor Carleton on the 3rd of January, 1775, expressly ordered 'that the Society of Jesuits be suppressed and dissolved, and no longer continued as a body corporate and politic, and all their rights and possessions and property shall be vested in Us for such purposes as we may hereafter think fit to direct and appoint'. It was not, however, until 1800 that the Crown took full possession of the estates. In the meantime, in or about 1770, King George III had given some promise of these estates to Lord Amherst as a reward for his services in Canada, and the claim of the Amherst family was not finally extinguished until 1803. In Canada it had always been contended that the proceeds of the Jesuits' estates ought to be devoted to education, and eventually, in 1831, Lord Goderich handed over the revenues from this source to the Quebec Legislature for educational purposes. In the following year that Legislature passed an Act applying the funds in question to education, and by a later Canadian Act of 1856 the Jesuits' estates were appropriated to form 'The Lower Canada Education Investment Fund'. Many years afterwards, subsequent to the Confederation Act, the provincial Legislature of Quebec passed in 1888 the Jesuits' Estates Act, under which a sum of $400,000 was paid in compensation for the property which the Jesuits had once owned.[1]

It will be observed that Lord Durham criticizes the British Government on the ground that 'it has applied the Jesuits' estates, part of the pro-

[1] See *The Seigniorial System in Canada*, Munro, p. 250, note 4.

perty destined for purposes of education, to supply a species of fund for secret service; and for a number of years it has maintained an obstinate struggle with the Assembly in order to continue this misappropriation' (ii. 136). From the Report of the Commissioner of Inquiry into the State of Education in Lower Canada (vol. iii, App. D), and from Mr. Dunkin's special Report upon the Jesuits' estates, it is clear that this criticism applies wholly or mainly to the years between 1800 and 1831, Mr. Dunkin's account being that 'the revenues of the estates during the interval between this period (1800) and the year 1831, when they were surrendered by the Provincial Parliament for the support of education, were appropriated by the local executive as a part of the property of the Crown, and no report as to the mode of their application was made public '.

The Seminary of St. Sulpice had never, like the Jesuits, fallen under the ban of the British Government. On the contrary, the Sulpicians had been allowed to retain undisturbed possession of their estates, and in consequence it was held by the law officers of the Crown in England, who were consulted in the matter during Sir James Craig's Government, by Lord Goderich in 1831, and by Lord Gosford and his fellow commissioners, who made a special Report upon the question in October 1836, that the Crown could not without great hardship disregard their proprietary rights. The Sulpicians owned three seigniories in the district of Montreal, one of which included nearly the whole island of Montreal, and the object of Lord

Gosford and his colleagues, as well as of Charles Buller's later recommendations, was to facilitate commutation of these feudal rights, which were felt to be a growing encumbrance in proportion to the growth of the city of Montreal. No time was lost in dealing with the matter after Buller had reported. In April 1839 the Special Council of Lower Canada passed an ordinance incorporating the seminary, confirming its title to its seigniories, and providing for the commutation of the seigniorial rights, thereby—to quote the words in which the objects of the ordinance were described —'relieving a wealthy and enterprising community from the encumbrances and drawbacks of a feudal tenure'. The ordinance contained a clause providing that it should not take effect, until confirmed by an Imperial Act, or other legislative authority competent—which the Special Council was not—to give it perpetuity. Sir John Colborne from Canada, and Lord Durham in England, earnestly pressed that the matter should be settled without delay; and in the following year, 1840, by duly authorized local legislation this long outstanding question was set to rest.[1]

[1] What happened was rather complicated. The Special Council for Lower Canada was created by the Imperial 'Constitutional Act Suspension Act, 1838.' That Act provided that any laws passed by the Council should expire on November 1, 1842, 'unless continued by competent authority.' Therefore the Council could not in any case—apart from the reservation clause in the ordinance referred to in the text—legislate in perpetuity for the Seminary of St. Sulpice. But in August 1839 the Imperial Parliament passed the Suspension Act Amendment Act, 1839, which repealed the provision making laws passed by the Special Council expire on November 1, 1842, and the same Act, while prohibiting the Special Council from legislating on the temporal or spiritual rights of

PUBLIC LANDS

In all new countries, as a general rule, land companies play a prominent part, and Canada was no exception to the rule. Two companies deserve special mention, one of which went to work in Upper Canada, the other in the eastern townships of the Lower Province. The former, the Canada Company, was the elder of the two, and was given legal recognition by an Act of the Imperial Parliament, passed in June 1825,[1] which was followed by a Royal Charter incorporating the company and bearing the date of the 19th of August 1826. The preamble of the Act shows clearly that the object which the Government had in view in passing it, was the settlement and cultivation of the Crown and clergy reserves in Upper Canada by sale within limits to a chartered company; and Buller, in his Report on Public Lands, wrote that 'The sale to the Canada Company, though in form an exceptional method of disposing of public lands, was in effect, and was intended to be, a delegation of the powers of Government in this important

ecclesiastics, or the law of tenure, made a special exception in favour of legislation for commuting the seigniorial rights of the Seminary of St. Sulpice. When the Act had been passed, Lord John Russell, who was then Secretary of State for the Colonies, returned the ordinance to be revised and re-enacted. Meanwhile there had been considerable opposition to it in Canada on the ground that it was too favourable to the Seminary. Poulett Thomson therefore passed a new ordinance through the Council in 1840, following more closely the lines laid down by Buller, and less favourable to the ecclesiastics. There was still some opposition both in Canada and in England, but the ordinance was allowed to stand. When the Canadian Act 'for the abolition of feudal rights and duties in Lower Canada' was passed in 1854, the settlement which had been made was safeguarded, but further provisions with regard to the Seminary and its tenures were included in the Seigniorial Amendment Act of 1859. [1] An amending Act was passed in 1828.

particular to a private company' (Appendix B, iii. 55).

The quantity of land sold to the company, and the terms on which it was sold, are given as follows in the evidence of John Radenhurst, chief clerk of the Surveyor-General's office in Upper Canada, who appeared before Buller's Commission.

'The company at first contracted for the purchase of 1,384,413 acres of Crown Reserves and 829,430 of Clergy Reserves at 3s. 6d. per acre. The Government were, however, unable to perform their contract, so far as related to the Clergy Reserves, and, as a substitute, the company were allowed to select 1,100,000 acres in a block on the shores of Lake Huron, at the same price for the whole as was to have been paid for 800,000 acres of Clergy Reserves, making the whole of their purchase 2,484,413 acres; the purchase money was to be paid in the following annual instalments, viz. In the year ending July 1827, £20,000; 1828, £15,000; 1829, £15,000; 1830, £15,000; 1831, £16,000; 1832, £17,000; 1833, £18,000; 1834, £19,000; 1835, £20,000; and £20,000 a year for the next seven years. The company was to be at liberty to expend one third part of the purchase money of the block of 1,100,000 acres in public works and improvements within such block of land, such as canals, bridges, roads, churches, wharfs, and school houses, &c.'

John Galt, the Scotch novelist, had much to do with the inception and the early work of the Canada Company. He was the founder of Guelph, and the town of Galt bears his name. The main sphere of the company's operations was the Huron district, due west of Toronto, between Lakes Huron and

Ontario; and undoubtedly much was done to develop and settle this part of Upper Canada. In 1856 an Imperial Act was passed giving facilities for winding up the company; but when the Colonial Land and Emigration Commissioners issued their last colonization circular in 1877, they reported that the company had still 400,000 acres to sell or lease. A further Imperial Act was passed in 1881, and the Company is still in active operation.

The British American Land Company made an agreement with Stanley, afterwards Lord Derby, then Secretary of State for the Colonies, on the 3rd of December 1833. Under this agreement the Government sold to the company 847,661 acres in the eastern townships for £120,000, payment being at the rate of 3s. 6d. an acre for Crown reserves and surveyed land, and 3s. for unsurveyed land. The company was incorporated by Royal Charter on the 20th of March 1834, and the charter was confirmed by Act of Parliament dated the 22nd of May 1834. The charter extended to the whole of British North America, including Newfoundland, and the company was empowered to hold lands purchased from the Crown or from private persons up to three millions of acres at any one time in the British North American provinces. One section of the Act authorized the commutation of any feudal rights on lands acquired under seigniorial tenure into free and common soccage. The company's operations were, as a matter of fact, confined to the eastern townships, where the actual amount of land acquired from the Crown seems not to have been quite as large as was specified in the first contract with the Government. The colonization circular of 1877, to which reference has been made above, states that the company purchased from the Crown in the eastern townships, where its head-quarters were at Sherbrooke, about 767,000 acres, and that the directors were then offering for sale nearly 500,000 acres. The company met with bitter opposition from the French Canadian majority in the Quebec Legislature, and repeated demands were made that the charter should be cancelled and the Act repealed. The introduction of British immigrants, which was welcome in Upper Canada, was resented by the French of Lower Canada as part of a policy designed to denationalize the province. It was contended that the Executive Government had no right to dispose of the waste lands of the province without the authority of the Legislature; and that, in the sale to the company of so large a tract of land, the rights of the Canadian people had been disregarded in favour of monopolists in the United Kingdom, and the rights of cultivators in favour of landlords. There were two Acts of Parliament which were constant sources of complaint against the Imperial Government by the Quebec Legislature, both connected with land—one was the Tenures Act, the other was the Act which confirmed the charter of the British American Land Company. The Imperial Government, however, refused to entertain any proposals which involved repudiating their contract, and the company is still in existence, working under the provisions of successive Imperial Acts, the latest of which was passed in 1894.

A troublesome and long-standing question connected with land in Canada was that of claims to land by those who had served in the militia in the war of 1812. So far as Lower Canada was concerned, this question formed the subject of a special Report by Charles Buller, which is given in App. A (vol. iii); and Lord Durham embodied in his own main Report (ii. 225–30) the instructions which he gave to the commissioners whom he appointed to settle the claims, after receiving Buller's recommendations. Some time after the war of 1812, free grants of land in the Lower Province were promised by Royal Instructions to militiamen who had served in the war, the boon being intended for the six battalions of embodied militia, as opposed to what was known as the sedentary militia, though some of the latter also preferred claims. The grants were to range from 100 acres to the privates to 1,200 to the commanding officers. They were to be made on condition of settlement; but sufficient facilities for settlement were not given, and the land claims were in large measure disposed of by the militiamen to land speculators. There resulted, in Buller's words, 'the maximum of injury to the province with the minimum of benefit to the militiamen'; and, on his recommendation, Lord Durham appointed a board of commissioners to investigate the claims, and to pay off those claimants who had made good their title by orders representing the money value of the land to which they were entitled, at the average selling price of Crown lands during the last ten years. There had been similar trouble in Upper

Canada in the years after the war; and John Richards, who had been specially deputed by the Imperial Government in 1830 to visit the British North American provinces and make a Report in connexion with Waste Lands and Emigration,[1] wrote:

'The Province of Upper Canada appears to have been considered by Government as a land fund, to reward meritorious servants. Lots are given to reduced officers; say, 1,200 acres to a Colonel, 1,000 to a major, 800 to a captain, 500 to a lieutenant, 200 to a serjeant, and 100 to a disbanded soldier, and to the United Empire Loyalists, their sons and daughters, 200 acres each.'

The interest of the matter lies in noting not merely or mainly the abuses which arose from making free grants of land to disbanded soldiers, but rather the great part which the practice played in the history of Canada. Thus in the days of Louis XIV, when Colbert and Talon were busy colonizing Canada, discharged soldiers of the famous Carignan Salières regiment were planted out on the land under feudal tenure. After the cession of Canada to Great Britain, by the Royal Proclamation of 1763, grants of land were offered to soldiers and sailors who had served in America in the previous war on conditions of settlement; similar grants were offered after the war of American Independence. It was in principle a good and sound method of rewarding those who had fought for their country, and attaching to the soil colonists

[1] The report was made in January 1831, and laid before the House of Commons in March 1832, No. 334. See p. 4.

who had shown that they could defend it. But in the case in point, the militiamen had already their homes in the land, and there was no question of attracting them to remain in it as settlers. Moreover, as Buller pointed out, in Lower Canada ' the majority of the militia were French Canadians, who have not hitherto been, and are not now, an emigrating people' ; the result, therefore, of giving them grants of land would at best only have transferred them reluctantly from one district of the province to another, while the actual outcome was to make the land claims the subject of traffic and speculation.

Various other questions connected with lands in the two Canadas might be noted. There was a difficulty caused by squatters who had settled on the waste lands of the Crown without any legal title. Their case is referred to in Buller's Report, and Lord Durham met or proposed to meet it by naming a date, and giving to all bona fide settlers, who had established themselves on Crown lands without title before that time, a right of pre-emption at the price which had been fixed for Crown lands in their neighbourhood. He wrote a separate dispatch on this matter, and it formed the subject of later correspondence between Lord John Russell and Poulett Thomson. There was again the subject of the lands assigned to the Six Nation Indians in Upper Canada ; but, without further reference to these specific questions, it is time to comment upon the general subject of Crown lands in Canada, and upon Buller's scheme, which was Wakefield's scheme, and which Lord Durham adopted for dealing with the lands in the public interest.

Buller's, or rather Wakefield's, scheme was designed partly to remedy the evils which had resulted from the profusion of land grants in the past ; partly to provide a sound working system for disposing of public lands in the future. In the past the Government had parted with a vast amount of land to private owners, with the result that much was locked up and uncultivated. In order to bring these lands into cultivation, Buller proposed that a tax at the rate of 2d. an acre should be levied upon all wild lands, and that the proceeds of the tax should be applied, either directly or by being made part security for a development loan, to making roads, improving communications, and facilitating the settlement of the country. Proprietors were to be allowed to pay the tax in land, such land 'to be taken by the Government at the rate of 4s. per acre, in lots of not less than 100 acres' (App. B, iii. 88). Thus the Government would recover some of the land which had been alienated in the past, and the proprietors who paid the tax would be recouped for losing some of their land, by the increased value which would accrue from the proceeds of the tax to the lands which they still retained in their own hands. The tax was to be imposed and its continuance guaranteed by a central authority, the Imperial Parliament. As regards the future, Buller recommended that all public lands should be sold not by auction, but at a fixed price ; that this fixed price should be uniform, one and the same in all parts of British North America, and that the money should be paid at the time of sale. The price, he suggested, might be 10*s.* an acre, though he doubted whether it was not too low. ' Even at that price, there is great reason to fear that labouring emigrants may be induced to become purchasers before they have either the requisite capital or knowledge to qualify them for the position they will thus assume. The produce of the fund, also, will be scarcely adequate to the objects to which it ought to be applied, the construction of public works and the promotion of emigration' (iii. 113). He named the sum in question as a compromise, noting that the neighbourhood of the United States must be an element in determining the price, and that the question therefore was perhaps one to be left to and settled by the authority to which the administration of the public lands would be confided. He recommended that no limit should be placed to the amount of land which any one man might buy; that all reserves of every kind, including the clergy reserves, should be thrown open to purchase and settlement; and that ' public land in all the North American colonies should be open to purchase by all persons to whatever country they may belong, requiring, if necessary, that the subject of a foreign power should at the time of purchase take the oath of allegiance' (iii. 108). This provision he considered to be especially desirable, in order to encourage settlers from the United States; and both he and Lord Durham criticized, with some inaccuracy,[1] the

---

[1] See note 1 to ii. 172.

measures which had been taken in Upper Canada after the war of 1812, to prevent land being held by American citizens, for Buller laid great stress on the value to Canada of American settlers— 'none form such efficient pioneers of civilization.'

The funds derived from land sales, and from licences for cutting timber, in addition to the proceeds from the tax on wild lands belonging to private proprietors, were to be applied to making roads, railways, and canals, and to introducing emigrants, who were rather to work for wages on first arrival than to take up land for themselves; and at the outset loans were to be raised upon the security of the funds, partly for public works and partly for emigration. The whole scheme was to be embodied in an Act of Parliament; and when the principles had been laid down and ratified by law, the practical working was to be entrusted to a central commission in the United Kingdom, with subordinate commissioners in the North American colonies, all acting under the supreme control of the Secretary of State for the Colonies.

Similarly, guided by Wakefield, as Lord Durham and Buller were guided, the Select Committee of 1836 had recommended, with regard to the Australian and West Indian colonies and the Cape, 'that the whole of the arrangements connected with the sale of land, including both the price and the precise mode of sale, should be placed under the charge of a Central Land Board, resident in London, and made responsible either to some existing department in the Government, or to Parliament directly, as may be deemed expedient'. The outcome was the appointment in 1840 of the Board of Land and Emigration Commissioners, who worked in subordination to the Secretary of State for the Colonies and the Lords of the Treasury.

Thus the public lands in British North America were to be administered upon a definite system, for the benefit alike of the colonies and of the mother country; but the authority, under which the system was to come into being, was the Imperial Parliament and not the Colonial Legislatures; and, though Reports of the proceedings of the commissioners were to be laid before the Colonial Legislatures as well as before the Imperial Parliament, the Executive was to be directly responsible not to any colonial authority but to the Secretary of State.

Further and separate reference will be made below to emigration and improvement of means of communication, to which the funds derived from public lands were to be applied; but it will be borne in mind that these two subjects were from Lord Durham's and Buller's point of view inseparably connected with the disposal of public lands, and were an integral part of a great scheme of colonization. Towards the end of his Report (ii. 327–31) Lord Durham summarizes the whole. On the 'management of public lands' he writes, 'The plan, which I have framed for the management of the public lands, being intended to promote the common advantage of the colonies and of the mother country, I therefore propose that the entire administration of it should be confided to an Imperial authority.' Then, passing on to the 'measures to promote emigration', he says, 'In conjunction with the measures suggested for disposing of public lands, and remedying the evils occasioned by past mismanagement in that department, they form a plan of colonization to which I attach the highest importance. The objects, at least, with which the plan has been formed, are to provide large funds for emigration, and for creating and improving means of communication throughout the provinces. . . .' Then, reviewing the prospective 'benefits of a judicious system of colonization', he lays down that 'it is by a sound system of colonization that we can render these extensive regions available for the benefit of the British people. . . . The experiment of keeping colonies and governing them well, ought at least to have a trial, ere we abandon for ever the vast dominion which might supply the wants of our surplus population, and raise up millions of fresh consumers of our manufactures, and producers of a supply for our wants.'

It has been noted that Lord Durham was a strong and convinced Imperialist, and that, in the matter of public lands, he kept his eyes fixed on the mother country at least as much as on the colony. This point of view was characteristic of the group of public men to which he and Buller and Gibbon Wakefield belonged. They were, in modern phraseology, Radicals, but the reverse of Little Englanders; and their attitude will be better appreciated, if it is contrasted with the views on public lands in the colonies which are contained in Cornewall Lewis's *Government of Dependencies*, published in 1841, two years after Lord Durham's Report was given to the press and to Parliament. In the chapter on 'The advantages derived by the dominant country from its supremacy over a dependency', Lewis [1] discusses the advantage accruing to the people of a dominant country from the possession of a dependency, 'in the facilities for emigration and for the acquisition and cultivation of land which it may afford to them'; and he argues that 'the system of defraying the expenses of emigrants from the proceeds of the sale of public lands in the colony does not necessarily suppose that the new settlement is a dependency of the country which sends out the emigrants', that 'there is nothing in the colonial relation which implies that the colony must be a dependency of the mother country, nor generally is it expedient that such a relation should exist, even in the case of a newly founded settlement.' Lord Durham had no sympathy with this point of view. He wished to give responsible government to Canada, and so far to remove it from the category of dependencies; but at the same time he would have emphatically rejected the reasoning which treated the political connexion between Great Britain and Canada, in the matter of public lands and emigration, as of no real advantage to either party.

Sir William Molesworth spoke in high praise of the passages in Lord Durham's Report which refer to public lands, and of Buller's special Report on the subject. It is true that no part of the whole

[1] 1891 ed., pp. 225-9.

inquiry was more detailed, more elaborated, or more complete, but, in the light of subsequent experience, it must be added that no part was so academic or so divorced from living realities. On paper the principles which Wakefield laid down were sound and broadly based; his reasoning was logical and conclusive; and indirectly his doctrines produced no little practical good. But new countries and the English race do not lend themselves to cut-and-dried systems. English emigrants go out to live as they think best, and not as they are ordered, and colonization and uniformity have little in common. The success which Lord Durham credited to the Wakefield system was nowhere attained; indeed the system was never fully and consistently tried; and whatever scope there may have been for its application in Australia, in British North America the field was already too much occupied, the conditions which past history had evolved were too various, to make a uniform system for all the British North American provinces even a remote possibility. Uniformity was impossible; and even more impossible, in the light of the political controversies which had taken place, more especially in Lower Canada, was the proposed combination with the grant of responsible government of Imperial control over the public lands.

It will be remembered that when, in 1831, the proceeds of the taxes which were raised under the Quebec Revenue Act were handed over to the Legislatures of the two Canadian provinces, the casual and territorial revenues of the Crown were still reserved;

that the control of these revenues formed one of the main issues between the Imperial Government and the Legislature of Lower Canada; and that the position taken up by the Imperial Government was, roughly, that these funds would be handed over to the local Legislature when certain conditions had been complied with, principal among which was the provision of a Civil List. In February 1831 Lord Aylmer, then Governor-General, in a message to the Quebec House of Assembly, classified the casual and territorial revenues of the Crown under the following heads [1] :—

(1) Rents, Jesuits' estates.
(2) Rent of the King's Posts.

[1] See the House of Commons Paper of July 15, 1831, Canada Crown Revenues. These funds were enumerated by Mr. John Davidson, Commissioner of Crown Lands in Lower Canada, in his evidence before Buller's Commission, as follows :—

Of what does the landed property of the Crown in this Province consist ?

All the estates which were held by the King of France at the time of the conquest, which may be arranged as follows :

1st. Certain fiefs in the city of Quebec and town of Three Rivers, whereof the censitaires held immediately under the Crown.

2nd. The forges of St. Maurice, which were established by the old French Government and have been let for different terms to private persons.

3rd. The King's trading posts, which signifies that portion of the Province of Lower Canada between the settled lands on the north bank of the St. Lawrence and the land held under the Charter of the Hudson's Bay Company, and which tract is held by that Company under a lease that secures to them the sole right of hunting, fishing, and trading on that territory. The lease expires in 1842.

4th. The King's Wharves in Quebec, which were originally formed by the old French Government, and have been improved by the British Government, and are now let upon lease to individuals.

5th. The estates held at the time of the conquest by the late order of Jesuits, which upon the extinction of that order in the Province were reserved by the Crown, and which consist of extensive seigniories and

(3) Forges of St. Maurice.
(4) Rent of King's Wharf.
(5) Droit de Quint.[1]
(6) Lods et Ventes.[1]
(7) Land fund.
(8) Timber fund.

The average receipts from these sources in Lower Canada amounted at this date to no more than upwards of £7,000 per annum, whereas the revenues which were raised under the Quebec Revenue Act, and which in this year, 1831, were handed over to the Quebec Legislature, were estimated, on an average, at £38,000 per annum. In other words, the public lands in Lower Canada, even after 1830, only formed one item, or, including timber, two items in a list of Crown receipts the sum total of which was not more than about one-fifth of the sum which had been derived from taxes levied under Imperial Acts, and which the Imperial Government had controlled prior to 1831. In specifying the items of the casual and territorial revenues, Lord Aylmer, as already stated, insisted that these

of other property, including buildings in the city of Quebec and town of Three Rivers.

6th. All the beaches and water lots upon all navigable rivers.

The beaches consist of the land on both sides of the rivers between the highest and lowest water-mark, and the water lots extend from the lowest water-mark into deep water.

7th. The whole of the waste and unappropriated land within the Province.

In addition to this the Crown is entitled to a mutation fine upon the sale of seigniories, varying from the maille d'or, which is a nominal acknowledgement, to one-fifth part of the purchase, which is the more common fine, and payable in either case before the seignior is admitted to perform fealty and homage.

[1] The 'Quint' and the 'Lods et Ventes' were mutation fines, the former paid by the seignior, the latter by the censitaire. See Munro's *Seigniorial System in Canada.*

revenues were the property of the Crown. 'They stand upon a perfectly different ground from taxes, properly so called. They are enjoyed by the Crown, by virtue of the Royal Prerogative, and are neither more nor less than the proceeds of landed property, which legally and constitutionally belongs to the Sovereign on the throne.' This account of the funds would have been strictly accurate, if it had been given before William IV came to the throne; but it was overlooked at the time when Lord Aylmer addressed the Quebec Legislature, and apparently it was more or less overlooked for many years afterwards,[1] that by the Civil List Act which was passed when King William IV became king, and again by the Civil List Act of Queen Victoria, all the casual revenues of the Crown, whether within or without the United Kingdom, were made part of the Consolidated Fund. Thus in 1831, and afterwards, the casual and territorial revenues of the Crown in British North America, including the waste lands, were not the property of the Crown, but the property of the Imperial Government. The confusion on the subject was finally cleared up in the year 1852, when the Imperial Parliament passed 'An Act to remove doubts as to the lands and casual revenues of the Crown in the colonies and foreign possessions of Her Majesty.'

Buller, in his Report (iii. 37), spoke of the waste lands as 'in name the property of the Crown'; and Lord Durham wrote (ii. 209) that 'the whole

[1] The point, however, was appreciated by Lord Gosford and his fellow commissioners, and noticed in the first of their reports, which dealt with the Crown revenues in Lower Canada. See the House of Commons Paper of February 20, 1837, No. 50, p. 12.

of the public lands have been deemed the property of the Crown'; but there is little or no indication in Buller's Report or in Lord Durham's that these waste lands, to which they attached such great importance, and from which under proper management they hoped so much, had been included and more or less hidden away in the list of casual and territorial revenues of the Crown: and Lord Durham makes no specific mention of public lands when, in referring to the sources of public revenue in Lower Canada, he writes: 'With the exception of the small amount now derived from the casual and territorial funds, the public revenue of Lower Canada is derived from duties imposed partly by Imperial and partly by provincial statutes' (ii. 141). Lord Glenelg, on the contrary, had fully appreciated the position, when in his instructions to Lord Gosford and his colleagues in July 1835, he indicated that while he was prepared to hand over to the Quebec Legislature the casual and territorial revenues in return for an adequate Civil List, the concession would include the right of appropriating the revenues arising from Crown lands, but would not include the management of those lands which would be retained in the hands of the Executive Government. On this basis Lord Gosford and his fellow commissioners made their recommendations; but Lord Durham and Buller practically ignored what had gone before, and discussed the question of the disposal of public lands very much as though the time-honoured dispute as to the control of the territorial revenues of the Crown had never existed. The result was that whereas in Lower Canada these revenues were to have been handed over to the local Legislature in return for the grant of a Civil List, Lord Durham proposed to withhold from the United Legislature of the two Canadas both the management of public lands and the funds accruing from land sales and land taxes, and further to insist ' on the concession of an adequate Civil List' (ii. 327) as the price of giving up to the Legislature the remaining revenues of the Crown. The recommendation was a curious pendant to the grant of responsible government. While anxious to give free institutions, to create a national spirit and a national pride, while pleading the cause of self-government with rare eloquence and cogent reasoning, Lord Durham, at the same time and in the same scheme, withheld from the proposed national Legislature more than the Imperial Government for years had contemplated withholding.

It was in no narrow or timid spirit that he put forward his scheme. He was broad-minded in withholding as in granting; he withheld, because in the matter of public lands he conceived that Imperial interests were at stake; but his recommendation was impossible in view of what had gone before in Canada, and more impossible when coupled, as it was, with the grant of responsible government. To ignore in this matter previous political controversies and previous conditional promises was only to invite a recrudescence of bitterness against the Imperial Government and the mother country. To give free institutions, but at the same time to withhold the control of the soil and the revenues arising from it, was little better than a contradiction in terms.

Hence it must be summed up that, however broad was Lord Durham's conception of the rightful disposal of public lands, however suggestive was the form in which his views were embodied, under the actual conditions of place and time, and under the political conditions which he proposed to create, his scheme was wholly impracticable.

EMIGRATION.

In an interesting and often quoted Parliamentary Paper, to which Lord Durham refers (ii. 115), and which was laid before the House of Commons in March 1832, entitled ' Copy of the Report of Mr. Richards to the Colonial Secretary respecting the Waste Lands in the Canadas and Emigration ', the author of the report writes that ' much was said to me in the colonies upon the two questions of spontaneous and regulated emigration ; and the great evil of which they complain was the entire absence of wholesome regulation. I feel, therefore, fully convinced, whatever course may be ultimately adopted, even if the present loose mode is to go on, that the necessity of reducing it to a system will be forced upon us '.[1] In the interval between Mr. Richards' visit to British North America and Lord Durham's mission, something had been done by the Government in the direction of safeguarding emigrants, including the passing in 1835 of an amended Passengers' Act ; but, according to

[1] No. 334. Canada, Waste Lands, p. 23. See above, p. 174.

Durham and Buller, who as disciples of Wakefield were entirely in favour of 'systematic emigration', very much more remained to be done, and the parts of their reports which deal specially with emigration are mainly devoted to pointing out existing evils, and emphasizing the need of further regulation by Government. Lord Durham concludes his comments on the subject with the remark, 'All the gentlemen, whose evidence I have last quoted, are warm advocates of systematic emigration. I object, along with them, only to such emigration as now takes place—without forethought, preparation, method, or system of any kind' (ii. 259). In this, as in other respects, Durham had no sympathy with the coming Manchester school. He believed in Government intervention, and, as will be further noted, both he and Buller criticized the view which the Government Commission on Emigration in 1831 had upheld, that the direct interference of the State was not required in connexion with emigration to British North America.[1]

The close of the Napoleonic wars was the beginning of the modern history of emigration from the British Isles. The Report of May 1838, to which Durham and Buller refer, and which was written by Mr., afterwards Sir T. F. Elliot, in his capacity of Agent-General for Emigration from the United Kingdom, states that for the first ten years after the Peace the average annual number of emigrants to Canada was about 9,000, that for

[1] See ii. 253-5 of Lord Durham's Report and note, and Buller's Report, Appendix B, iii. 119.

the five years ending with 1831 the average was 20,000, and that in the year 1831 over 50,000 passed through the port of Quebec. Between 1816 and 1834 the emigration from the United Kingdom to British North America was as a rule much larger than to the United States, but with the year 1835 the tide turned and ran strongly in favour of the United States, where the Irish now went by preference, having previously emigrated or been assisted to emigrate largely to British North America.[1] The first Imperial grants in aid of emigration seem to have been made in the years 1821, 1823, and 1825, to assist emigrants from the South of Ireland to Canada and the Cape, and the first vote for an emigration establishment was in 1834, when a small sum was provided to cover the pay of emigration agents at Liverpool, Bristol, Dublin, Belfast, Cork, Limerick, and Greenock. In 1826 and 1827 committees of the House of Commons considered emigration at very great length; and the committee of 1827, among other recommendations, advised that a Board of Emigration should be constituted 'under the direct control of an executive department of the State'. In 1831 Lord Goderich appointed the Government

[1] But even in the year 1837, if the figures given in an Appendix to Elliot's report are correct, out of 29,884 emigrants who left the United Kingdom for British North America, the emigrants from Irish ports numbered 22,463, against 7,421 from Great Britain, while out of 36,770 who left for the United States, they numbered only 3,871, against 32,899 from Great Britain. Elliot's Report was printed for the House of Commons on May 14, 1838, No. 388, 'Copy of a report to the Secretary of State for the Colonies from the Agent-General for Emigration from the United Kingdom.' Reference is made to it on pp. 248 and 253-4 (vol. ii) of Lord Durham's Report, and on p. 119 (vol. iii) of Buller's report.

Commission on Emigration, to which reference has been made, and which consisted of five members, including the Parliamentary Under-Secretary of the Colonial Office, Lord Howick (afterwards Lord Grey), and the Permanent Under-Secretary, Mr. Hay, while the secretary of the commission was Elliot, also a member of the Colonial Office. This commission was dissolved in 1832, and the Colonial Office was left to carry out its recommendations, until in 1837 Elliot was appointed Agent-General for Emigration; and finally in 1840, after Durham's and Buller's Reports had been published, the Board of Colonial Land and Emigration Commissioners was established, Elliot being one of the three commissioners. This Board was not wholly abolished until the year 1878.[1]

Such legal provision as had been made in past times for the protection of emigrants on the outward voyages, was largely embodied in clauses of the Customs Acts. The first Act, which was definitely known as the Passengers' Act, was passed in 1825, though an Act of the kind had been passed as early as 1803. The Act of 1825 was repealed in 1827 upon the recommendation of the House of Commons Committee on Emigration, apparently because the Committee considered that it involved unnecessary interference with oversea transit. It was, however, re-enacted, as far as concerned British North America, in 1828; and in

[1] See the Paper on Emigration and the Land and Emigration Board, which forms Appendix XVII to the Report of the Departmental Committee on Agricultural Settlements in British Colonies, vol. ii, Minutes of Evidence, &c., Cd. 2979, 1906, p. 327.

1835 an amended Passengers' Act was passed. This was the Act which was in force when Durham and Buller reported. Several later Acts were passed, notably in 1842, 1849, and 1855, and now the provisions of the Passengers' Acts are included in the Merchant Shipping Acts, the principal of which is the Act of 1894.

Various strains of emigrants contributed to the peopling of Canada in the earlier years of the nineteenth century, as they contribute to it now. The House of Commons Committees of 1826 and 1827, the later of which called Malthus as a witness, and largely relied on his evidence, invited special attention to the condition of the Irish labouring classes, and to the terrible distress which had been caused among the weavers in Lancashire and other parts of the North of England, as well as in the South of Scotland, by the substitution of machinery for handlooms. It was held that emigration from Ireland to the king's dominions beyond the seas ought to be encouraged and assisted, in order to prevent the emigration which was already taking place from Ireland to England and Scotland, thereby lowering the already too low wages of the English and Scotch labourers; and there had been an object-lesson in emigration from Ireland in 1823 and 1825, when Peter Robinson, with the help of Government funds, took out emigrants from County Cork and successfully planted them in Upper Canada. On the first occasion he had some difficulty in inducing between 500 and 600 to emigrate; on the second, according to his own evidence before the 1827 Committee, he selected

2,000 out of 50,000 who were ready to emigrate. The starving handloom weavers supplied a large number of emigrants, many of whom were Scotchmen from Lanarkshire and Renfrew. Numbers of emigration societies came into existence from 1820 onwards; and private individuals, landlords, and others, gave money to promote emigration, among them being Lord Egremont, who, in 1832, started an emigration scheme at Petworth in Sussex, and the excellence of whose arrangements for the care of the emigrants on the ships which he sent out is extolled in the evidence appended to Buller's Report.

The emigration from the United Kingdom to British North America, during the twenty years prior to Lord Durham's mission, was pre-eminently the outcome of bitter poverty and distress. The poor in their misery were anxious to emigrate, their better circumstanced fellow countrymen were anxious to help them, emigration was generally recognized as the true remedy for a great and pressing evil, and British North America, though far away in the absence of steam, was near as compared with Australia. Given the most destitute of emigrants, given the desire to put no restriction on their emigration, given a British territory not as distant as some other parts of the British dominions, where there was unbounded room for British immigrants, and where State policy made British immigration especially desirable; given again a time when modern appliances were unknown, and views of life were less enlightened than our own; there is then no room for wonder that the emigrants took with them on the middle passage, as Lord Durham termed it [1] (ii. 253), and to the other side, hardship and suffering which reached its climax when the emigrant ships brought cholera from England in 1832. As far back as 1819 a Quebec Emigrants' Society had been formed for the relief of emigrants on arrival; from time to time the Quebec Legislature voted money for the same purpose; and in 1832, more especially, two important Acts were passed. One was a Quarantine Act, being 'An Act to establish Boards of Health within this province and to enforce an effectual system of quarantine'. It was an Act consisting of forty sections, but, in accordance with a most mischievous practice of passing temporary laws which the Assembly of Lower Canada had adopted in its crusade against the Government, it was only passed in the first instance for one year, becoming law on the 25th of February 1832, and remaining in force till the 1st of February 1833. It was passed in consequence of a warning from the Imperial Government that cholera had reached England, and would probably pass on to Canada; and under its provisions a quarantine station was established at Grosse Isle, rather more than thirty miles below the port of Quebec. It was passed none too soon. In June an emigrant ship brought the cholera, which caused terrible mortality,[2] and supplied a fresh and not wholly

[1] The actual words are, 'the yet unhealthy mid-passage.'

[2] 'On June 8 it declared itself in Quebec, and the following day at Montreal. An almost decimation of the inhabitants of both cities took place before it ceased its ravages.' From 'Remarks on the Quarantine Station, Grosse Isle, from its establishment in 1832, by Sir John Doratt,

unreasoning grievance against England among the French Canadians, in that emigration from England had brought death to Canada.

The second Act was 'An Act to create a fund for defraying the expense of providing medical assistance for sick emigrants and of enabling indigent persons of that description to proceed to the place of their destination'. This Act again was a temporary Act, expiring on the 1st of May 1834,[1] and, like the Quarantine Act, had been suggested by the Imperial Government. It levied a tax on immigrants of 5s. a head, and the proceeds of the tax were divided into fourths, between the Quebec Emigrant Hospital, the Montreal General Hospital, the Emigrant Society at Quebec, and the Emigrant Society at Montreal, the main object being to forward destitute emigrants on arrival to their destination. It was a tax which Buller criticized on the score of equity. 'To tax the whole body of emigrants for the purpose of providing a remedy

M.D.', included in Appendix A to Lord Durham's Report. This has not been reprinted.

[1] The inconvenience caused by this temporary legislation is shown by the following extract from Buller's Report (iii. 121): 'In the year 1837, when from the prevalence of the cholera the necessities of the emigrants were greatest, the societies in question had absolutely no public money at their disposal, on account of the expiration of the Provincial Act under which the fund had, till then, been raised.' An Act was passed in March 1834, prolonging the operation of the 1832 Act until May 1, 1836, but the prolonging Act was reserved for the King's pleasure, and did not receive the Royal assent till August, 1834, and the royal assent was not notified by proclamation of the Governor-General till January 1835, when the Act came into force. There were subsequent Acts which prolonged the original Act till 1839. As to Acts for the relief of emigrants in Lower Canada, see the General Report of the Assistant Commissioners of Municipal Enquiry, Appendix C, iii. 169, 170.

for evils which no adequate means have been adopted to prevent, and thus to compel the most prudent of that class to bear the burden of imprudence or negligence in others, is surely a measure of very doubtful justice' (Appendix B, iii. 122).

That Durham and Buller did good service in calling attention to existing abuses in connexion with emigration from the United Kingdom to British North America, and in demanding more effective control by the Government, cannot be doubted; nor is there any doubt that their representations bore fruit, when in the following year the Board of Colonial Land and Emigration Commissioners was created, and Lord John Russell formulated their instructions. But the main interest of the subject lies in comparing the views which are propounded in their reports with those which are set out in Elliot's Report of 1838. According to Elliot's Report, a strong distinction had been drawn by the Commission of 1831 between emigration to Australia and emigration to British North America, emigration to Australia requiring direct State aid, which was held not to be required in the case of emigration to British North America; and Elliot summed up the Government emigration policy, in regard to British North America, in the words 'that although no direct aid is given to the resort of people to North America, every effort is made for the ease and safety of their transit, so that while the emigration to that quarter is left to flow from natural springs, no pains are spared to keep the channels free through which it takes its course'.[1]

[1] p. 10.

The official view, in short, was that emigration to British North America need not be subsidized or stimulated, though the emigrants must be and actually were safeguarded. Durham, on the other hand, strongly contended that sufficient safeguards were not applied, and that the existing amount of Government control was not adequate. But, with Buller, he went further; he disputed the whole thesis that while the Wakefield system was applicable to Australia, it was not applicable to British North America, and that in the case of British North America Government interference should be strictly limited. To Durham and Buller emigration was only one part of a great scheme for colonizing the Empire; and though they appreciated the difference between the conditions of the Australian colonies and those of British North America, yet the scheme which they contemplated was to be as far as possible uniform for the whole Empire, and in carrying it out the agency of the Imperial Government was to be omnipotent and omnipresent. 'There is not indeed any obvious reason why the Government should take less effectual measures to regulate emigration to the American than to the Australian colonies,' writes Buller (iii. 120), 'there may be a difference in the character and circumstances of emigration to the two regions, but none so great as to free the former from all interference, while the latter is in several cases to a great extent, and in one entirely, regulated by Government.' It will be borne in mind that the time was one when a strong body of public opinion was being formed antagonistic to State interference, and about to result in Free Trade; that the great Poor Law Amendment Act of 1834 had been a practical pronouncement in favour of self-help and of restricting aid from public funds; that Durham, as the apostle of self-government for the colonies, seemed to be in harmony with the trend of opinion which made for *laissez-faire* in the case alike of individuals and of peoples. Yet it was at this time, and by this man, that the strongest possible pronouncement was made, in connexion with public lands in the colonies and emigration to the colonies, in favour of interference by the Government with the individual, and by the Imperial Government with the colonial community. The explanation is that Durham, when he recognized what he considered to be abuses, was not tied by *a priori* doctrines, and that he had above all a great and overpowering sense of the unity of the Empire.

Means of Communication

It has been seen that the funds derived from the tax upon wild lands, from the sale of lands, and from timber licences, were, according to Buller's scheme, to be applied partly to assisting and safeguarding emigration, and partly 'to such works as would improve the value of land and facilitate the progress of settlement. Of such works', writes Buller, 'I may mention the construction of leading lines of road, the removal of obstructions in the navigation of rivers, and the formation of railroads and canals. In some of

CHAP. V   MEANS OF COMMUNICATION   199

these works, the whole of the cost will be defrayed out of these funds; in others, it will only be necessary to afford a limited amount of assistance in aid of works in which private capital may be invested, though not to a sufficient amount to complete the undertaking. Of the class in which only a partial assistance would be required are the railroads and canals, which have been projected to connect the different colonies with each other; or to improve existing or create new means of transport for passengers and merchandise to the Western States of the Union; and to which the resources of the colonies are as yet unequal. Of these, I may mention the projected canal between the Bay of Fundy and the Baie Verte, referred to in the evidence of Mr. Mackay; the canal connecting the River Ottawa and Lake Huron by means of Lake Nipissing and French River, referred to in the evidence of Mr. Shirreff; a projected railroad connecting Lake Ontario with Lake Huron; and the railroad from Halifax to Quebec ' (iii. 116). It will be noted that Buller suggests that railroads and canals should be constructed, not so much directly by the State, as by supplementing and subsidizing private enterprise from Government funds. Such a course had been adopted in regard to the Welland Canal; and the Canadian Pacific Railway may be taken as one of the most striking of many instances in which private citizens have carried out great public enterprises in Canada with the aid of State subsidies. In this respect Canada differs from the self-governing dominions in Australasia, where the means of communication have been supplied almost entirely by the State. In Canada, for instance, the great railway systems of the Canadian Pacific, the Grand Trunk, and the Canadian Northern are all owned by private companies, though they have been largely aided and strongly backed by the Government. Of the four public works to which Buller referred as in contemplation, the two last have been carried out. Various railways connect Lake Ontario with Lake Huron, and the Intercolonial Railway links Halifax to Quebec. But the Baie Verte Canal has never been made, and the great, much-considered scheme of the Georgian Bay Canal is still for the future. Buller wrote of improving or creating means of transport for passengers and merchandise to the Western States of the Union, but he made no mention of the great North-West of Canada. Nor is there any mention of it in Lord Durham's report, for far-seeing as Lord Durham was, and great as was his confidence in the resources of the coming time, the future grain lands of the prairies were hidden from his eyes.

For any empire, for any great territory within or without an empire, means of communication are all important; but perhaps throughout the whole world, no land tells so well as Canada to what extent the life of a country and of its people is a question of communication. Nowhere have communications been more essential to national existence than in Canada; nowhere has nature offered greater facilities for communication; nowhere has man supplemented nature in this respect with more conspicuous courage and enterprise.

Early in his Report Lord Durham, in a splendid passage, bears witness to Canada as he saw it, recounting that 'trade with other continents is favoured by the possession of a large number of safe and spacious harbours; long, deep, and numerous rivers, and vast inland seas, supply the means of easy intercourse; and the structure of the country generally affords the utmost facility for every species of communication by land' (ii. 12, 13). Towards the end of his Report he lays down, as beyond dispute, that 'the great discoveries of modern art, which have throughout the world, and nowhere more than in America, entirely altered the character and the channels of communication between distant countries, will bring all the North American colonies into constant and speedy intercourse with each other. The success of the great experiment of steam navigation across the Atlantic opens a prospect of a speedy communication with Europe, which will materially affect the future state of all these provinces'; and he prophesies that with the construction of a railway from Halifax to Quebec, and with steamers running across the Atlantic, 'the passage from Ireland to Quebec would be a matter of ten or twelve days, and Halifax would be the great port by which a large portion of the trade, and all the conveyance of passengers to the whole of British North America, would be carried on' (ii. 316–19).

The line of length in Canada, like the line of life, has been from east to west. 'The great natural channel of the St. Lawrence,' to use Lord

Durham's words, runs south-west and north-east. While Canada belonged to France, the story of Canada, excluding Acadia and Hudson's Bay, was the story of the St. Lawrence, the story of a waterway, and that waterway ran in the main east and west. In later times expansion was still mainly east and west, still from one meridian of longitude to another, not from one parallel of latitude to another, although the fur traders roamed north and south as well. It was otherwise in the case of the United States. There the earlier settlement was for the most part north and south along the Atlantic seaboard ; and, when in the course of years settlement expanded inland to the west, the great river which was secured for the American Republic, the Mississippi, was a river which ran north and south, not east and west.

By the severance of the United States from the British Empire, Canada gained a future as a nation ; but its national existence and its national growth became almost entirely a matter of longitudinal expansion, for the treaty of 1783 gave to the British provinces, which now form the Dominion of Canada, a southern boundary, which hemmed them in, and in a sense prolonged their line by making the length of habitable land—before the North-West was opened up and known—out of proportion to the breadth. The line was threatened at this point and at that, notably on the Maine boundary, by the unnatural results of the treaty of 1783, and communication became beyond all things vital to the existence of Canada.

Further, the coming into being of the American

boundary, with a not too friendly people on the other side, gave prominence to military considerations in the matter of Canadian lines of communication. Military men desired to impede rather than to promote communications between Canada and the United States, and within Canada they desired to construct communications as far removed as possible from the frontier. It was for military, not, as Lord Durham read the history,[1] for political reasons, that it was attempted, after the war of 1812, to prohibit settlement and keep a belt of bush between Canada and the United States on the south side of the St. Lawrence; and the construction of the Rideau Canal was entirely due to the soldiers' wish to have water communication, for military purposes, between Montreal and Lake Ontario, beyond striking distance from the American frontier. In the first of these two cases, after the government reversed its policy, we find a military man expressing regret that the bush was allowed to be cut down in these frontier districts and settlement to be promoted; while correspondence which has been published on the subject of the beginnings of the Rideau Canal,[2] shows that that work was so entirely the outcome of military considerations, that Colonel By, the skilful engineer who carried out the undertaking, himself a soldier, with difficulty induced the Government to consent to making the canal and its locks large enough for commercial as well as for military purposes. A prize essay on the

[1] See the Report, ii. 65, and note, and below, p. 278.
[2] See the Report on the Canadian Archives for 1890, Appendix D.

canals of Canada, by Mr. Keefer, published in 1850, comments severely upon the military canals in Canada, and speaks of 'those unfortunate military considerations which have ever been a bar to our advancement'; [1] but it was under a soldier governor, and in time of war, that the canals of Canada began; and Canada has owed not a little to the military instinct which has sought for lines of communication remote from the international boundary.

Coming down to later times, the confederation of Canada was more than anything else a question of communication. The 145th section of the British North America Act provided that, 'Inasmuch as the provinces of Canada, Nova Scotia, and New Brunswick have joined in a declaration that the construction of the Intercolonial Railway is essential to the consolidation of the union of British North America, and to the assent thereto of Nova Scotia and New Brunswick,' a railway connecting the river St. Lawrence with the city of Halifax should be begun within six months of the date of union; and as this Intercolonial Railway, the railway which Lord Durham foreshadowed, was an essential condition to the union of the maritime provinces with Canada, so the consideration for which in 1871 British Columbia joined the Dominion, was that a railway linking that province with Eastern Canada should be begun within two years, and completed within ten years from the date when the province entered

---

[1] Prize Essay: *The Canals of Canada*, by Thos. C. Keefer, Civil Engineer, Toronto, 1850.

the Union. In 1885, a little later than the promised time, the Canadian Pacific Railway spanned the continent, and to a greater extent than any other single work of man in any part of the world contributed to the making of a nation.

Although airships have been invented, communication has so far been carried on either by water or by land. Nature gives communication by water, though there are usually flaws in the connexion which need to be remedied by the handiwork of man. By land, at best, she does not prohibit it. Lord Durham, in the passage which has been quoted above, notes that in Canada ' the structure of the country generally affords the utmost facility for every species of communication by land'; and his statement holds true, although, when he made it, he had in view at most but half the continent. Stupendous as was the work of carrying the first railway through such a desert as lies on the north shore of Lake Superior, the prairies beyond are formed for roads and railways, and the Rocky Mountains and the Selkirks were traversed without burrowing underground as in the Alps. From Montreal to Vancouver the Canadian Pacific Railway runs for 2,900 miles; along its whole course there is still no St. Gothard or Simplon tunnel, and but few tunnels, as at Field, of appreciable length.

In the matter of waterways Nature has been wonderfully bountiful to Canada. It would be difficult to find a parallel in other parts of the world, if account is taken both of inland waters and of outlet to the sea. This is perhaps the greatest advantage that Canada possesses, as compared with the other self-governing dominions of the King. There is continuous water communication for 2,200 miles from the Straits of Belle Isle to Port Arthur at the western end of Lake Superior. The difference in level between the sea and Lake Superior is about 600 feet. Along this great waterway there are some 73 miles of canal; and between Montreal at the head of ocean navigation, 986 miles from the Straits of Belle Isle, and Lake Superior, there are 48 locks. The beginning of Canadian canals was in the years 1779–83, years of the War of American Independence, when General Haldimand governed Canada. They were constructed for military purposes, and consisted of short cuts with locks on the St. Lawrence above Montreal, between Lakes St. Louis and St. Francis, at the Cascades, the Cedars, and Côteau du Lac, which were subsequently merged in the Beauharnois Canal. In 1797–8 some kind of canal appears to have been made by the North-West Company on the Canadian side of the Sault St. Marie. The Lachine Canal, which, with a length of $8\frac{1}{2}$ miles and five locks, carries vessels past the Lachine rapids and across the southern part of the Island of Montreal, was early projected; and after the second American war, in 1815, the Quebec Legislature, on the suggestion of the Governor, Sir George Prevost, passed an Act appropriating a sum of money to its construction. The canal, however, was not completed till 1824, at a cost of over £107,000, and the first ships went through it in 1825. Of the other canals which were in existence in Lord Durham's time, the Rideau Canal from Ottawa to Kingston, 126 miles in length, a military w rk constructed entirely at the expense of the Imperial Government, was begun in 1826 and opened in 1832; while the Welland Canal, 27 miles long, correcting the break in navigation caused by the Falls of Niagara, and therefore of the utmost importance to Canadian waterborne trade, though begun before the Rideau Canal, was not available for traffic till 1833. In 1834 the Cornwall Canal, to which Lord Durham refers, and which rectifies the navigation of the St. Lawrence past the Long Sault Rapids, was begun, but it was not opened for traffic till 1843. One of the early projects in connexion with inland navigation in Canada was the improvement of the waterway of the Richelieu River, connecting the St. Lawrence with Lake Champlain. In 1818 an Act was passed in Lower Canada, empowering a company to construct the Chambly Canal on the line of this river; but it was not until 1843 that, after various vicissitudes, the canal was opened, having a length of 12 miles with 9 locks.[1] Meanwhile, the Richelieu River had been connected with the St. Lawrence over against Montreal by a little railway of 15 miles in length, running from La Prairie to St. John's on the Richelieu, above the Chambly Rapids. This was the line to which Lord Durham refers in his Report (ii. 212–13) as the 'one railroad in all

---

[1] One of the best accounts of the Canadian canals up to the date of the report is the *Historical Sketch of the Canals of Canada,* given in the report of the Canal Commission of 1871, Canadian Sessional Papers, 1871, No. 54.

British America', and it had only been opened for locomotive traction in 1837.

As compared with the great canals and railways which throughout Canada, as Canada was in Lord Durham's time, make the transit of men and merchandise sure and speedy, and which beyond the limits of his horizon are making a new world in the West and North-West, carrying communications to the northern as well as to the western seas, the public works of Canada in Lord Durham's day appear puny and insignificant. But not a little had been done, and out of all comparison with the accomplished facts was the recognition of what was coming in the future. On the 13th of July, 1826, Colonel By, when contending for larger dimensions in the scheme of the Rideau Canal, wrote : 'The number of the steamboats now building on the banks of the St. Lawrence is one of the great proofs of the increasing trade and prosperity of this country.'[1] Lord Durham notes how the province of Upper Canada had become involved in financial difficulties through entering on a bold policy of public works, and it has been seen that the first vessel to cross the Atlantic by the help of steam alone had been built in and started from Canada. In spite of political troubles and antagonisms, possibly to some extent because of them, Canada was instinct with the sense of possibilities, and Lord Durham shared it to the full. It is the common failing of political thinkers and writers to devote their whole attention to laws and constitutions, and what is called political science, and

[1] Report on Canadian Archives for 1890, Appendix D.

to overlook the tremendous effect which science in the stricter sense, invention, and engineering, has had and will have in an increasing degree upon politics and history. It was one of Lord Durham's supreme merits that, politician as he was, and devoted to constitutional reform, he appreciated public works present or future at their full value, and appreciated them not merely for their direct material results, but also, and in a greater degree, because of their bearing on politics. They appealed to his constructive mind as being communications, as making divided parts into one, as making small things into great, as linking one home to another, one little town to another little town, one province to another, one united group of provinces to the mother country. He notes as one among various objections to the system of clergy reserves, that they were an obstacle to communication and to continuity of settlement (ii. 220-2). Here are words in which he condemns the policy of the Legislature of Lower Canada (ii. 99-100): 'While the Assembly was wasting the surplus revenues of the Province in jobs for the increase of patronage, and in petty peddling in parochial business, it left untouched those vast and easy means of communication which deserved, and would have repaid, the application of the provincial revenues. The state of New York made its own St. Lawrence from Lake Erie to the Hudson, while the Government of Canada could not achieve, or even attempt, the few miles of canal and dredging, which would have rendered its mighty rivers navigable almost to their sources.' And here are words which show

how well he understood the bearing of public works on politics, and how he looked to roads and railways to help on confederation : ' The completion of any satisfactory communication between Halifax and Quebec would, in fact, produce relations between these Provinces that would render a general union absolutely necessary ' (ii. 318).

It has been noted that Lord Durham's horizon did not include the North-West and beyond, but assuredly if ever a man deserved to see what our eyes have seen in Canada, a dominion from sea to sea as the direct result of railways, it was the man who could feel as he felt, and write as he wrote, with regard to the importance of means of communication.

MUNICIPALITIES AND LOCAL GOVERNMENT

How close was the connexion in Lord Durham's mind between means of communication and local government may be seen from the Commission which he issued to Buller, authorizing an inquiry into the municipal institutions of Lower Canada. The Commission recites, ' Whereas it is highly expedient and desirable that the counties, cities, towns, parishes, and townships in our province of Lower Canada should respectively enjoy as extensive a control as may be consistent with their own improvement, and with the general welfare of our said province, over all matters and things of a local nature, to the end that intercourse may be facilitated, industry promoted, crime repressed, education appreciated, and true liberty understood and advanced.' The first place among the objects for which local self-government should be given is assigned to facilitating intercourse; and similarly Charles Buller, in his letter of instructions to the Assistant Commissioners of Municipal Inquiry, places in the forefront 'increased facilities of internal communication'. ' You will inquire and report about the provision which has been made for the formation and maintenance of those internal communications, which, as they concern only local divisions, can never be the objects of interest to a central government. The system by which the roads and bridges of the province have been managed will be one of the first and most important subjects of investigation.'

The General Report of the Assistant Commissioners of Municipal Inquiry is of great value for students of Canadian history, embracing as it does a large variety of subjects, and illustrating, for instance, such anomalies as had been caused by the mischievous practice of temporary legislation, which the Quebec Assembly had reduced to a fine art. The Report, however, deals with Lower Canada only, and in their Preliminary Report the Commissioners state that they had been compelled to modify their plan of investigation, and curtail their labours, by 'events untoward for the settlement of these colonies' (Appendix C, iii. 138), in other words, by Lord Durham's resignation. The Commission authorizing the inquiry is dated the 23rd of August 1838, the General Report is dated the 14th of November 1838, and from what Lord Durham says (ii. 113), it is clear that he had not received the Assistant Commissioners' Report, when he wrote his own.

In their Preliminary Report the Assistant Commissioners record that 'there is no such thing as systematized local self-government in Lower Canada' (Appendix C, iii. 139); and the paragraph in their General Report, headed 'Existing Means for Local Self-Government in Lower Canada', begins with the statement that 'The only machinery for the working of a plan of municipal government in the province is to be found under the operation of the road law and collateral enactments' (Appendix C, iii. 227). In reference to the same province, Lord Durham writes of 'the utter want of municipal institutions giving the people any control over their local affairs' (ii. 113). Municipal corporations had come into existence in Quebec and Montreal in 1832, in pursuance of Acts passed in the previous year, but they went out of existence again in 1836, in consequence of the temporary Acts under which they had been created not being renewed by the cross-grained Assembly of Lower Canada; and Lord Durham tells us, that he found it necessary to organize police forces for the two cities (ii. 132). Throughout the country, under the old French régime, the militia had been, in Lord Durham's words, 'so constituted and used, as partially to supply the want of better civil institutions' (ii. 98), but the force was now practically annihilated. In short, in Lower Canada, in both town and country, there was administrative chaos.

On the subject of local government in Upper

Canada Lord Durham has little to say; though, in the part of his Report which refers to that province, he notes that 'there is no adequate system of local assessment to improve the means of communication' (ii. 184); and on the other hand, that 'the Province has already been fortunately obliged to throw the whole support of the few and imperfect local works, which are carried on in different parts of the Province, on local assessments' (ii. 190). Buller, in his instructions to the Assistant Commissioners, gives Upper Canada as an instance of a country in which 'a very perfect municipal machinery exists without being rendered available for the most important municipal purposes' (Appendix C, iii. 136); and from a Report which was supplied to Poulett Thomson in January 1840, and forwarded by him to Lord John Russell,[1] it appears that, while the country townships of Upper Canada had their local machinery and elected their officers, they had no power of raising money for local improvements. On the other hand, the same Report states that 'Nearly all the towns in Upper Canada have obtained corporate powers, namely Toronto, Kingston, Hamilton, Cobourg, Niagara, Prescott, Cornwall, and London'. Toronto had been incorporated in 1834, and with its incorporation regained its original name, and discarded the name of York which it had borne since 1793. The first Mayor of Toronto, elected

[1] Report by Captain Pringle on Land Tax, Roads, and Municipal Institutions, dated Toronto, January 20, 1840: House of Commons Paper, 147, March 23, 1840. Copies or Extracts of Correspondence relative to the Re-union of the Provinces of Upper and Lower Canada, p. 41.

by his fellow citizens, was William Lyon Mackenzie.

Bearing in mind that what is stated in Lord Durham's Report and its Appendixes on the subject of municipalities and local administration has special reference to Lower Canada, Lord Durham's views on the subject will be best appreciated, by giving what are more or less obvious answers to the question, Why did he set so much store by municipal institutions and local self-government? The first and most obvious answer is, that the want of such institutions was so painfully apparent; but it is unnecessary to labour this point, or to multiply quotations showing how great and pressing was the actual need for adequate municipal and local administration in Lower Canada; and Lord Durham, while he lost no time in providing for security of life and property at Quebec and Montreal, had views beyond merely meeting the wants of the moment.

He was a strong Liberal, he was a strong Imperialist, and he had an eminently constructive mind. From all these points of view he was concerned to endow Canada—especially French Canada—with a proper system of municipal and local institutions. It has been already noted that municipal reform was one of the planks in the Whig programme, and in 1835 Lord Melbourne's Government had carried the celebrated Municipal Corporations Act. Lord Durham was not a member of the Government at the time, but he was a leading member of the party; and it may well be believed that he was in full sympathy with the movement for giving self-government to the great cities of England, and wished to create similar institutions in Canada. But even more as an Imperialist than as a Liberal, he was anxious to further the policy of local self-government in Lower Canada, for he wished to anglicize Lower Canada, and he regarded local and municipal institutions as peculiarly Anglo-Saxon. ' Lower Canada remains without municipal institutions of local self-government, which are the foundations of Anglo-Saxon freedom and civilization' (ii. 98-9); and again, referring to the United States, ' In the greater part of the States to which I refer, the want of means at the disposal of the central executive is amply supplied by the efficiency of the municipal institutions ; and even where these are wanting, or imperfect, the energy and self-governing habits of an Anglo-Saxon population enable it to combine whenever a necessity arises. But the French population of Lower Canada possesses neither such institutions, nor such a character. Accustomed to rely entirely on the government, it has no power of doing anything for itself, much less of aiding the central authority ' (ii. 112-13). Lord Durham's contention was in effect, that under the old French régime local liberties and responsibilities had been unknown; that, when Great Britain took over French Canada, French centralization and despotism had been abolished without substituting for it Anglo-Saxon municipal and local institutions; and that French Canada could only be made British by being given these liberties, while conversely the liberties could only be appreciated and put to proper use, if French Canada were anglicized. A similar train of reasoning will be found in the Report of the Assistant Commissioners. 'The simple question at issue is, whether the province shall remain French, or stand still until pushed forward by the aggressive movements of the United States, or become English in the progressive and prosperous action, as well as in the outward and visible character of its institutions' (iii. 230).

Apart from his desire to convert Lower Canada into a British province, Lord Durham, as a constructive statesman, as a man who wished to create and to build up, attached the greatest importance to municipal institutions. He regarded, and rightly regarded, municipal and parish work as a training ground for higher politics, and he criticized the action of the British Government in giving to the people of Lower Canada representative government without at the same time giving them municipal institutions. 'If the wise example of those countries in which a free representative government has alone worked well, had been in all respects followed in Lower Canada, care would have been taken that, at the same time that a Parliamentary system, based on a very extended suffrage, was introduced into the country, the people should have been entrusted with a complete control over their own local affairs, and been trained for taking their part in the concerns of the Province, by their experience in the management of that local business which was most interesting and most easily intelligible to them. But the inhabitants of Lower Canada were unhappily initiated into self-government at exactly the wrong end, and those who were not entrusted with the management of a parish, were enabled, by their votes, to influence the destinies of a State' (ii. 113). Holding municipal institutions to be an integral part of the structure of a well-organized community, he embodied in his own scheme for the union of the two Canadas ' a plan of local government by elective bodies subordinate to the General Legislature' (ii. 324); and, in discussing the possibility of a union of the whole of the British North American provinces, he expressed his opinion that the formation of municipal bodies would be 'an essential part of any durable and complete Union' (ii. 322).

But again, it was not only as a Liberal Imperialist, intent on building up a community, that Lord Durham expressed this opinion and advocated so strongly municipal institutions. He advocated them also as what might be styled a Conservative reformer; for, as has been pointed out already, he regarded the creation of municipal and local institutions as a necessary check upon the general legislature which he proposed to call into being, and to which he intended to entrust the powers of responsible government; and he took this view very especially because, having under his eyes the abuses of which the Quebec Assembly had been guilty, he wished to remove from the General Legislature of the future the opportunities for local jobbery. It was with the same object that he laid down that money votes should be initiated only by the ministers of the Crown. How right he was in this view, and how essential it was to create municipal machinery for the purpose, is shown by the dispatch in which, at the end of 1839, his successor, Poulett Thomson, afterwards Lord Sydenham, made his recommendations to Lord John Russell on the subject of the coming Union Bill. He wrote that:

'One of the most important provisions in the plan proposed last session, one on which the Earl of Durham has justly laid the greatest stress, and of which I find the strongest approbation expressed in the Canadas, is that which restricts the initiative of money votes in the House of Assembly to the Government, and which is calculated to put an end to the disgraceful system of local jobbing for Parliamentary grants, which has prevailed in both provinces. But if this provision be adhered to—and without it I should think the Bill of little comparative value—it is absolutely necessary to provide machinery by which local taxation can be raised for local purposes. Thus the establishment of municipal institutions becomes a necessary part of the Union Bill.' [1]

A man who was, as Lord Durham was, a heart-whole believer in responsible government, but who was, as Lord Durham was not, purely a political theorist, might well have argued, Give the people the right to govern themselves, and they will at once see the necessity of having local institutions, and forthwith call them into existence. Lord Durham thought otherwise, for his political doctrines were leavened with common sense. It was

[1] House of Commons Paper, 147, March 23, 1840. Copies or Extracts of Correspondence relative to the Re-union of the Provinces of Upper and Lower Canada, p. 31.

not that he doubted whether the popular Legislatures, if left to themselves, would do the right thing in the matter of local institutions ; he was quite certain that at the outset they would not, for he recognized the limitations and shortcomings of democracy, in small, untrained communities. And being thus persuaded in his own mind, he would have none of the ordinary Whig platitudes as to trusting the people, but held it to be incumbent upon the Imperial Government to withhold from the Colonial Legislatures the power of mischief.

'The establishment of a good system of municipal institutions throughout these provinces is a matter of vital importance. A general legislature, which manages the private business of every parish, in addition to the common business of the country, wields a power which no single body, however popular in its constitution, ought to have. . . . It is in vain to expect that this sacrifice of power will be voluntarily made by any representative body. The establishment of municipal institutions for the whole country should be made a part of every colonial constitution ; and the prerogative of the Crown should be constantly interposed to check any encroachment on the functions of the local bodies, until the people should become alive, as most assuredly they almost immediately would be, to the necessity of protecting their local privileges ' (ii. 287).

That his views on this point were accurate and true has been shown by subsequent colonial history,[1] as it had already in effect been proved by

[1] Reference should be made to the second edition of Merivale's *Lectures on Colonization and Colonies*, Appendix to Lecture XXII, pp. 651-4. See above, pp. 151-2 and note, and below, pp. 297-8.

the history of Lower Canada; for it was due to the representative Legislature of Quebec, not to any want of goodwill on the part of the Imperial Government, that municipal institutions were not existing and flourishing in Lower Canada. Lord Durham blamed the Home Government for not having insisted on such institutions, for not having brought them into being at the time when representative government was given to the province in 1791, and it is a little difficult to decide how far this criticism was well founded. He does not notice that the Quebec Act of 1774, which gave to the province of Quebec, as it then was, a nominated Legislative Council, while withholding from it the power of taxation, gave it explicitly full powers to authorize towns and districts to levy local rates 'for the purpose of making roads, erecting and repairing public buildings, or for any other purpose respecting the local convenience and economy of such town or district'.[1] In 1786 the magistrates of Cataraqui, afterwards Kingston, in what was a few years later the province of Upper Canada, represented that ' the election or appointment of proper officers in the several townships to see that the necessary roads be opened and kept in proper repair, we conceive, would be of great utility, by facilitating the communication with all parts of the settlement ';[2] and though the constitutional Act of 1791 was silent on the subject of

[1] Section XIII.
[2] See Shortt and Doughty, *Documents relating to the Constitutional History of Canada*, p. 643. The note at the bottom of the page is, ' This is the beginning of the agitation in the western settlements for the introduction of municipal government.'

municipal institutions, as the Union Act of 1840, save in the matter of authorizing the constitution of townships,[1] was silent also, there was nothing to forbid the Legislatures of the two provinces from inaugurating municipal institutions, and as a matter of fact, in Upper Canada, the machinery of local administration was actually brought into existence.

But Lord Durham, it must be repeated, was not satisfied with permissive legislation. Municipal institutions were with him a vital necessity. It was his creed that a community should be given self-government in balanced proportions; that as the Act of 1791 erred in granting representative institutions without responsible government, so it erred in granting those institutions to the whole province, without at the same time granting them within defined limits to the towns and districts of the province. For the absence of local liberties, which meant local responsibilities, he blamed, rightly or wrongly, the Imperial Government. Possibly he overlooked the fact that the legislators of 1791 had not at their command the valuable experience in colonial matters which since that date had been painfully accumulated; and possibly too he did not sufficiently bear in mind the difficulty of passing a Bill, overloaded with detail, through the House of Commons.

But it should be noted that his view, that the Home Government had been remiss in not establishing municipal institutions in the British North American provinces, was shared by the Assistant

[1] Section LVIII.

Commissioners of Municipal Inquiry, and also by Charles Buller. The former wrote of Lower Canada 'that although long under the rule of England, the province has participated far too sparingly in the benefits of sound British institutions' (Appendix C, iii. 139); while Nova Scotia, that most British province, is described by Buller as a country from whose institutions 'every vestige of the municipal system of the old colonies was jealously excluded' (Appendix B, iii. 76).

In the administration of their Empire, it was the policy of the Romans to respect municipal liberties, and encourage municipal life. They did so, it would seem, partly because the towns were convenient units of administration, and partly in order to provide their subjects with a substitute for political freedom and national life. At their best—and their best was very good—the Romans were despots; they always had in mind the maxim *Divide et Impera*; they did not regard municipalities either as a training ground for higher freedom, or as an integral part of an edifice of constitutional government; least of all did they contemplate in them a necessary check upon the central authority. If what Lord Durham wrote in his Report upon the subject of local self-government is contrasted with what the historians tell us in this regard of Roman provincial administration, and if it is borne in mind that in the matter of the *municipia* the Romans came nearest to encouraging freedom, we can form some fair estimate of the extent to which British Imperialism is broader than the Imperialism of Rome.

Administration of Justice

The General Report of the Assistant Commissioners of Municipal Inquiry contains a good deal of matter relating to the administration of justice in Lower Canada. To this subject Lord Durham devoted several pages of his Report, commenting severely upon 'the mischievous results prominently exhibited in the provision which the Government of Lower Canada makes for the first want of a people, the efficient administration of justice' (ii. 116). His criticisms are almost entirely confined to the case of Lower Canada, where difference of race, law, and custom had led to complication and confusion; and only one paragraph, on pp. 182–3, refers to administration of justice in the Upper Province.

The British Government had begun by introducing, or trying to introduce, into the Province of Quebec the law of England, both in criminal and in civil matters. By the terms of the Royal Proclamation of 1763, the Governor in Council was empowered to constitute Courts of Justice, 'for hearing and determining all causes, as well criminal as civil, according to law and equity, and as near as may be agreeable to the laws of England.' On this basis, in September 1764, Governor Murray passed an ordinance establishing a superior Court of Judicature or Court of King's Bench, and an inferior Court of Judicature, or Court of Common Pleas, and introducing trial by jury, Justices of the Peace, and Quarter Sessions. The Quebec Act of 1774, while continuing the law of England in criminal matters, restored as a whole [1] French law and custom in civil matters, thereby abolishing in civil cases trial by jury; and this compromise in the main prevailed down to the date at which Lord Durham wrote. It is obvious that under the circumstances some confusion was inevitable, and that technical difficulties must have arisen in the endeavour to deal fairly by two races with separate customs and traditions in one province; but the interesting point to note is how in the matter of administration of justice, as in regard to other subjects dealt with in his report, Lord Durham held the Imperial Government responsible. The Imperial Government, and the Governors who were sent to Canada, had no other object or desire in connexion with the administration of justice than to give to the province of Lower Canada the laws and procedure which the time and place seemed to demand. They were not the obstacle to adequate and efficient administration of justice; the blame rested with the Quebec Legislature; but Lord Durham censured the Home Government at once for not giving larger powers to the Legislature, and for not insisting upon that Legislature doing its duty. Presumably he would have contended that, had responsible government been in existence, little or no blame would have attached to the authorities in England for shortcomings in administration of justice, or in any other matter; but that, inasmuch as under the constitution of 1791 the ultimate responsibility still remained with the

[1] Section IX excepted lands granted or to be granted in free and common soccage. See what Lord Durham says on pp. 69 and 116 (vol. ii) of the Report.

CHAP. V ADMINISTRATION OF JUSTICE 225

Imperial Government, that Government was to blame in giving so much latitude to the representative assembly in the province, and not at the same time ensuring that the French Canadian legislators passed the measures which were obviously required for the good of the community. From the time of Sir James Craig the Quebec Legislature had instituted a regular crusade against the judges. Jonathan Sewell, who was appointed Chief Justice of Lower Canada in 1808, and who only retired at the time of Lord Durham's Mission, had been the object of special hostility, but other judges also had been arraigned one after another in spiteful and vindictive fashion. One reason probably was that the judges were mainly British, and in earlier days, at any rate, imported from outside, not always with much regard to suitability for their work. Another reason was that they stood rather especially for independence of the votes of the popular assembly; while a third and potent reason was that they were not held aloof from politics. In the early stages of a colony, a man who has been selected to hold the post of Chief Justice, may well, by his training and standing, be a valuable public asset to the Government and to the community, apart from his judicial functions; and a good case may be made for not excluding him from the advisory council or the Legislature, provided that he is not subject to popular election. Even at the present day, in some Crown Colonies, the Chief Justice is a member of the Executive Council, or of the Legislative Council, or of both. Sewell was Speaker of the Legislative

Council in Lower Canada, as Beverley Robinson was of the Council in the Upper Province, and the stronger and more efficient the particular judge was, the more he tended to attract the opposition of the popular party. In 1831 Lord Goderich, as Secretary of State, instructed the Governor 'to communicate to the Legislative Council and Assembly His Majesty's settled purpose to nominate on no future occasion a judge either as a member of the Executive or Legislative Council of the Province', with one exception, that exception being the Chief Justice of Lower Canada, whose presence in the Legislative Council was thought advisable in connexion with legislation, but who was to be instructed to hold aloof from all party proceedings.[1] Lord Goderich, at the same time and in the same dispatch, proposed that, as in England so in Lower Canada, the judges should be given by Act of the Legislature permanent salaries and complete independence—pending good behaviour—both of the Royal pleasure and of the popular assembly. But independence of the judges was abominable to the Quebec Assembly,[2] and the question was still outstanding at the time of Lord Durham's Mission, with the result that one of his recommendations was (ii. 327) that 'the independence of the Judges should be secured, by giving them the same tenure of office and security of income as exist in England'.

[1] See Christie, vol. iii, p. 366, and see above, p. 59.
[2] See ii. 88 of the Report, in which Lord Durham gives an instance of the Quebec Legislature having resort to 'tacking', in order to defeat legislation for securing the independence of the judges.

CHAP. V   ADMINISTRATION OF JUSTICE   227

It is very noteworthy in the history of Canada, how anxious the Imperial Government and the Colonial Ministers were to reproduce in Canada the conditions which prevailed in England, in the honest belief that what suited England must suit Canada; whereas it was inevitable that much that was suitable and congenial to an old and purely British country was not adapted to a new land in which a large proportion of the inhabitants were not British. Thus provision was made in the Constitutional Act of 1791 for enabling the Crown to connect hereditary titles of honour with membership of the Legislative Council, and the correspondence which preceded the passing of the Act showed that the Government would have desired to go farther in the direction of giving distinction to members of the Upper Chamber, and introducing the hereditary principle; but the man on the spot, the experienced Governor, Lord Dorchester, discouraged the attempt to reproduce in one form or another a House of Lords. 'Many advantages,' he wrote, ' might result from an hereditary Legislative Council, distinguished by some mark of honour, did the condition of the country concur in supporting this dignity ; but the fluctuating state of property in these provinces would expose all hereditary honours to fall into disregard ; for the present therefore it would seem more advisable to appoint the members during life, good behaviour, and residence in the province.' [1]   His advice was

[1] Shortt and Doughty, p. 675. Similarly in the summary of recommendations at the end of his Report, speaking of the Legislative Councils, Lord Durham says, ' The analogy which some persons have

not followed so far as to omit from the Act all mention of the subject, but it was followed in that the sections which referred to it remained a dead letter. The same Act contained the sections which constituted the clergy reserves and endowed the Church of England, and on this subject Lord Durham took up his parable in words which have been already quoted, pointing out that 'the apparent right which time and custom give to the maintenance of an ancient and respected institution cannot exist in a recently settled country, in which everything is new' (ii. 178). But apparently one of the most unfortunate attempts to reproduce English institutions in Lower Canada was the introduction of the system of unpaid Justices of the Peace. 'The system of unpaid magistracy, as incidental to the criminal law of England, was naturally introduced into the province with that law; and the utter unfitness of the people for such an institution is a striking instance of the imprudence of unadvisedly engrafting the code of one country on that of another' (Appendix C, iii. 160). This was the verdict of the Assistant Commissioners of Municipal Inquiry, who further pointed out that the Provincial Legislature, by enacting that every

attempted to draw between the House of Lords and the Legislative Councils seems to me erroneous. The constitution of the House of Lords is consonant with the frame of English society; and as the creation of a precisely similar body in such a state of society as that of these colonies is impossible, it has always appeared to me most unwise to attempt to supply its place by one which has no point of resemblance to it, except that of being a non-elective check on the elective branch of the Legislature' (ii. 325).

CHAP. V   ADMINISTRATION OF JUSTICE   229

Justice of the Peace must possess a certain amount of landed property, in accordance with the precedent set in the English counties, practically excluded from the Commission of the Peace British merchants who lived in the towns and did not own land. Lord Durham was equally emphatic as to the unsuitability of an unpaid magistracy to the case of Lower Canada. 'When we transplant the institutions of England into our colonies,' he wrote, 'we ought at least to take care beforehand that the social state of the Colony should possess those peculiar materials on which alone the excellence of those institutions depends in the mother country' (ii. 131), and he suggested that under existing conditions, a small stipendiary magistracy would be preferable not only in Lower Canada but in Upper Canada also.

Bad, however, as had been the result of introducing the system of unpaid Justices of the Peace into Lower Canada, Lord Durham laid down (ii. 126) that 'the most serious mischief in the administration of criminal justice arises from the entire perversion of the institution of juries, by the political and national prejudices of the people'. Early in the Report, when illustrating the intense animosities of race in Lower Canada, he shows how the jury system had been used to obstruct justice, a conspicuous instance being the acquittal of the murderers of Chartrand[1] (ii. 52–4); and he returns to the point, when he deals especially with the subject of administration of justice in Lower Canada. In the paragraph, which has for

[1] See above, p. 95, and see note (2) to vol. ii, p. 54.

its side-note 'perversion of juries' (ii. 126), he points out how the practical effect of following English practice in the selection of juries had been to give the French an entire preponderance, to produce miscarriage of justice, and to destroy public confidence in the administration of the criminal law. His summary is (ii. 130) that 'The trial by jury is, therefore, at the present moment, not only productive in Lower Canada of no confidence in the honest administration of the laws, but also provides impunity for every political offence'; and it seems strange that he did not make any definite recommendation that the system should for the time be suspended. But though trial by jury, which the English had brought into Lower Canada, proved under conditions of extreme race bitterness to be a temporary failure, it was not, in criminal matters at any rate, like various other English institutions, permanently out of place in the province. It failed utterly for the time being, as it has failed at times of political excitement in various other countries, notably Ireland; but it must not be classed with the misfits with which the English, in good intention, have from time to time endowed one or another province of the Empire.

On the subject of Appeal Courts, reference should be made to a note which has been appended to the passages in the Report which deal with this subject (ii. 121). From the dispatches which were laid before Parliament in 1839, it would seem that Durham, while in Canada, was credited or discredited in England with having created a new

CHAP. V ADMINISTRATION OF JUSTICE 231

Court of Appeal for Lower Canada; whereas he left the Executive Council, as he found it, the Court of Appeal for the province, but made it more effective for the purpose by swearing in an additional number of judges as Executive Councillors, and by not summoning to the Council, when it sat as a Court of Appeal only, those Executive Councillors who had no legal training.[1]

At the same time, in the dispatch which he wrote on the subject from Canada to Lord Glenelg, he said plainly: 'Had I possessed the means and the power, I should have been glad to have given the province a completely competent and permanent Court of Appeals, consisting entirely of lawyers, for it is much wanted and called for, and forms one feature of the plan which I had in view for the future government of the provinces.' The summary of his recommendations at the end of the Report does not include a new Court of Appeal for Lower Canada or for the two Canadas only, but it includes, as has been already noticed, 'a supreme Court of Appeal for all the North American colonies' (ii. 325). The 101st section of the British North America Act of 1867 empowered the Dominion Parliament to provide such a general Court of Appeal for Canada, and in 1875 that Court came into existence under the name of the Supreme Court of Canada.

[1] See the Report, ii. 123, and see Lord Durham's dispatch to Lord Glenelg of September 29, 1838. House of Commons Paper, British North America, February 11, 1839, p. 194. See also Buller's Sketch of Lord Durham's Mission, iii. 351, 352.

Education

In the matter of education in Lower Canada, Lord Durham criticizes the Government very severely. He tells us early in his Report (ii. 27–34) that under the French régime no general provision was made for education, and goes on to speak of the entire neglect of education by the British government. Later on (ii. 136) he writes: 'I am grieved to be obliged to remark, that the British government has, since its possession of this Province, done, or even attempted, nothing for the promotion of general education.' Similarly Arthur Buller, the commissioner whom he appointed to inquire into the state of education in Lower Canada, and whose Report forms Appendix D, writes (iii. 246) : ' Up to this moment the only acts of the British government, in respect of Canadian instruction, have been the wholesale seizure and the partial restoration of the Jesuits' estates.' How far were these criticisms well founded ?

The education Report gives instances of education Acts being passed by the local Legislature, sent home for the Royal Ascent, and never being heard of again. Both Arthur Buller and Lord Durham censure—with evident reason—the dealings of the Home Government in connexion with the Jesuits' estates. On the other hand, instances might be quoted to show that neither Governors nor Secretaries of State were unmindful of the importance of education; and Lord Glenelg, when inviting ' the most serious attention ' of Lord Gosford and his colleagues to the state of educa-

CHAP. V   EDUCATION   233

tion in Lower Canada, speaks of 'the earnest endeavours of my predecessors on this subject', which had been repeatedly frustrated; although, at the same time, he seems to admit that the Imperial Government might not have been sufficiently prompt in devising a well-considered system of education[1] for the province.

The education Report, as a whole, seems to show that the Quebec Assembly was mainly responsible for the want of a good educational system in Lower Canada, and that, if the Imperial Government was to blame, its fault consisted in not having made the local Legislature do its duty. Arthur Buller advocated, as strongly as Lord Durham himself, the Anglifying of Lower Canada; and this process was to be carried out by a system of common schools, instead of letting French and English children learn their lessons and play their games apart. 'Until Canada is nationalized and Anglified, it is idle for England to be devising schemes for her improvement. In this great work of nationalization, education is at once the most convenient and powerful instrument' (iii. 273). Similarly, before the Constitutional Act of 1791 was passed, in October 1784, Hugh Finlay, the Postmaster-General of the Province of Quebec, wrote: 'Before we think of a House of Assembly for this country, let us lay a foundation for useful knowledge to fit the people to judge of their situation, and deliberate for the future wellbeing of the Province. The first step towards this desirable

[1] See House of Commons Paper, No. 113, March, 1836, Copy of the Instructions given to the Earl of Gosford, &c., p. 15.

end is to have a free school in every parish. Let the schoolmasters be English, if we would make Englishmen of the Canadians.'[1] If then the British Government was to be blamed for the want of a sound system of education among the peasantry of Lower Canada, and if the essence of a sound system of education was the establishment of common schools, in which the children were to be brought up to be British and not French, then it must be summed up that the fault of the Imperial Government consisted in not over-riding popular wishes, traditions, and prejudices, in not forcing a French people and a Roman Catholic Church—the latter distinguished, as Arthur Buller is careful to tell us, by 'the most undeviating allegiance to the British Crown' (iii. 241),—to extinguish their nationality and give up the principle of separate schools.

Lord Durham, as well as Arthur Buller, saw the difficulty of the position and the obstacles which the clergy, not of the Roman Catholic Church alone, would place in the way of non-sectarian education. He expresses his confidence, notwithstanding, 'that the establishment of a strong popular government in this province would very soon lead to the introduction of a liberal and general system of public education' (ii. 136); and then, in the words which have been quoted, he goes on to blame the British Government for having done nothing in the matter.

The Report of the Commissioner of Inquiry

[1] Finlay to Nepean, Quebec, October 22, 1784 (Shortt and Doughty, p. 500); but Finlay would have allowed the masters to be Roman Catholics.

into the state of Education in Lower Canada is dated Quebec, 15th November 1838; but, from the wording of the Report, it is clear that it was not written, at any rate in part, until a later date; and it was not laid before Parliament until June 1839, whereas Lord Durham's own Report was presented in the previous February. Lord Durham, therefore, speaks of the results of the Education Inquiry as not complete (ii. 134), and his own comments are mainly confined to emphasizing the very defective state of elementary education in Lower Canada, and in one passage (ii. 94) enlarging upon the extent to which political jobbery had entered into educational grants. It may be noted that Lord Gosford and his fellow commissioners also dealt very briefly with this thorny subject in their General Report on Lower Canada in November 1836, and in regard to religious instruction, confined themselves to generalities and to a pious hope ' that a system of education founded on the truly Christian principle of toleration and general charity would not be unattainable '.[1]

Lord Durham's Commissioner of Inquiry, Arthur Buller, was the younger brother of Charles Buller, and, like the latter, had been a pupil of Carlyle. The family ability is evident in his Report, and though his work was cut short by Lord Durham's resignation, he collected and embodied in the Report a great amount of valuable information, which was supplemented by a very exhaustive Report on the

[1] Reports of Commissioners on Grievances complained of in Lower Canada. House of Commons Paper, No. 50, February 20, 1837, General Report, p. 50.

Jesuits' estates, compiled by Mr. Dunkin, the Secretary to the Education Commission. Buller comments on the dealings or misdealings of the British Government with the Jesuits' estates, which were in 1831 handed over to the Colonial Legislature for the purposes of education. He gives some account of the education Acts which were passed by that Legislature, and of the education Bills which did not become law; and he sums up (iii. 265) that education in Lower Canada 'languished under systems where the masters were illiterate and needy; the supervision careless and dishonest; the school-houses unfit for occupation, and ill supplied with fuel; the children unprovided with books; and parents utterly indifferent to an institution of which they could not appreciate the importance, and the trouble and cost of which, at all events, they deemed the province of the legislature'. This deplorable result he attributed mainly to the fact that education had been made by the House of Assembly subservient to politics. 'The moment they found that their educational provisions could be turned to political account, from that moment those provisions were framed with a view to promote party rather than education' (iii. 266). The utter breakdown of all previous education schemes, however, had in his eyes the merit that it left the field clear for a wholly new system, which he proceeded to recommend, the basis of his proposals, as has already been stated, being that 'the principle of Anglification is to be unequivocally recognized, and inflexibly carried out' (iii. 288).

He tells us that, in making his proposals, he took for his models the educational systems in force in Prussia and the United States; and it may be noted that the Gosford Commission mentions 'that the Report of M. Cousin on the state of education in Prussia, as well as several works on the subject of education in the United States, are beginning to attract notice in the Province '.[1] The chief features of the proposals were, that there should be common elementary schools for the children of all denominations, in which undenominational Christianity should be taught from an approved book of Bible extracts, denominational teaching being allowed out of school hours. The elementary schools were to be supplemented by a certain number of model schools, giving a rather higher education, and offering scholarships to the best boys from the elementary schools. These model schools were to supply pupils to three normal schools, in which the future schoolmasters were to be trained; and to the normal schools, and if possible to the model schools also, farms were to be attached, in which the pupils should learn the most approved methods of agriculture.

The elementary and model schools were to be supported on the principle which had been adopted in the United States, viz. by requiring 'each school district to furnish, by assessment, among

[1] House of Commons Paper, February 20, 1837, General Report, p. 49. The Cousin referred to was Victor Cousin. He was in 1831 commissioned by the Government of Louis-Philippe to go to Germany to examine the state of education there, and in 1832 he published his 'Rapport sur l'état de l'instruction publique dans quelques pays de l'Allemagne, et particulièrement en Prusse'.

its inhabitants, an amount at least equivalent to the sum apportioned to it from the public funds' (iii. 279). The sum to be granted from public funds, which was to include the whole cost of the normal schools, and also a grant for the encouragement of superior educational institutions, was to be charged upon a permanent education fund, which fund was to be supplied from the proceeds of the Jesuits' estates and the clergy reserves, supplemented by direct grants from the provincial treasury. Popular or local control over the schools was to be secured in the following manner (iii. 285). Lower Canada was to be divided into municipalities, and the municipalities into districts. Three school commissioners were to be elected for each municipality, and three trustees for each district. The commissioners were to have vested in them all the legal estate of the elementary schools in their respective municipalities, to receive the money allotted by the Government for education, and to distribute it to the trustees in the districts. The trustees were 'to manage the daily concerns' of the schools, to receive the Government grants, to collect the money raised by local assessment, to pay the masters, and in conjunction with the ministers of religion to appoint the masters. In each municipality there was to be a board of school visitors, consisting of 'the resident ministers of religion, two residents appointed by the Inspector, and two annually by the municipality'. There were to be slightly different arrangements for the three large towns. There were to be three inspectors for the whole province, and over all, at the seat of government, a superintendent or chief officer of instruction, who, as well as the three inspectors, was to be kept completely aloof from politics.

Finally, the proposed system, if and when adopted and embodied in law, was to be 'gradually put in force by a board of Commissioners somewhat similarly constituted to that of the Board of Poor Law Commissioners in this country' (iii. 293).

Bearing in mind that the root principle of the scheme was to make Lower Canada English, that the Roman Catholic Church was whole-hearted in opposition to it, and had petitioned Lord Durham for separate Roman Catholic schools (iii. 277), that the Church of England clergy were almost unanimously hostile, and the Presbyterians divided (iii. 277, 278), that the Canadian peasantry were indifferent to education, and strongly objected to being taxed to pay for it, it is difficult to regard Buller's proposals as in any sense practicable, or to look upon his Report as other than an interesting essay on what might have been ideally the best scheme of education for Lower Canada, if the actual conditions had not presented insuperable difficulties to its adoption. It is true that not many years had passed since Catholic emancipation had been carried in England, that in Canada and elsewhere under Protestant rule the Roman Catholics did not hold so assured a position as they do at the present day, and that by common consent tolerance and forbearance between the rival denominations was conspicuous in Lower Canada. 'It is indeed an admirable feature of Canadian society,' Lord Durham writes (ii. 39), 'that it is entirely devoid of any religious dissensions. Sectarian intolerance is not merely not avowed, but it hardly seems to influence men's feelings.' It might therefore not be safe to estimate the strength of the opposition to Buller's recommendations by the feeling which was aroused in later years, when the Manitoba schools question was faced by Sir Wilfrid Laurier. But, just as Canada had been divided into two provinces in 1791, largely in the hope of preventing friction between the two rival races, so it is probable that the kindly feeling between the different denominations was in great measure due to their holding apart from each other in educational matters ; and it is impossible to doubt that any British Government, which had resolved to carry out what Buller proposed, would have been practically committed to replacing tolerance with religious bitterness, to alienating a loyal church, and to coercing the whole French Canadian people. Lord Durham, it has been seen, had not Buller's full Report before him when he wrote his own, and contented himself with contemplating that the laity would be too strong for the clergy, and that the grant of a popular Government would bring in its train a liberal system of public education. He cannot therefore be held responsible for Buller's views; and yet it can hardly be doubted that those views largely reflected his own, especially as the Anglifying of French Canada was one of the main themes of his Report. We come back then once more to the point of view that Lord Durham was prepared to take a high hand in carrying through

CHAP. V   EDUCATION   241

the reforms that he deemed to be necessary, to the conclusion that possibly he did not always sufficiently count the cost, and that, had he been placed in the position not to recommend merely but to carry out his recommendations with a free hand, it is possible that French Canada might not have been redeemed by responsible government, but by the measures which were to be co-temporaneous with responsible government, might have been converted into the Poland of the British Empire.

It is interesting to note how Buller contrasts the character of the two sexes among the French Canadians, as the result of the better education which the girls received. ' The difference in the character of the two sexes is remarkable. The women are really the men of Lower Canada. They are the active, bustling, business portion of the habitants, and this results from the much better education which they get, gratuitously, or at a very cheap rate, at the nunneries which are dispersed over the province ' (iii. 267, 268). Very noteworthy too are his comments on ' the too great abundance of means of superior education enjoyed by the French Canadians ' (iii. 270), as compared with the almost total want of facilities for higher education in the case of the British population in Lower Canada. Lord Durham also refers to this point. ' I know of no people among whom a larger provision exists for the higher kinds of elementary education, or among whom such education is really extended to a larger proportion of the population ' (ii. 32) ; and again (ii. 134), ' I have described the singular abundance of a somewhat defective education which exists for the higher classes, and which is solely in the hands of the Catholic priesthood.' On the other hand, 'There exists at present no means of college education for Protestants in the province; and the desire of obtaining general, and still more, professional instruction, yearly draws a great many young men into the United States.' Buller gives a list of the institutions for higher education which had been established by and under the control of the Roman Catholic Church, including 'the two large seminaries of Quebec and Montreal', founded in the seventeenth century, the former by the great Bishop Laval, the latter by the Sulpicians; [1] and he explains the use of the words 'too great abundance of means of superior education', by pointing out, as Lord Durham also points out, that the children educated at these colleges and seminaries, many or most of them children of habitants, were too numerous for them all to reap the advantages of their education in after life. The priesthood was open to them, but the military and naval professions were closed. They overstocked the professions of advocate, notary, and surgeon. Sprung from the ranks of the people, they led the people. 'To this singular state of things,' writes Lord Durham, 'I attribute the extraordinary influence of the Canadian demagogues' (ii. 33). As far back as 1768, Carleton had impressed upon the

[1] The letters patent of the French Crown, which authorized the seminary of Quebec, were dated April, 1663; this seminary was the parent of Laval University, created in 1852. The letters patent of the French Crown, which authorized the Sulpician seminary at Montreal, were dated May 1677.

British Government in the strongest terms the impolicy of excluding Canadians, more especially the Canadian gentry, from employment under Government; Lord Durham notes the kindred but somewhat different evil, of peasant children being educated for higher work than that of a peasant, and finding in after life that they had been taught and trained in vain.

Meanwhile, for the Protestant children of Lower Canada, two grammar schools were in the year 1826 established at Quebec and Montreal respectively, to which the Government, under the authority of the Secretary of State, with no great tact or consideration for Roman Catholic feelings, gave small annual grants from the proceeds of the Jesuits' estates. There was also one Protestant endowment at Montreal, of which the world was to hear in the days to come. In 1801 a provincial Act was passed 'for the establishment of Free schools and the advancement of Learning in the province'. Under this Act a corporation, entitled 'The Royal Institution for the advancement of Learning', was constituted for the management of the schools. This corporation was in fact, or was regarded by the Roman Catholics and French Canadians as being, exclusively British and Protestant; and in consequence the system was a failure. When Buller wrote his Report, he stated that 'The corporation has now no other function than the trusteeship of McGill's college' (iii. 249). This college, he tells us, was not yet open, the building was not yet erected, and the endowment was not sufficient to raise the college to the rank of a university.

The will of the founder, a Scotchman, James McGill, had been made in 1811, nearly three years before his death. A Royal Charter had been granted to the college in 1821; but it was not until an amended charter had been obtained in 1852, that the college began to develop into the great McGill University, which is now one of the Universities of the world. In the meantime, Buller suggested that if the British North American provinces should be united, a university jointly endowed by them might be established at Quebec.

Buller's Education Report referred to Lower Canada only, and Lord Durham has little to say on the subject of education in Upper Canada. He comments on the paucity of schools in the province, and notes that of the lands which had been originally appropriated for the support of schools throughout the country, the most valuable part had been diverted to the endowment of a university at Toronto (ii. 184). But there had been no indifference to the cause of education in Upper Canada. Private effort had been abundant, and the Government and Legislature had at least attempted to do their duty. The Lieutenant-Governors, from Simcoe onwards, had for the most part taken a warm personal interest in education, especially in higher education. Sir Peregrine Maitland was Lieutenant-Governor, when a Board of Education was established; and Sir John Colborne, who while Lieutenant-Governor of Guernsey had regenerated Elizabeth College in that island, conferred a similar boon upon Upper Canada, by replacing the Home district school of Toronto with

Upper Canada College, which was opened in 1830. The religious forbearance, which was so much in evidence in Lower Canada, did not exist to the same degree in the Upper province. Lord Durham (ii. 179–82) criticizes strongly the spirit of Orange intolerance towards the Roman Catholics, who formed one-fifth of the population of Upper Canada. It was the more marked, inasmuch as Upper Canada was the home of the Roman Catholic Glengarry Highlanders, and of Bishop McDonell, conspicuous in loyalty to the British Government. The feeling between Protestants and Roman Catholics on the one hand, and on the other between the Church of England and the non-Episcopalian Protestant bodies which centred round the question of the clergy reserves, was reflected in the denominational colleges which were established for higher education. Elementary education was dealt with by a provincial Act of 1816, which provided annual grants for the establishment of common schools throughout the province. The Act was to be in force for four years: it was renewed with modifications in 1820, and in 1824 it was made permanent. The Act of 1824 mentioned for the first time a General Board and district boards of education, and also extended the provisions of the Education Acts to schools for Indian children. Provision for higher education had been made at an earlier date. In 1797, when Peter Russell was administering the government, the Legislature of Upper Canada petitioned the Crown to appropriate a certain amount of Crown lands, for the establishment and support of grammar schools in the different districts, and of a college or university. The result was that some 550,000 acres were allotted for the purpose. In 1807 an Act was passed to establish public schools in the districts of the province, £800 being provided to pay £100 per annum to the master of each school in eight districts. These public schools were the district grammar schools of the province. Simcoe had contemplated a university for Upper Canada connected with the Church of England; the petition of the Legislature to the King in 1797 had asked for lands to endow a college or university as well as grammar schools, and the strong feeling in the province in favour of a university was shown by the fact that a provincial Act of 1820, for increasing the number of members of the House of Assembly, provided for future university representation. Eventually, in 1827, King's College at Toronto obtained a Royal charter, and was endowed with some 225,000 acres of the Crown land which had been appropriated for the purposes of higher education. Dr. Strachan, who had himself been a schoolmaster, the strong and able leader of the Church of England in Upper Canada, had much to do with obtaining the charter; and, although no religious tests were imposed upon the students, the college was placed entirely under the control of the Church of England, the president being the Archdeacon of Toronto, who at the time was Dr. Strachan himself. This exclusive control gave rise to complaints from the other Protestant bodies, and the House of Commons Committee of 1828 upon the Civil Government of Canada recommended that the Constitution should be widened. This was effected by a provincial Act of 1837, and eventually in 1843 the college, no longer a purely Anglican institution, began its work. In 1849 it was made entirely secular, and its name was changed to that of the University of Toronto. Its place as a Church of England college was taken by Trinity College at Toronto, which was established in 1852, and received a Royal charter in 1853; and meanwhile other denominations had also formed colleges of their own, the Wesleyans at Coburg, the Presbyterians at Kingston, and the Roman Catholics also at Kingston, the colleges being known as Victoria College, Queen's College, and Regiopolis respectively.

Lord Durham was not specially concerned with education, and he was specially concerned with the political condition of Upper Canada and its constitutional disorders. But, had he given closer attention to the province and spent a longer time in it, he might have found space in his Report to note the efforts which citizens and rulers alike had made in the cause of education, and might have placed on record that no little credit in this connexion was due to Tory Lieutenant-Governors who had old-fashioned views as to Church and State, and to the members of the Family Compact.

GENERAL UNION OF BRITISH NORTH AMERICA

Reference has already been made to Lord Durham's views as to a future general union of the British North American provinces. 'On my first arrival in Canada,' he writes (ii. 304), 'I was strongly inclined to the project of a federal union, and it was with such a plan in view, that I discussed a general measure for the government of the Colonies, with the deputations from the Lower Provinces, and with various leading individuals and public bodies in both the Canadas.' Buller tells us, in his sketch of the Mission, that Lord Durham had prepared the outline of such a scheme before he left England, that Roebuck had suggested it in the House of Commons, and that it had been well received. He tells us too that Durham had contemplated forming three provinces out of the two Canadas, constituting a new province out of the district of Montreal, the adjacent part of Upper Canada, and the eastern townships. Recognizing the objections to any plan of federal government, Durham had none the less contemplated that a federation formed under a monarchial government would gradually grow into a complete legislative union. But, on further consideration, and with longer experience of the conditions of British North America, he came to a different conclusion. He reasoned that the time was past for gradual measures in the case of Lower Canada; that the co-operation which would alone make a federal constitution practicable, would be wanting in the case of the French Canadians, if they were left, as they would be under a federal system, in a majority in their provincial Legislature; 'that tranquillity can only be restored by subjecting the province to the vigorous rule of an English majority; and that the only efficacious government would be that formed by a legislative union' (ii. 307).

On the other hand, while complete and immediate fusion of the two Canadas under one Legislature was, in his opinion, a vital necessity, and while therefore a federal system, at any rate as between the two Canadas, was rendered impossible, he did not consider that the conditions of the Maritime Provinces were such as to make it either just or expedient to force upon these latter provinces legislative union, until their Legislatures and peoples had been given ample time for deliberation and consent (ii. 322–3). This train of reasoning led him to recommend immediate legislation by the Imperial Parliament, 'restoring the union of the Canadas under one legislature, and reconstituting them as one province' (ii. 323–5); but 'the Bill', he continued, 'should contain provisions by which any or all of the North American colonies may, on the application of the Legislature, be, with the consent of the two Canadas, or their united Legislature, admitted into the union on such terms as may be agreed on between them'; and he goes on to recommend in terms which are not quite clear, that 'a general executive on an improved principle should be established, together with a Supreme Court of Appeal, for all the North American colonies', as though the executive and the judicial powers respectively were to be united in advance of legislative union. Possibly, by a general executive prior to legislative union, he intended no more than that a governor-in-chief or governor-general should be appointed, who should be in fact and not merely, as had been the case, in name, Governor of the whole of British North

America, having one or more secretaries who would correspond with all the provinces.

The conclusion of the whole matter then was that the condition of French Canada at the time determined Lord Durham's views with regard to British North America generally. But for the critical state of Lower Canada, he would have recommended a federation of the British North American provinces. He would have recommended it, however, not as a final and permanent solution, but as a preliminary to complete union. As things were, he concluded that the two Canadas must at once be fused, not federated; and thus, having begun with union, he proposed that the union should gradually be extended, without the preliminary stage of federation. But, though he thus advocated union and not federation, he must be regarded as having in the essence foreshadowed the future dominion. The soundness of his reasoning that the Maritime Provinces should not be hurried into combination with the Canadas, was illustrated by the difficulty which was experienced in carrying confederation in those provinces; and his proposal to include Newfoundland in the political system of British North America was revived, when the makers of confederation were drafting their first schemes. No part of his Report is more vivid or more cogent than the passages in which he sets out the gains which would accrue to British North America from being made one, his words speak for themselves, they would be spoiled by paraphrase, and one or two points only seem to call for comment and elucidation.

He starts by distinguishing between the two kinds of union which had been proposed, and which he terms federal and legislative (ii. 302–8); he defines federal union as a system under which 'the separate legislature of each province would be preserved in its present form, and retain almost all its present attributes of internal legislation; the federal legislature exercising no power, save in those matters of general concern, which may have been expressly ceded to it by the constituent Provinces'; and a few lines lower down he mentions as an objection which might be urged against a federal system, 'that a colonial federation must have, in fact, little legitimate authority or business, the greater part of the ordinary functions of a federation falling within the scope of the Imperial legislature and executive'. Similarly, Lord Glenelg, when, as has already been noticed,[1] he suggested to Lord Durham, in January 1838, that some kind of federal legislative body might be established for the two Canadian provinces, spoke of it merely as 'some joint legislative authority, which should preside over all questions of common interest to the two provinces, and which might be appealed to in extraordinary cases to arbitrate between contending parties in either; preserving, however, to each province its distinct legislature, with authority in all matters of exclusively domestic concern'. Lord Durham then clearly contemplated that a Federal Legislature in British North America would have little or no real power, inasmuch as British North America would not be

[1] Dispatch of January 20, 1838. See above, pp. 113, 132.

an independent State or nation. The real power would rest, partly with the Provincial Legislatures, and partly with the Imperial Government. Though it is the barest justice to his memory to regard him as the prophet of the coming Dominion, he did not contemplate what actually came to pass under the British North America Act, viz. that a Federal Legislature could and would be constituted of such a kind that, while its powers were necessarily only those which had been 'expressly ceded to it by the constituent provinces', yet the constituent provinces would cede to it all the powers which were not expressly reserved to themselves. Unlike the constitution of the United States, and unlike the constitution of the Commonwealth of Australia, the constitution of the Dominion of Canada makes the Federal Government and not the provincial governments the residuary legatee of political power in Canada. Neither in its relation to the constituent provinces, nor in its relation to the Imperial Legislature and Executive, is the Dominion Legislature a shadow without the substance: on the contrary it is in this Federal Legislature that the real power over Canada resides. To appreciate Lord Durham's point of view, it is necessary, on the one hand to bear in mind that what he had to guide him in forming his opinions on the subject of federation was the one great existing example of federation in the United States, and on the other hand to remember the lines which he laid down for responsible government. In the case of the United States he saw how strong had been and still was the basis of State rights, and to his mind a Federal Legislature with substantial power had only been rendered possible, because there was no further sovereign power outside and beyond. On the other hand, he had drawn a distinct line beyond which responsible government should not be extended, the line being between what he held to be matters of domestic and what he considered matters of imperial concern. The matters of domestic concern were matters for the domestic Legislature, and that meant, as long as the provinces were not made one, the Legislature of each single province. The matters of imperial concern were to be regulated outside Canada altogether, by the Imperial Legislature and Executive. Where, he argued, was there a place for an intermediate Legislature, except as a transitory form preliminary to substantial union. But what actually happened was the creation of a Legislature which took over a large proportion of the matters of domestic concern, and which either from the first possessed, or, as years went on, gradually gathered, many or most of the powers which Lord Durham conceived to be outside the sphere of purely Canadian politics. He was wrong and yet he was right : he was right and yet he was wrong. He wanted to create a nation, and that was achieved by the British North America Act. The Act really brought union into existence under the guise of federation. But when a nation was made, it was not possible to set bounds to national aspirations, or to uphold the limits within which he proposed to grant responsible government.

There is one aspect of a Federal Legislature, not

of great importance now, but important enough in earlier days, which he rather left out of sight. In discussing the future union of British North America, he quotes a letter which Chief Justice Sewell had received from the father of Queen Victoria, the Duke of Kent, on proposals for a union of the British North American provinces, which Sewell had submitted to the Duke. When the Bill, which eventually became the Constitutional Act of 1791, was under consideration, a predecessor of Sewell, Chief Justice Smith, wrote to Lord Dorchester a memorable letter in which he commented on the absence in that Bill of any provision for a General Legislature for all the British North American provinces. To the want of such a Legislature the writer attributed in large measure the loss of the old American colonies. It was in his view hopeless to have expected ' wisdom and moderation from near a score of " petty Parliaments ", with which Great Britain had had to deal.' 'All America was thus, at the very outset of the Plantations, abandoned to Democracy. And it belonged to the Administrations of the days of our fathers to have found the cure, in the erection of a Power upon the Continent itself, to control all its own little Republics, and create a Partner in the Legislation of the Empire, capable of consulting their own safety and the common welfare '.[1] Chief Justice Smith confined himself to the subject of legislation, and apparently did not contemplate responsible government; and Lord Durham,

---

[1] Chief Justice Smith to Lord Dorchester, February 5, 1790. See *Canadian Constitutional Development*, Egerton and Grant, pp. 104-6.

while going beyond him in the matter of granting responsible government, equally with him saw the advantage of creating a united Legislature, which would give a wider field for political ambitions than the ' petty parliaments' afforded, and create more equality and more sense of partnership with the Parliament of the United Kingdom. But Durham did not appreciate, as Chief Justice Smith did, or at any rate he did not enlarge upon the advantage, under the existing conditions of the British Empire, of a Federal Legislature, as contrasted with a Legislature which absorbed, instead of retaining in some sort, the Provincial Legislatures, in that it would have been 'a power upon the continent itself' controlling all its own little republics. In other words, he does not seem to have appreciated the advantage of a buffer between the little republics and the Imperial authority, against which, in lieu of the Imperial authority, the petty irritation of the provincial communities, the inevitable friction between the lower and the higher, would mainly have been directed.

In the earlier stages of the Empire, when distance was all powerful and knowledge and wisdom lingered, a Central Legislature on the spot, controlling but not wholly absorbing, and therefore not inheriting but restraining the small causes of bitterness in subordinate Legislatures, would have been, as in later times it has proved to be, a wonderful improvement in the machinery of a world-wide system.

There is one thing wanting in Lord Durham's

forecast of a united Dominion. It has been referred to already more than once. He foreshadows a Dominion, but it is not a Dominion from sea to sea. If he had not seen so far and so wide, there would be no room for wondering that he did not see still further and wider. But he had so much statesmanlike imagination, that it is matter for surprise that Upper Canada always bounded his western view. The territories of the Hudson Bay Company, the North West, the Pacific Coast were not within the scope of his mission, but yet they need not have lain beyond his horizon. The international line had long been drawn, though with outstanding points of dispute, as far as the Rocky Mountains; and the boundary from thence to the Pacific had been matter of negotiation. Possibly the difficulties with the United States, including the Maine Boundary question, to which he refers, and which at the beginning of 1839 reached its most acute and dangerous stage, made him hesitate to look too far afield, into what might be held to be debatable territory; but the result is to leave his picture of the future British North America foreshortened and incomplete. Yet it is a splendid picture, a great conception embodied in noble words. Once more stress may well be laid upon the writer's creativeness, his imperialism which held that England should make what was small and petty into what was worthy and great, his unerring perception that there was one way and one way only to prevent British North America from being permanently overshadowed, and ultimately absorbed, by the United States, and that

CHAP. V   GENERAL UNION   257

was by making it one and raising it to be a nation. Such a community, strong and self-governing, he held, and rightly held, would be less likely than the ' petty republics ' to sever the connexion with Great Britain.

REFERENCES TO THE UNITED STATES

As the whole course of Canadian history has been dominated by the proximity of the United States to Canada, so Lord Durham's Report abounds in references to the United States and its citizens, made for purposes of illustration, contrast, example, and warning. In 1837 Martin Van Buren succeeded General Jackson as President, and inherited a legacy of unrest. The year 1837 was in the United States a year of financial crisis and of bank failures. The anti-slavery movement was rapidly gathering strength. Texas, settled largely by American citizens, had in 1836 declared its independence of Mexico, and in 1837 applied for admission into the Union ; thenceforward the Texas annexation question troubled and divided American statesmen and politicians until 1845, when Texas became a State of the Union, and war with Mexico followed as a necessary consequence. Relations between Great Britain and the United States were very strained. The Maine Boundary question was outstanding, accentuated since the admission of the State of Maine to the Union in 1820. The Fisheries Convention of 1818 between Great Britain and the United States had given rise to disputes ; and, writing to Lord Durham in September 1838 on the state of Nova Scotia,

Mr. William Young referred to 'the oppressive and systematic encroachments of the Americans upon our fisheries'.[1] Along the international frontier further west than the Maritime Provinces, the rebellions in Lower and Upper Canada had led to breaches of the peace and violations of territory. Reference has been made to the case of the *Caroline* and the bitterness which it caused in the United States, while a few hours after Lord Durham's landing at Quebec, the *Sir Robert Peel*, a Canadian steamboat on the Upper St. Lawrence, putting into the American shore, was taken, looted, and burnt by a band of American pirates, to use Lord Durham's words. Writing to Lord Glenelg a few days afterwards, he reported that the population on the frontier of the State of New York was 'of the worst class and description—squatters, refugees, and smugglers, and that the executive power of the United States Government is a perfect nullity'.[2] He had thus given him, immediately after arrival in Canada, a practical illustration of the 'necessary weakness of a merely Federal Government' (ii. 270). One of his first acts, in consequence of the *Sir Robert Peel* incident, was to send his brother-in-law, Colonel Grey, to Washington, to carry remonstrances, coupled with assurances of friendship and co-operation, to President Van Buren, with the result that the President, honestly anxious to keep the peace, took steps to prevent as far as possible a recurrence of similar

[1] See Appendix A, iii. 14.
[2] House of Commons Paper, February 11, 1839. British North America, p. 114.

CHAP. V   REFERENCES TO UNITED STATES   259

outrages, though the later recrudescence of Canadian rebellion led to further fillibustering on the frontier. Lord Durham fully realized how little was wanting to bring on war between England and the United States, and to what extent the condition of the two Canadas made for war between the two countries. In his dispatch of the 9th of August 1838, which was marked secret at the time, but was subsequently published, almost *in extenso*, in the Blue Book of the 11th of February 1839, he summed up the causes which were exciting American animosity against Great Britain. He noted how, among the ill-informed in the United States, the French Canadians appeared to be struggling for the same rights which the Americans had secured by the War of Independence; how the bitterness of the British party in Canada against the United States, reflected in the colonial newspapers, had caused corresponding irritation; and how the American mind was becoming familiarized to the prospect of war. He commented upon the practical inconvenience and expense caused, alike to the States on the frontier and to the Federal Government, by the disturbances in Canada and the weakness of British administration; upon the added political difficulty of the boundary question; and lastly upon the restless, enterprising, lawless character of the frontier population, who had a precedent for successful invasion and seizure in the events which had taken place in Texas. These considerations are set out again at length in his Report, and he traces with clearness and insight how among the British loyalists in Lower

Canada, exasperation against American sympathy with the French Canadians was combined with an undercurrent of feeling that incorporation with the United States would once for all swamp the French majority, and further the material interests of the English-speaking population; and how in the Upper Province traditional loyalty to the British Government, if not supported by stable administration and constitutional reform, might be undermined by race sympathy, facility of intercourse, and the object lesson of abounding prosperity which discontented eyes in Canada beheld across the frontier.[1]

It was not the least of Lord Durham's services to his country that, when he reviewed the state of Canada, took action on the spot, and made recommendations for the future, he had always in mind British and Canadian relations with the great republic that lined the southern frontier of Canada; and Buller, in his account of the Mission, emphasizes the change of feeling between England and the United States, which was the result of Lord Durham's prompt measures, and his dignified courtesy to American citizens, producing alike greater friendliness to the country which he represented, and marked personal respect for himself.

Comment has been made already upon the outspokenness of Lord Durham's Report. He writes plainly and fearlessly on the situation from an international point of view. The side-note to one of his paragraphs is 'Importance of preserving

[1] See ii. 59-64 and 261-3.

the sympathy of the United States', and it runs:

'The maintenance of an absolute form of government on any part of the North American Continent can never continue for any long time, without exciting a general feeling in the United States against a power of which the existence is secured by means so odious to the people; and as I rate the preservation of the present general sympathy of the United States with the policy of our Government in Lower Canada as a matter of the greatest importance, I should be sorry that the feeling should be changed for one which, if prevalent among that people, must extend over the surrounding provinces' (ii. 297).

He argued in effect, that one reason for giving responsible government to the Canadas was that it would be congenial to the United States—a very good reason, but not one which at a time of crisis was likely to be attractive to loyalists in Canada. Again he writes (ii. 311–12) in the plainest words of the ever present, ever increasing, all surrounding influence of the United States in relation to Canada and the Canadians, and uses it as a powerful argument for the union of British North America, reasoning that 'If we wish to prevent the extension of this influence, it can only be done by raising up for the North American colonist some nationality of his own; by elevating these small and unimportant communities into a society having some objects of a national importance; and by thus giving their inhabitants a country which they will be unwilling to see absorbed even into one more powerful'.

Throughout his Report he draws a contrast between the American and Canadian sides of the frontier, in the matter of material development and prosperity, attributing the backwardness on the Canadian side mainly to the want of free institutions and firm and wise administration. 'It is not politic to waste and cramp their resources, and to allow the backwardness of the British provinces everywhere to present a melancholy contrast to the progress and prosperity of the United States' (ii. 262). In an earlier passage (ii. 212–13), with special reference to the disposal of public lands, he elaborates the contrast in forcible and picturesque language. 'On the American side all is activity and bustle. . . . On the British side of the line, with the exception of a few favoured spots, where some approach to American prosperity is apparent, all seems waste and desolate. . . . There, on the side of both the Canadas, and also of New Brunswick and Nova Scotia, a widely scattered population, poor, and apparently unenterprising, though hardy and industrious, separated from each other by tracts of intervening forest, without towns and markets, almost without roads, living in mean houses, drawing little more than a rude subsistence from ill-cultivated land, and seemingly incapable of improving their condition, present the most instructive contrast to their enterprising and thriving neighbours on the American side.' This last passage elicited an angry protest from the Select Committee of the House of Assembly in Upper Canada, who quoted it in their Report, and called on the Canadian farmers living by the

St. Lawrence and on the Niagara frontier to 'read this degrading account of them, and ask themselves whether they would feel perfectly safe in submitting their future political fate, and that of their children, to the dogmas of a man who has so grossly misstated their character and condition'.[1]

Lord Durham may have used exaggerated terms, but for many years after his time the contrast between the Canadian and American sides of the frontier was a favourite theme, and it has been reserved to the twentieth century to exhibit Canada—perhaps rather the North-West than the Canada of Lord Durham's vision—as more than rivalling the United States in attractiveness for settlers. Moreover, in view of the emphasis which Lord Durham laid upon misgovernment in Canada, it is interesting to note that no little element in this attractiveness has been the better administration of law in the Canadian Dominion than in the United States. On the other hand, it is a question whether Lord Durham did not overestimate the effect of defective institutions and inadequate administration, as accounting for the comparative backwardness of Canada. He did not take into account the fact that British settlement in Canada was in its infancy, whereas the vast development which he noted in the United States was the outcome of forces which generations had helped to bring to maturity. Unless gold or diamonds are brought to light, British colonization is wont to be a slow growth, but there comes a time, which has already

[1] See Parliamentary Paper, No. 289, June, 1839. Copies or Extracts of Correspondence Relative to the Affairs of Canada, p. 30.

come in Canada, and which seems to be nearly due in Australia, when harvest succeeds to seed time, when the young country comes of age, and when men enter in not by tens but by thousands, to open the lands and build up a nation.

In points of detail Lord Durham holds up the United States as a model to Canada. In the matter of public lands, for instance, he contrasts the efficiency of the system in the United States with the absence of any system in the British North American colonies (ii. 211). The words have already been quoted, in which he refers to the Erie Canal, and points out that 'the state of New York made its own St. Lawrence from Lake Erie to the Hudson, while the Government of Lower Canada could not achieve, or even attempt, the few miles of canal and dredging, which would have rendered its mighty rivers navigable almost to their sources' (ii. 99–100). He notes the 'noble provision' made by the northern States of the Union for education, as against the absence of any general system of instruction in Lower Canada (ii. 133); he speaks of the efficiency of the municipal institutions in these same northern States, whereas such institutions were wholly wanting in French Canada (ii. 91–92 and 112); and in a very interesting passage he writes at some length on Louisiana, giving that State as an instance, which he considered might well be copied in the case of Lower Canada, of a French population being successfully absorbed in a wider nationality (ii. 299–302); in the same connexion he refers to the fusion of the Dutch element in the State of New York.

He emphasized the bright side of American institutions and American initiative, and rather left in the background the counterbalancing defects. Even in the matter of public works, Canada had not all to learn from the United States. A note to the Report of the Assistant Commissioners of Municipal Inquiry runs, ' Persons who are disposed to regard the local administration of the United States as a model for other countries, will probably be unwilling to believe that in the State of New York, whose prosperity has been immensely increased by its canal and railroad communications, the management of the roads is extremely defective, although there is a large population, possessing abundant resources.' [1] Mr. Young, of Nova Scotia, saw nothing to gain from American citizenship: ' I know not of a single individual of influence or talent, who would not regard a severance of our connection with the mother country, and our incorporation, which would soon follow, into the American Union, with its outrages on property and real freedom, its growing democratic spirit and executive weakness, as the greatest misfortune that could befall us.' [2] To Lord Durham the United States were a bright illustration of the blessings which flow from responsible government, coupled with wise treatment of public lands. It is true that, as has been pointed out already, he did not look closely into the American constitution or examine how far the Americans enjoyed what he meant by responsible government. It was enough for him that they had free institutions, and from

[1] Appendix C, iii. 194 note.   [2] Appendix A, iii. 13.

these institutions, in his view, flowed material blessings. He over-rated the shortcomings of men and things in Canada, he drew too rosy a picture of men and things in the United States, but his conclusion was sound and true. If British North America was to be kept for Great Britain, instead of succumbing to the powerful attraction of the great and growing republic which was and is its everyday neighbour, then the British North American provinces must be given self-government, and be raised by union from the level of separate petty communities to the higher plane of a single nation.

COLONIAL OFFICE AND COLONIAL ADMINISTRATION

In connexion with, but over and above, the main subject of responsible government, Lord Durham's views on the Colonial Office and colonial administration are worthy of note. It has been seen that, at the time when he wrote, the Colonial Office was, from the nature of the case, mainly a Crown Colony Office; that the head of the permanent staff in the office was an unusually strong official, serving a Secretary of State who, from the public point of view, was exceptionally inadequate; and that Charles Buller, the sworn foe of the Colonial Office, was Lord Durham's right hand man. Further, whereas, in the Liverpool administration, Lord Bathurst had been Secretary of State for the Colonies for fifteen years, from 1812 to 1827, holding the office for a longer period continuously than any Secretary of State for the

Colonies before or since, in the next ten years the appointment had changed hands no fewer than eight times. These frequent changes were, in the Report of a Select Committee of the House of Assembly of Upper Canada, which Lord Durham quotes and endorses (ii. 104), alleged to be ' one of the chief causes of dissatisfaction with the administration of Colonial affairs '.

How strongly the Colonial Office was criticized and condemned by men of the Buller school, can best be judged by reading the speeches of his friend Sir William Molesworth, who eventually became for a few months before his death Secretary of State for the Colonies. Molesworth's criticisms of the office were not confined to the régime of Lord Glenelg, whose colonial administration he attacked in the House of Commons in 1838, but continued pretty well to the end of his own life in the fifties. His theme was mainly the maladministration of the present self-governing dominions, but he also held that the Crown Colonies were misgoverned; and, when in 1849 he moved for a Royal Commission to inquire into the administration of the colonies, while laying down that ' the Commission should draw a broad distinction between those colonies which have or ought to have representative institutions, and those of the Crown Colonies which are unfit for free institutions ', he expressed the view that ' In both cases the more the government is local, the better I believe it will be. It will, therefore, be an important subject for inquiry by the Commission, what is the best form of local government for those Crown Colonies which are unfit for free institutions'.[1] In an earlier speech he contrasted the Government of India, still under the East India Company, most favourably with Colonial Office mismanagement of the Crown Colonies. On another occasion he asserted that 'the tendency of every Executive, and especially of a Colonial Office Executive, is towards excessive expenditure, and therefore towards excessive taxation';[1] and from first to last he argued, and so did Buller, that the Colonial Office system, as it existed in his time, was not merely faulty but absolutely impossible, for it consisted in arbitrary power exercised by ignorant and irresponsible men at a distance. The Secretaries of State were constantly changing, and could therefore have no real grip of colonial administration: they were nominally responsible to Parliament, but practically irresponsible, for Parliament neither knew nor cared about colonial matters: the real power was in the hands of under secretaries and clerks, and the result of the whole was ignorance, negligence, and vacillation as 'three inseparable accidents of our system of colonial government', and a Colonial Office characterized by 'rashness, ignorance, indiscretion, incapacity'.[1]

As against this wholesale condemnation, it is interesting to note the passages in the *Government of Dependencies*, in which Cornewall Lewis, a contemporary of Molesworth and Buller, refers to the advantage of having a Colonial Office. He points out that the States of ancient times had no public

[1] *Selected Speeches of Sir William Molesworth*, edited by Professor Egerton, pp. 13-14, 232, 239-40, 325, 353.

office, and no public officer, specially charged to superintend and control the governments of their dependencies, and the conduct of the governors; and considers that such an office or such an officer would have made for amelioration of the government of the dependent communities, and therefore for consolidation of the Empire to which they belonged. 'The industry and ability of Cicero would have been employed far more advantageously to the provincials, if he had filled an office of this sort, than they were in his prosecution of Verres.'[1] It is a commonplace of Roman history that the provinces fared better under the Empire than under the Republic, and under the Emperor than under the Senate, partly because there were not such frequent changes of governors, but mainly because there was a stronger and more sympathetic control over them at head-quarters. Lewis goes on to mention the Spanish Council of the Indies as the first Colonial Office, 'the first example of a separate public department in a dominant country for the management of dependencies,' and credits it with at any rate some measure of efficiency and regard for the native races. He then sums up the value of a Colonial Office in the following passage:

'If it be assumed that colonial and other dependencies are to remain in a state of dependence, it cannot be doubted that they, on the whole, derive advantage from the existence of a public department in the dominant country, specially charged

[1] *Government of Dependencies* (1891 ed.), pp. 162-4; see also pp. 119 note and 149.

with the superintendence of their political concerns. The existence of such a department tends to diminish the main obstacles to the good government of a dependency, viz. the ignorance and the indifference of the dominant country respecting its affairs ; and to supply the qualities requisite for its good government, viz. knowledge of its affairs and care for them. If the existence of such a department tends to involve the affairs of the dependency in the party contests of the dominant country, it is to be remembered that this very evil has its good side ; inasmuch as the public attention is thereby attracted to the dependency, and the interest of some portion of the dominant people is awakened to the promotion of its welfare.'

Lewis wrote of a Colonial Office in the abstract, while Molesworth castigated the actual Colonial Office of the day. Moreover, Lewis was considering only the case of dependencies which are to remain dependencies, in other words, Crown Colonies, whereas Molesworth dealt mainly, though not exclusively, with the case of what are now the self-governing dominions. Still the difference in the two men's views is striking and instructive. To Molesworth, control from Downing Street was an abomination, to Lewis it was, at any rate in capable hands, a beneficial safeguard. It need not be said that Lord Durham, prompted no doubt by Buller, approached more nearly to Molesworth's point of view than to that of Cornewall Lewis, but on the one hand Durham was not concerned in any way with Crown Colonies, and on the other his condemnation of the Colonial Office is not so wholesale nor so bitter as that of Molesworth. He deals with the subject more especially in relation to Lower Canada (ii. 101–10), and characteristically attacks the existing system on account of the weakness which resulted from it. The side-note to the beginning of the passage is ' Want of vigorous administration of Royal Prerogative ', and the argument runs : The Governor of the colony is supposed to represent the Sovereign, but he is in fact a mere subordinate of the Secretary of State, receiving instructions not only as to the general line of policy to be pursued, but also as to details. Being the tool of the Home Government, he is the centre of attacks from the popular party in the Colony, and naturally throws the responsibility as far as possible upon the Home Government, and does little or nothing without referring home for instructions. Thus the Executive on the spot loses all vigour and initiative, action is enfeebled by distance and delay, ' and the colony has, in every crisis of danger, and almost every detail of local management, felt the mischief of having its Executive authority exercised on the other side of the Atlantic.' On the other side of the Atlantic again, the British public are wholly ignorant of colonial conditions, so are the large majority of members of Parliament ; and, except on the occasion of some great colonial crisis, ' responsibility to Parliament, or to the public opinion of Great Britain, would be positively mischievous, if it were not impossible.' The Secretaries of State are being constantly changed on party grounds, which have nothing whatever to do with the colonies : they therefore have no time to learn their business, and consequently the management of the colonies rests with 'the permanent but utterly irresponsible members of the office'. Thus, in the first place, there is no responsibility anywhere for colonial administration under the existing system; in the second place, the business of the Colonial Office is so multifarious that, in his short tenure of office, the Secretary of State cannot master it himself; in the third place, his advisers have no first-hand local knowledge; and in the fourth place, the constant changes of Secretaries of State mean constant change of policy, so that to ignorance is added vacillation as an accompaniment of colonial administration; finally, there is superadded a general secrecy as to the motives and purposes of the rulers, resulting (to quote the side-note to the passage) in 'ignorance of the people as to the proceedings of their government'.

In a later passage (ii. 192) referring more especially to Upper Canada, Lord Durham reverts to the injury done to a colony by allowing the policy of its administration to depend upon political changes at home. The general feeling in the province was, he tells us, that 'they ask for greater firmness of purpose in their rulers, and a more defined and consistent policy on the part of the government; something, in short, that will make all parties feel that an order of things has been established to which it is necessary that they should conform themselves, and which is not to be subject to any unlooked for and sudden interruption consequent upon some unforeseen move in the game of politics in England'.

COLONIAL ADMINISTRATION

Many years have now passed since all parties and all schools of thought in this country recognized, that in the case of the white communities in the British Empire, responsibility for good or bad government must be vested in the people on the spot; but, though Lord Durham treated of the Colonial Office only in reference to these communities, it is impossible to estimate how far the Colonial Office deserved the blame which men like Molesworth attached to it, without taking into consideration the Crown Colonies also. In the first place, it is difficult to suppose that this office, under the guidance of Sir James Stephen, and with men like Sir Henry Taylor and Sir T. F. Elliot, either in it or connected with it, was abnormally bad, worse than other public offices in England at the time. The age was ripe for a change of system as regards Canada and Australia, and the change was carried out; but it does not follow either that responsible government could usefully have been granted at a much earlier date, or that the Colonial Office in particular was to blame for withholding it till Lord Durham's time. In the second place, the grounds on which Molesworth condemned the Colonial Office as absolutely hopeless and impossible have, as regards the Crown Colonies, continued to exist in a greater or less degree down to the present day, and, notwithstanding, England, and the Empire, and the Colonial Office, and the world generally have gone on very comfortably all the same. There are still the obvious disadvantages arising from constant changes of Secretaries of State: the duties thrown on each

Secretary of State in turn are infinitely more multifarious than whose which Molesworth declared that no one man could adequately discharge : as a necessary consequence, much responsibility still devolves, and must always devolve, upon the permanent advisers of the Secretary of State ; and in their case want of first-hand personal knowledge of local conditions is still—though not to so great an extent as before—almost inevitable as regards some outlying parts of the Empire. It is true that steam and electricity are minimizing distance so far as it is a factor in misgovernment; but the same forces have infinitely multiplied the facilities for constant interference from home, whether by the Colonial Office or by the House of Commons. Molesworth, in his hatred of an irresponsible bureaucracy at a distance, advocated, even in the cases of Crown Colonies, establishing responsibility in the colony rather than at home ; but he admitted that such colonies were not suitable for representative institutions, and therefore, on his own showing, the power, if removed from the Home Government, must have been vested either in a despotic governor, or in a governor advised by a white oligarchy, with the prospect of reproducing the evils of Roman provincial administration under the republican régime. It is too often left out of sight that government from a distance is not all evil, especially where coloured men are concerned. It means, or ought to mean, government of coloured races without being influenced by colour prejudices ; and if it is coupled, as it is in the case of the British Crown

Colonies, with the grant of wide discretion to the governors and officers on the spot, a form of government results which, tried by the test of the greatest happiness of the greatest number, will bear comparison with any political system in the history of the world.

The British Empire contains probably a greater number of diverse elements than any association of peoples and races has ever contained, and the essence of the Home Government is the party system. The interests of the whole require, on the one hand, that full play for the diverse elements should be combined with some general rules, some approach to uniformity in the main lines of public administration; and on the other, that the constant changes at head-quarters, which the party system involves, should be counterbalanced by one or more institutions which make for tradition and continuity. Under the Crown, which is the one great bond of the Empire, an office like the Colonial Office, putting its value at the lowest, and omitting all its work of direct administration, discharges an absolutely necessary function in supplying some measure of uniformity and of continuity. The Colonial Office has always been and always will be easy to attack, but to those who stop to think it is no less easy to defend.

CHAPTER VI

RETROSPECT, FORECAST, AND SEQUEL

THE questions, how far Lord Durham read the past correctly, how far he formed a correct forecast of the future, and how far his recommendations were adopted, have to a large extent been answered already. Omitting points of detail, and instances of exaggerated language, and noting once more that the accuracy of Lord Durham's account of parties and conditions in Upper Canada was most strongly and categorically challenged by both Houses of the provincial Legislature at the time,[1] it seems fair to say that the main fault in his retrospect was the amount of blame which he attached to the British Government, especially in regard to Lower Canada, although he speaks of 'the uniform good intentions which the Imperial Government has clearly evinced towards every class and every race in the colony' (ii. 100). It cannot be too often repeated that he had in him something of a Strafford or a Cromwell: he understood despotism and he understood self-government, but he had no patience with half-way compromise; and from

---

[1] The Report of the Select Committee of the House of Assembly is given in the Parliamentary Paper No. 289, June 1839, 'Copies or Extracts of Correspondence relative to the Affairs of Canada,' and the Report of the Select Committee of the Legislative Council will be found at pp. 173-88 of *Canadian Constitutional Development* (Egerton and Grant).

CHAP. VI RETROSPECT, FORECAST, SEQUEL 277

this point of view he reviewed and censured back history, judging the men of 1791 or earlier in the light of 1838. ' It is difficult to conceive,' he writes (ii. 76), ' what could have been their theory of government, who imagined that in any colony of England a body invested with the name and character of a representative Assembly, could be deprived of any of those powers, which, in the opinion of Englishmen, are inherent in a popular legislature.' In this passage he talks of the Assembly being deprived of powers which it had never possessed. There is no hint or suggestion that the constitution of 1791 was a distinct step forward; that representative institutions without responsible government were not unknown elsewhere in the British Empire, as for instance in the West Indies; that the constitution of 1791 may have been, and probably was, a wise preparatory stage, especially in view of the fact that French Canadians had never in the whole course of their history known any kind of political representation. It was enough for him that the system was faulty, as tried by the standard of his own day, and, this being the case, he took up the position that the people of Canada had been deprived of rights which all men ought to enjoy.

Still more open to criticism is the interesting passage (ii. 62–71) in which he condemns the division of Canada into two provinces, and the policy pursued towards French Canada, as a policy which was mistaken in the first place, and in the second place not consistently followed up.

He lays down that, after the United States

had become independent, the British Government adopted towards their remaining possessions in North America a policy of *Divide et Impera* : that their object was ' to isolate the inhabitants of the British from those of the revolted colonies ' : to govern the colonies which still belonged to Great Britain ' by means of division, and to break them down as much as possible into petty isolated communities, incapable of combination, and possessing no sufficient strength for individual resistance to the Empire '. As an illustration of the intent to isolate Canada from the United States, he quotes instructions which were given by the Government to prohibit settlement and maintain a belt of woodland on the American frontier south of the St. Lawrence, whereas these instructions were given on military advice, and for purely military reasons, in the light of the war of 1812.[1] To the same imaginary intention of keeping up division and preventing consolidation, he attributes the division of the Province of Quebec by the Act of 1791, and then he proceeds to attack the Government for not having fully carried out the policy of separation which was embodied in the Act. His argument is, either French Canada might have been left entirely to the French, or it might have been gradually but surely denationalized and incorporated in British colonization. The latter was the course which he maintained should have been adopted; but, the other alternative having been chosen, the policy of French Canada for the French Canadians should have been rigidly adhered

---

[1] See above, p. 203, and note 2 to vol. ii, p. 65.

CHAP. VI RETROSPECT, FORECAST, SEQUEL 279

to. ' The province should have been set apart to be wholly French, if it was not to be rendered completely English.' The Home Government, however, while trying to preserve the French character of the Lower Province, encouraged British immigration into it; there was a mixture of French and British laws and land tenures and religions and so forth; with the result that the province became neither one thing nor the other, and was the scene of discord of races.

It was hardly true to facts, or fair to the Government of Great Britain, to represent it as inspired by the principle of *Divide et Impera* in its dealings with the British North American provinces; nor was this policy in the minds of those who framed and carried the Act of 1791. It is true that that Act divided Canada into two provinces, one mainly French, the other British; but the object which was aimed at was, not so much isolation of the French Canadians, as gradual assimilation of the two races to each other, by letting them grow up side by side, without overlapping too much, until they knew each other better. Again, it was not true to facts, though it was convenient as a generalization for a treatise, to lay down that there are only two methods of dealing with a conquered territory—either the whole of this or the whole of that. Practical statesmen find it necessary to compromise; a thorough policy is not often desirable, and, when a House of Commons has to be consulted, almost impossible. Lord Durham, beyond question, put his finger upon the weak spot in British colonial policy, when he emphasized the evils which arise from not following out one course consistently, but this weakness had not been exceptionally conspicuous in the case of British North America. There had been, no doubt, change and vacillation, as for instance in regard to the abortive Bill of 1822 for re-uniting the two Canadas; but there had been no violent reversals of policy, such as have marked the history of South Africa. On the whole, one Secretary of State after another, on either side of the House, had striven to conciliate the French Canadians, while not conceding their full demands. They had compromised, they had tried to hold the balance even between the contending parties and races, they had not pronounced for one or for the other. Lord Durham blamed them for not having steadily and with a whole heart taken the British side, and subordinated the French; but such a policy could have succeeded only on two hypotheses, first, that the Home Government had determined to run counter to the British instinct of fair play and generosity to the conquered, which after all is nearly the most valuable asset that a ruling race can possess; and secondly, that party government in England would have permitted the continuance for at least a generation of a policy of coercion in Canada. Neither hypothesis would ever have come to pass, and the practical impossibility of what Lord Durham would have advised invalidates his criticism of what actually was done.

The Home Government showed little strength and little foresight in dealing with Canada, but they were consistent in letting natural forces have their play, and in giving as much rope as possible to the French Canadians short of self-government. Lord Durham saw when the time had come for self-government; and he saw what might have been an ideal solution, if England had not been England, and the French Canadians had not had a natural desire to remain French Canadians; but, if the actual conditions of the case are taken into consideration, his retrospect of the past is not good history.

If Lord Durham were now alive, he would probably maintain that, so far as he failed to forecast the future of Canada correctly, it was because his recommendations were not fully carried out; but in any case it must be admitted that he wholly underrated the strength and the tenacity of the French Canadian race. He looked upon absorption into Anglo-Saxon surroundings as the inevitable fate of the French Canadians. He writes of ' the vain endeavour to preserve a French Canadian nationality in the midst of Anglo-American colonies and states ' (ii. 70); and again, ' It is but a question of time and mode; it is but to determine whether the small number of French who now inhabit Lower Canada shall be made English, under a Government which can protect them, or whether the process shall be delayed until a much larger number shall have to undergo, at the rude hands of its uncontrolled rivals, the extinction of a nationality strengthened and embittered by continuance' (ii. 292). It is interesting to contrast this view with the forecast made by Governor Carleton in the year 1767. There were then but few English in French Canada, for Canada had only lately been transferred to British keeping, yet Carleton contemplated that the superiority of the French to the English in numbers would not decrease but increase. 'Barring a catastrophe shocking to think of,' he wrote to Lord Shelburne, 'this country must, to the end of time, be peopled by the Canadian race, who already have taken such firm root, and got to so great a height, that any new stock transplanted will be totally hid, and imperceptible amongst them, except in the Towns of Quebec and Montreal.'[1] Lord Durham notes the fecundity of the French Canadians, but notes it only as leading to further subdivision of estates and deterioration of the people, and he speaks of the race as destitute of invigorating qualities. His British predilections, his imperialism, and his political views, all, it would seem, coloured his vision in regard to the French Canadians. He stated in so many words that their race was in a condition of hopeless inferiority to the English: he desired to submerge it, for constructive reasons, in order to produce one great uniform British nationality: and, as a Radical, he had no hope of any good thing coming out of the intense conservatism and feudal institutions of French Canada.

Possibly he might have modified his views, had he stayed longer in Canada and studied the French Canadians in normal times. He came and went at a time when race animosity was unduly accentuated; and probably on the one hand he exaggerated the intensity of the feeling, while on

[1] Shortt and Doughty, p. 198. See note 1, vol. ii, p. 70.

CHAP. VI RETROSPECT, FORECAST, SEQUEL 283

the other he erred in thinking that it could be extinguished by a policy which aimed at eradicating the nationality. The analogies, which he quotes, seem to show that he did not sufficiently estimate how much the preservation or the extinction of nationality is a question of degree. He takes the case of Louisiana, but the French in the province of Quebec held it by far greater numbers and by far longer tenure than they held Louisiana; while the Dutch in New York, to whom Lord Durham also refers, had only a fifty years' tenure of Manhattan Island and the Hudson valley before they were brought under British rule. He might have noted that the Dutch in South Africa absorbed the handful of Huguenots who settled among them, but this illustration also would not have been in point. From the dawn of colonization in North America the valley of the St. Lawrence had been the home of the French, and the history of Canada had testified abundantly to their stubbornness and their strength. In the year 1838 or 1839 it was too late to talk of denationalizing a people who had made the land their own; and it was hopeless to think that efforts to do so would extinguish the bitterness of race feeling. It was left to Lord Elgin, while carrying out in full Lord Durham's views of responsible government, and sharing Lord Durham's confidence that responsible government would make for loyalty and not for separation, to repudiate at the same time his father-in-law's doctrine that the French should be denationalized, and to advocate free play for their language and their usages. Later history has proved how far from the fact was Lord Durham's estimate that the French Canadian nationality must necessarily be absorbed; for, having been left to its destiny under a system of popular government, it has more than held its own within and even beyond the province of Quebec.

How far race antagonism in Canada has been diminished since Lord Durham's time, and to what degree French and English have come closer to each other, it would be difficult to estimate with any approach to accuracy. French are French, and British are British, and will remain so till the end. On the other hand, modern life makes for greater courtesy and forbearance as between peoples and races. French and English have lived side by side for seventy more years since Lord Durham wrote, and have acquired habits and traditions of co-operation; and—most important point of all—the confederation of Canada by the British North America Act of 1867 has completely altered the position, for, to quote once more the words of Chief Justice Smith's wise letter of 1790, that Act has erected 'a Power upon the Continent itself, to control all its own little Republics',[1] and race difficulties are not increased by appeal to, and resentment against, a Legislature on the other side of the Atlantic.

A second point in regard to which, if Lord Durham were, so to speak, to be pinned down to the wording of his Report, he did not form a correct forecast of the future, is the extent to which he held that colonial self-government can be limited,

[1] *Canadian Constitutional Development* (Egerton and Grant), p. 105.

CHAP. VI RETROSPECT, FORECAST, SEQUEL 285

and a line be drawn between matters of imperial concern. It may well be answered that it is not fair to criticize his words in this respect, as being intended to hold true for all time; that he took conditions as they were; and under those conditions laid down limits to the freedom of the colony on the one hand, and the interference of the mother country on the other; but that it does not follow that, under the altered conditions of later times, he would have upheld those limits as unalterable. It has been seen that he enumerates (ii. 282) 'the constitution of the form of government—the regulation of foreign relations, and of trade with the mother country, the other British Colonies, and foreign nations—and the disposal of the public lands' as 'the only points on which the mother country requires a control'; and he notes that 'a perfect subordination, on the part of the colony, on these points, is secured by the advantages which it finds in the continuance of its connexion with the Empire'. He wrote in the light of his own day, when colonies were not dominions, when the small had not become great, and could not stand alone. It would be pettifogging to tie his memory to the exact words. But it is a fair criticism to say that, while he laid stress on self-government as creating a national existence, he did not seem fully to recognize that when once an oversea community has been endowed with national institutions, it is difficult, if not impossible, to set a limit to its growth as a nation, or permanently to withhold any subject as outside its scope. Free Trade had not come in

England when he wrote; he does not refer to it, but it was well on the way; and, when it came, it profoundly modified the colonial problem; but, apart from a particular national movement, the effects of which he might or might not have foreseen, there is no indication that he at all foresaw to what responsible government was going to lead, and to what it inevitably must lead. Cornewall Lewis's reasoning, in the passage which has already been quoted, is unanswerable. 'If the government of the dominant country substantially govern the dependency, the representative body cannot substantially govern it; and, conversely, if the dependency be substantially governed by the representative body, it cannot be substantially governed by the government of the dominant country. A self-governing dependency (supposing the dependency not to be virtually independent) is a contradiction in terms.'[1] After responsible government had been given to Canada, it was substantially governed by the representative body of Canada, and ceased to be substantially governed by England. Lord Durham, to judge from his words, seemed to think that the substantial government could be divided, and that Canada, while becoming a nation, could remain a subordinate nation; but history has abundantly shown that, starting from the grant of self-government, there can be but one line of movement, from subordination to complete equality. It is true—taking his reservations—that the Constitution of Canada still depends upon Imperial legislation; that the

---

[1] *Government of Dependencies*, p. 289.

CHAP. VI RETROSPECT, FORECAST, SEQUEL 287

external relations of Canada in political matters are still under Imperial control; that, while the self-governing dominions have for half a century and more been left to settle their own tariffs, it has never been admitted in principle that they can differentiate at will; that control of the Public Lands in Canada was not reserved to the Imperial government because that government was in effect already pledged to concede it. But the broad fact remains that the Canadian self-government of to-day is not what Lord Durham recommended, and the Canada of to-day is more nearly an allied than a subordinate nation.

A third point on which Lord Durham failed to forecast the future has been sufficiently laboured already. It relates to the actual extent of the Canadian Dominion. He contemplated a dominion, but consisting only of the present eastern provinces. He did not look from sea to sea, a vision to which even a lesser prophet than himself might have been moved. But without further criticizing his outlook, it is time to note how far his recommendations were adopted.

The recommendation that the two Canadian provinces should be reunited was carried out, but not as he had intended. He had expressed himself (ii. 323, 324) as entirely opposed to 'the mere amalgamation of the Houses of Assembly of the two Provinces', and also 'to every plan that has been proposed for giving an equal number of members to the two Provinces'. He had contemplated complete fusion of the two provinces, and new electoral divisions formed by a Parliamentary Commission, with a view to 'giving representation, as near as may be, in proportion to population'. He had, no doubt, in his mind the Union Bill of 1822, which had proposed to re-unite the two provinces on the basis of at first simply joining together the existing members of the two Legislative Councils and of the two Assemblies, with a provision for the future that the elected representatives for each province should not exceed sixty. To this method of reunion, which would continue to treat Canada as two provinces and not as one, Lord Durham was entirely opposed; and when the Melbourne Ministry first handled his Report and first drafted a Reunion Bill, they were inclined to share his views. On the 3rd of June 1839, Lord John Russell stated in the House of Commons that 'It is our opinion generally, that you ought not to lay down any precise number of representatives for Lower Canada and for Upper Canada',[1] but, after going through various drafts, and being recast in Canada, the Union Bill, as it became law in 1840, provided in its 12th section that in the Legislative Assembly of the new province of Canada, Lower Canada and Upper Canada should have an equal number of representatives, and the effect of the subsequent sections of the Act was to give forty-two members to either of the two late provinces. The Act empowered the new Legislature to alter the system of representation by a two-thirds majority in both houses, but the net result was to federate Lower and Upper Canada rather than to fuse

[1] Hansard's *Parliamentary Debates*, vol. xlvii, pp. 1264-6.

CHAP. VI RETROSPECT, FORECAST, SEQUEL 289

them; the line of least resistance was followed, and the complete union which Lord Durham had desired was not carried out. The only provision in the Act which at all reflected Lord Durham's attitude towards the French Canadian nationality, was the 41st section, which enacted that English alone should be the language of the legislative records, and this section was repealed by a Provincial Act of 1848, passed in Lord Elgin's time. From the outset both French and English were used in the debates, and the first Speaker of the Assembly, after the union had come into existence, was a French Canadian. Nor did the Act contain any provision such as Lord Durham had recommended, and such as was subsequently included in the Confederation Act of 1867, to enable other British North American provinces to enter the union. In short, the Act of 1840 was a compromise Act, falling far short of the root and branch policy which Lord Durham had sketched out.

It has been seen that his policy prescribed that the union of the two provinces should be accompanied by the grant of responsible government, limited by various restrictions, and that Lord John Russell and his colleagues were not prepared to accept in full either the principle or the practice of responsible government. Nor was Poulett Thomson, afterwards Lord Sydenham, whom the Whigs selected to be Governor-General and to carry through the union. But they were all moving in Lord Durham's direction : all were agreed to try and maintain harmony between the executive and the legislative authorities, by employing in the service of the Government men who had the confidence of the people. Lord John Russell went far towards responsible government when, in a dispatch of the 16th of October 1839, he laid down that the high executive officers, such as the Colonial Secretary and the Treasurer, must not in future be considered to hold their posts by a permanent tenure, but should be liable to be changed with the change of Governor, or to ' be called upon to retire from the public service, as often as any sufficient motives of public policy may suggest the expediency of that measure '.[1] In September 1841 the Assembly of United Canada passed resolutions, said to have been drafted by Lord Sydenham himself, the first of which laid down 'that the most important, as well as the most undoubted, of the political rights of the people of this Province is that of having a Provincial Parliament for the protection of their liberties, for the exercise of a constitutional influence over the Executive departments of their government, and for legislation upon all matters of internal government'; while a subsequent resolution declared that, in order to preserve harmony, 'the chief advisers of the representative of the Sovereign, constituting a Provincial administration under him, ought to be men possessed of the confidence of the Representatives of the people'.[2] No legislation was needed in order to take the

[1] See *Canadian Constitutional Development* (Egerton and Grant), pp. 270-2.
[2] See Houston's *Documents illustrative of the Canadian Constitution*, pp. 303-4.

further step, to make the executive a purely parliamentary executive, to give full scope to party government, and in purely Canadian matters to constitute the advisers of the Governor, as representing the majority of the people, the real rulers of Canada. This step was taken by Lord Elgin in or about the year 1848. The same date may be given to the completion of responsible government in the Maritime Provinces,[1] and it followed very shortly afterwards in Newfoundland, Australia, and New Zealand.

Among the restrictions on responsible government, Lord Durham designed reform of the Legislative Council, which should then ' act as an useful check on the popular branch of the Legislature ' (ii. 326-7); but, as has been noted, he left to others to decide on what lines the Council should be revised. The result was that no change was made, and that the Union Act left the constitution of the Second Chamber as it had been framed in the Act of 1791, the members of the Council being nominated for life. The section of the 1791 Act, however, which gave power to the Crown to attach to hereditary titles of honour a right to be summoned to the Legislative Council, found no place in the Act of 1840. This latter Act was amended in 1854 by another Imperial Act, which empowered the Canadian Legislature to alter the constitution of the Legislative Council; and under the authority thus given a provincial law was passed in 1856,

---

[1] 1848 in the case of Nova Scotia and New Brunswick; 1851 in that of Prince Edward Island; 1855 in that of Newfoundland. See Keith, *Responsible Government in the Dominions*, pp. 8-9.

making the Legislative Council an elective body. But under the British North America Act of 1867 the elective principle was discarded, for the members of the senate are, as were the legislative councillors under the Acts of 1791 and 1840, nominated to hold their places for life.

The 57th section of the Union Act embodied Lord Durham's recommendation that 'no money votes should be allowed to originate without the previous consent of the Crown' (ii. 328), and a similar provision was included in the British North America Act of 1867. The Union Act also followed his Report in charging against the consolidated revenue fund of the united provinces an ample Civil List. This list was divided into two schedules. The first schedule provided £45,000 in permanence to cover the salaries of Governor and Lieutenant-Governor, the salaries and pensions of the judges, and the general cost of administration of justice. The second schedule provided £30,000 during the life of the Queen and for five years afterwards, to cover the cost of the salaries and pensions of the principal executive officers.

In the year 1846 the Canadian Legislature passed an Act for granting a Civil List to Her Majesty, the provisions of which were in lieu of the Civil List sections and schedules of the Union Act; and in the following year, 1847, an Imperial statute [1] gave validity to this provincial Act, and thereby superseded, so far as the Civil List was concerned, the terms of the Union Act. On this footing the Civil List continued in existence until

[1] 10 & 11 Vict. c. 71.

the passing of the British North America Act of 1867, when it finally disappeared;[1] but the salaries and pensions of the judges, as well as the salaries of the ministers, are still guaranteed by permanent Acts of the Dominion Parliament, and the 99th section of the British North America Act provides that the judges of the superior courts shall hold office during good behaviour, removable only by the Governor-General on address of the Senate and the House of Commons. The judges therefore are given the independent position and the security of tenure upon which Lord Durham insisted.

In return for an adequate Civil List, Lord Durham proposed to hand over to the control of the Legislature all the Crown revenues except those derived from public lands; but in accordance with what had been a long standing offer of the Home Government, the 54th section of the Union Act surrendered in return for the Civil List the territorial and other revenues of the Crown, which included the public lands, and the same provision was included in the provincial Civil List Act of 1846, validated by the Imperial Act of 1847, to which reference has been made above. Finally, the complete control of the Canadian Government over the public lands of the province was assured by the Imperial Act of 1852, which cleared up a question of legal ownership, as has already been explained.[2] Thus the whole of Lord Durham's elaborate scheme for keeping the public lands of Canada under the authority of the Imperial

[1] Under sections 102 and 126 of the British North America Act.
[2] See above, p. 185.

Government, and disposing of them on the lines laid down by Gibbon Wakefield, was stillborn.[1]

Under the head of public lands should be noted the action which was taken with regard to the clergy reserves. Lord Durham, in discussing the subject (ii. 173–9), contented himself with the recommendation that all provisions in Imperial Acts relating to the application of the clergy reserves and the funds arising from them should be repealed, and that the disposal of the funds should be left to the local Legislature; and in the summary of his recommendations at the end of his Report, he suggested (ii. 326–9) that the same Imperial Act which carried out the union of the provinces and the accompanying changes, should repeal the existing provisions relating to the clergy reserves. Before, however, the Union Act was passed, Poulett Thomson had already moved in the matter. Shortly after his arrival in Canada, he

---

[1] The case was summed up as follows in Lord John Russell's instructions to the Land and Emigration Commissioners of January 14, 1840. 'With regard to British North America, the case stands as follows. In Upper Canada and in New Brunswick, the sale and management of waste lands is vested by local enactments in certain local authorities, with whom the Crown has no right of interference. In Nova Scotia and in Newfoundland, there is every reason to anticipate that similar laws will be shortly passed in pursuance of offers made by the Crown to assent to them. In the present state of affairs in Lower Canada, this, in common with many other questions, must be regarded as in abeyance. In general, therefore, it may be stated that you will have no power to contract for the sale of lands situate in British North America, or in any of the adjacent islands' (House of Commons Paper, Colonial Land Board, February 4, 1840, p. 5).

The Canadian Legislature in their first session after the Union, 1841, passed 'An Act for disposal of Public Lands', 4 & 5 Vict. c. 100, which, among other provisions, absolutely prohibited free grants of land.

CHAP. VI RETROSPECT, FORECAST, SEQUEL 295

induced the Upper Canada Legislature, in the session of 1839-40, to pass a Bill which devoted the revenues derivable from the sale of clergy reserve lands exclusively to religious purposes, and secured to the churches of England and Scotland one-half of the future proceeds, leaving the remainder to be distributed for the support of religious instruction among the different Christian denominations in the province, in proportion to the numbers of their respective adherents. This Bill, when sent home, was disallowed as being *ultra vires*; and in the session of 1840 the Imperial Parliament, in addition to passing the Union Act, the 42nd section of which dealt with ecclesiastical and Crown rights, passed also a special Act to provide for the sale of the clergy reserves in Canada, and for the distribution of the proceeds.[1] Under the provisions of this Act, two-thirds of the proceeds of the lands sold prior to the passing of the Act were assigned to the Church of England and one-third to the Church of Scotland ; while of the annual proceeds of future sales, one-third was appropriated to the Church of England, one-sixth to the Church of Scotland, and one-half was to be applied for purposes of public worship and religious instruction in Canada. Poulett Thomson, in sending home his own Act, had intimated that public opinion in Upper Canada considered it to be too favourable to the Church of England, and that the majority of the people were in favour of applying the proceeds of the reserves to education or to general State purposes ; and when he received the Imperial Act of 1840,

[1] 3 & 4 Vict. c. 78.

which was still more favourable to the Church of England, he expressed a strong opinion as to the injustice of the settlement. The sections of the Constitutional Act of 1791, which originally created the clergy reserves, gave power to the local Legislatures, under certain restrictions, to vary or repeal the provisions respecting the reserves; and, though this power was taken away by the Act of 1840, Lord Durham's view that the question was one to be settled in Canada was widely shared in England. Accordingly, in 1853, the Imperial Parliament passed a further Act [1] empowering the Canadian Legislature to deal with the matter; and in the following year, 1854, a Canadian law finally set to rest this long standing grievance and controversy, by secularizing the reserves and the moneys accruing from them. This law was entitled 'An Act to make better provision for the appropriation of moneys arising from the lands heretofore known as the Clergy Reserves by rendering them available for municipal purposes'. It was an uncompromising Act, for it recited that 'it is desirable to remove all semblance of connexion between Church and State', and it did not even provide that the moneys in question should be applied to education, but handed them over for municipal purposes. Still treating Canada as a federation of two provinces rather than as a single province, it provided that the revenues of the clergy reserves should be paid over to an Upper Canada and a Lower Canada municipalities fund, and should be divided among the municipalities in

[1] 16 Vict. c. 21.

proportion to population. On the day that this measure became law, the assent of the Crown was also given to another far-reaching Act passed by the Canadian Legislature, 'for the abolition of feudal rights and duties in Lower Canada ', which put an end to the seigniorial system.

Lord Durham proposed (ii. 323-6) that the Parliamentary Commission, which should be appointed to form the future electoral districts in United Canada, and to determine the number and allotment of members, should also form a plan of 'local government by elective bodies subordinate to the General Legislature.' It has been seen that he attached paramount importance to the introduction of a sound system of municipal and local institutions into Canada, and Poulett Thomson was, if possible, even more emphatic on the subject. In a passage which has already been quoted,[1] the latter wrote to Lord John Russell urging that the provision of machinery by which local taxation could be raised for local purposes was a necessary complement of the reform by which the initiative of money votes in the House of Assembly would be confined to the Government; and that the establishment of municipal institutions therefore became a necessary part of the Union Bill. Clauses creating district councils were accordingly embodied in the Bill; but, before it left the House of Commons, they were omitted, largely on the suggestion of 'Bear' Ellice; and the Bill, as it became law, contained one section only—the 58th—which referred to the constitution of townships. The omission of

[1] See above, p. 218.

the municipal clauses was bitterly resented by Poulett Thomson, who wrote in September 1840,[1] condemning in the strongest possible terms the abandonment of what he considered to be a most vital part of the Union Bill; but, before the Act was brought into operation, he passed a Local Government ordinance in the Special Council of Lower Canada, and followed it up, after the Union had been proclaimed, by carrying a similar Bill for Upper Canada through the Canadian Legislature. A few years later the elective element was introduced more largely into the municipal system which he had created in the two provinces.[2] Writing in 1861, Merivale referred to Upper Canada as the only British colony within his knowledge that had then an adequate municipal system. 'The same organization,' he added, 'is spreading in Lower Canada, but has far greater difficulties to contend with. Elsewhere, in British North America, municipal organization seems to remain in a most imperfect state; and instead of local rates, public works and improvements are effected by grants from the central legislature; a system leading both to improvidence and to corruption.'[3] Under the British North America Act of 1867, by the 92nd section, 'municipal institutions in the province'

[1] See his dispatch to the Secretary of State, September 16, 1840 (Egerton and Grant, pp. 280-7).

[2] See note to Egerton and Grant, p. 288, which states that the elective system for municipal officers was introduced for Lower Canada in 1845, and for Upper Canada in 1849, and that 'these Acts are still the foundation of the municipal systems of the Provinces of Quebec and Ontario'.

[3] *Lectures on Colonization and Colonies*, 1861 ed., Appendix to Lecture XXII, p. 653.

CHAP. VI   RETROSPECT, FORECAST, SEQUEL   299

are included among the exclusive powers of the Provincial Legislatures.

Lord Durham's comments and recommendations on the subject of emigration bore no fruit, so far as emigration was coupled with the disposal of public lands as a factor in a great scheme of imperial colonization.

In his instructions to Poulett Thomson, issued in September 1839, Lord John Russell referred to Lord Durham's Report, as only placing in a clearer light the difficulties which existed in the case of Canada in the way of raising an emigration fund from the sale of Crown lands.[1] But immigration into Canada—apart from the subject of public lands—formed the subject of much correspondence between the Governor-General and the Home Government; and in the speech with which he opened the Canadian Legislature in the summer of 1841, Poulett Thomson announced that the Imperial Government was prepared to assist in facilitating the passages of immigrants from the port of landing in Canada to the places where their labour would be made available.[2] By this time the Board of Colonial Land and Emigration Commissioners, established in January 1840, had been in operation for more than a year; and in Lord John Russell's initial instructions to them [3] may be traced the effects of Lord Durham's powerful criticism of the want of adequate safeguards for

[1] See Parliamentary Paper, 1840. Correspondence relative to the Affairs of Canada, Part I, p. 9.
[2] See Egerton and Grant, p. 291.
[3] House of Commons Paper, February 4, 1840, Colonial Land Board.

emigrants embarking from the ports of the United Kingdom. From this date onwards, the provisions of Passenger Acts and Merchant Shipping Acts, administered first by the Land and Emigration Commissioners, and subsequently by the Board of Trade, protected British emigrants when crossing the seas; and 'the collection and diffusion of accurate statistical knowledge' for the benefit of Intending Emigrants, which Lord John Russell included in the list of duties of the newly-formed Board, is now provided, not only by the representatives in this country of the dominions beyond the seas, but also by the Emigrants' Information Office, established in 1886 by the Imperial Government.

The first session of the United Legislature of Canada, at the close of which, in September 1841, Poulett Thomson, then Lord Sydenham, died, was rich in measures dealing with subjects which had found a place in Lord Durham's Report. In addition to the District Councils Act for Upper Canada already mentioned, an Act was passed to improve the administration of justice in minor civil cases in Lower Canada; and a Common Schools Act was also passed, Poulett Thomson having, in his opening speech to the Legislature, reminded its members that 'a due provision for the education of the people is one of the first duties of the State, and in this province, especially, the want of it is grievously felt'.[1] Under the provisions of this Act, the newly-created district councils of the province were constituted Boards of

[1] Egerton and Grant, p. 292.

Education, but separate schools for the different denominations were included under the heading of common schools. Various other Education Acts followed in later years, and at the present day, by the 93rd section of the British North America Act of 1867, education—under certain restrictions—is assigned to the Provincial Legislatures, the rights of denominational schools in the provinces of Ontario and Quebec being adequately safeguarded. Public works received at the outset of the Union as much attention as even Lord Durham could have desired. In this same first session, the Legislature passed an Act creating a Board of Works for the whole province; and an Imperial Act of 1842 guaranteed the interest on a loan of 1½ million sterling to be raised by the Canadian Government, for relieving the pressure of immediate financial difficulties, and carrying out the works which were so sorely needed for the development of Canada.

Lord Durham died in England in 1840. Lord Sydenham died in Canada in 1841. In either case, humanly speaking, the career was foreshortened, yet in a sense in either case the career was complete. Lord Durham preached his gospel and died; Lord Sydenham, before he too died, set the political machine running in the right direction. Then the machine went on, the way widened, the views widened, men grew up to contemplate a nation, and after contemplating to create it. Lord Durham's Report gave the inspiration. Sydenham, with his combination of strong popular sympathies and great business capacity, showed how to begin putting principles into practice. The history of Canada has been on the whole a history of singular good fortune; and not the least part of this good fortune has been, that Lord Durham should have been forthcoming at the particular time when he went to Canada, and that Lord Sydenham should have been available as his successor. It would be difficult to find in the chronicles of any country two men who, within little more than three years in all, did so much to help the coming time.

CHAPTER VII

THE REPORT AND THE EMPIRE

How far, it is proposed to ask in conclusion, are the doctrines or principles embodied in Lord Durham's Report of universal application? The answer consists in summarizing in a very few words, and to some extent repeating, what has gone before.

Though Lord Durham laid down in his Report far-reaching principles of colonial administration, it must always be borne in mind that he was primarily concerned with the objects of a special mission. He was not thinking of the whole world. He was not even thinking of the whole British Empire. He had his eyes fixed upon the British provinces in North America, to which he had been sent; and, when he raised his eyes, his gaze fell upon the adjoining part of North America which had once belonged to Great Britain, and the prosperity of which conveyed to his mind a contrast and a moral. Having this horizon, he propounded and set himself to answer the following question. Given a people living at a distance from the central authority, who are either of British race, or at any rate of European origin, bred up under British rule, and in some familiarity with British privileges and institutions, what under such circumstances is the best political constitution, designed at once with a view to giving contentment to the distant community, and with a view to maintaining and strengthening its connexion with the central authority? His answer was that, with certain very important and carefully defined reservations, the distant community should be left to govern itself on the lines on which representative and responsible government is understood and carried on in the United Kingdom.

It will be noted (1) that he prescribed for distant communities; (2) that he prescribed for communities which were either British, or Anglicized, or *ex hypothesi* to be Anglicized, and which already enjoyed representative institutions; (3) that his prescription was responsible government most carefully restricted. Each of these points require a few words of comment.

It has been pointed out that one of the most admirable features of the Report is the stress which is laid upon the importance of means of communication, and the almost prophetic insight which the writer possessed of the extent to which the forces of science might mould the future. If the question which has just been stated were propounded at the present day, the answer would be that in all probability, before many years have passed, there will be no distant communities. If we are to reason from the past to the future, the day will come, and may come in no very long time, when distance will cease to exist to any appreciable extent. The world moves so constantly and so fast that statesmen, and writers, and thinkers, never seem sufficiently to take stock of the advance

CHAP. VII THE REPORT AND THE EMPIRE 305

which has been made, or to appreciate that what science has done in the past it will probably do in the future, only at a perpetually accelerated pace. It is a little under a century and a half since, in his *Observations on a late state of the Nation*, Edmund Burke elaborately ridiculed the proposal that the American colonies should be represented in the British Parliament, working out the time that would be necessary in order to traverse the distance. His weeks have now become days or even less; if he were writing at the present time, he would have to recast his arguments; and if the next century and a half proves to be as fruitful in scientific discovery and invention as the interval since he wrote has been, distance at the end of that period will have vanished altogether.[1]

It does not follow that elimination of distance will necessarily produce unity within the Empire: there are instances to the contrary, which go to

[1] With reference to the great merit of Lord Durham's Report in appreciating what scientific invention would do for the Empire, there is an interesting passage in the Annual Register for 1838, written in reference to his Report, which shows similar confidence in the future of communications. 'The only conceivable course for bringing our colonial dependencies within the legitimate action of the constitution would be to summon them to send members to the Imperial parliament. This is a remedy which to some may seem worse than the evils which demand its application. Nor can it be dissembled that it would open the door to a multitude of ills, the nature of many of which may be perceived by the inconvenience which is produced by the presence of some of the Irish members in Parliament. . . . One considerable obstacle, at least, to the success of such a plan as we have been noticing, has to a great extent been removed by the speed and certainty of communication attained by steam navigation, so that it is probable that no great inconvenience to any party would now ensue from the delay and difficulties of the transit between Great Britain and her Atlantic colonies' (pp. 337-8).

prove that distance may in some cases lend enchantment; and, while the distant provinces of the Empire are year by year being brought into closer touch with each other, they are at the same time and by the same means being brought into closer touch with foreign nations; but the fact remains that the difficulty which faced Lord Durham, how to hold together communities at a distance from each other, is gradually becoming obsolete; and this particular problem is being superseded by new problems and new difficulties which did not exist in his time, or of which, in his Mission and in his Report, he was not called upon to take cognizance.

In the second place, he was only concerned with British communities, or, on his own showing, with communities which were to be completely anglicized, and which already had some measure of British institutions. Thus, one half of the British Empire lay entirely outside his ken. Now let us ask, what is the main difference between the British Empire and all other empires that the world has as yet known? The term 'Empire'[1] is used, in

[1] Sir G. Cornewall Lewis in *The Government of Dependencies* (1891 ed.), pp. 73–4, defined 'Empire' as follows: 'The entire territory subject to a supreme government possessing several dependencies (that is to say, a territory formed of a dominant country together with its dependencies) is sometimes styled an Empire, as when we speak of the British Empire. Agreeably with this acceptation of the word Empire, the supreme government of a nation, considered with reference to its dependencies, is called the Imperial government, and the English parliament is called the Imperial Parliament, as distinguished from the provincial parliament of a dependency.' The Roman word *Imperium* had no special military signification. It was, as Mommsen points out, the right to command the citizens in all matters within a given area (see Mommsen's *History of Rome*, Book II, chap. iii, vol. i, p. 297 note).

CHAP. VII THE REPORT AND THE EMPIRE   307

default of a better term, as simply equivalent to a people or collection of peoples owing allegiance to some one common head or central authority. Some prejudice, modern and ill-founded, has arisen against the use of this word, as implying despotism and military rule. It seems to be forgotten that, in the days of King Henry VIII, 'Empire' and 'Imperial Crown' connoted the Sovereign independence of England, not the rule of England beyond the seas.[1]

When ancient and modern political systems are compared, we are told that the main differences between them are, that in the ancient world nothing was known of representation in politics, and that slavery was an integral factor in every community. There is the further and most vital difference that the ancients had no knowledge of steam and electricity. Notwithstanding these differences, the Roman Empire, which by common consent was by far the greatest political creation of the Old World, is usually and rightly taken as the standard with which to compare the British Empire. So far as the world's history has gone, the Romans and the British have been the most successful empire builders; the two peoples have had to a large extent the same qualities, one of the notable features of the Romans being that, though dwelling in Southern Europe, they had rather the characteristics of a northern race. Like the Romans, the British have not been 'cursed with the passion for uniformity';[2] and Romans

[1] See the Oxford English Dictionary s.v. 'This Realm of England is an Empire,' 24 Hen. VIII, cap. 12.
[2] Arnold's *Roman Provincial Administration*, 2nd ed., 1906, p. 22.

and British alike realized to the full how essential to making and keeping an empire are adequate means of communication. Allowing then for the differences above mentioned as being the result of different stages of civilization, what is the main distinction to be drawn between this Roman Empire, which of all empires was most akin to our own, and the British Empire of the present day?

The Roman Empire seems to have resembled the Empire of Spain in America, in so far as it was created by conquest and held by despotism, while including in the conquered provinces a large amount of colonization from the motherland, which made the dominant feature of the provinces in one case Roman [1] and in the other Spanish. Neither in the Roman nor in the Spanish American Empire was there any distinction between the areas which were ruled and the areas which were settled. In the earlier system there were Roman colonies, and more or less self-governing *municipia*, scattered through a subject world. In the later system there was no part of Spanish America which, as a province of the Spanish Empire, differed widely in kind from the other parts. Herein is the great distinction between the British Empire and the Roman Empire, and between the British Empire and all other empires. In the British Empire, broadly speaking, the sphere of settlement is distinct from the sphere of rule. The British Empire includes in wholly

---

[1] This statement does not overlook the great part which Greek language and civilization played to the Roman Empire, but what was dominant as opposed to subordinate in that Empire was Roman.

CHAP. VII THE REPORT AND THE EMPIRE 309

different areas colonies which are not really dependencies, and dependencies which are not really colonies. Nor, as regards the first of these two categories, has any European people, ancient or modern, on anything like the same scale, made other parts of the world the permanent home of the colonizing race, without intermixture of coloured races, the closest parallels being the case of the French in Canada, and in a lesser degree, of the Dutch in South Africa, both of whom are now within the circle of the British Empire.

The great cardinal feature of the British Empire then is that it consists of two wholly different spheres, the sphere of rule and the sphere of settlement, and to the sphere of settlement alone Lord Durham's Report applies. He does not give us any guidance as to the great problem how to hold together as parts of one political system peoples and provinces, at present at a distance from each other, when the provinces show the utmost differences in climate, when the peoples differ in race, in colour, and in stages of development, when some provinces are and must be, self-governing, while others are despotically governed.

This problem lies outside the scope of the present Introduction; but, with reference to the statement made above that elimination of distance need not necessarily make for greater unity, it may be noted in passing, that better communication has already tended to accentuate what is perhaps the greatest present-day difficulty of the British Empire—a difficulty which does not appear to have existed in the Roman Empire—the colour question.

Lord Durham's outlook having been confined to what has been called the sphere of settlement, we next ask how far in that sphere were the principles which he laid down, and the reasoning which he employed, of general application. He prescribed, in the first place, for provinces which already had been given representative institutions. He says (ii. 278), ' We are not now to consider the policy of establishing representative government in the North American colonies. That has been irrevocably done; and the experiment of depriving the people of their present constitutional power is not to be thought of.' In the second place, he prescribed more especially for communities which bordered on a self-governing nation of British origin, though the government of that country was not the particular form of self-government which he advocated for Canada. In the third place, as has been abundantly pointed out, he postulated as a necessary preliminary to self-government, that the community, so far as it was not British, should be made British, that every foreign element in it should be submerged. Suppose that Canada, instead of adjoining the United States, had been, like Australia, far removed from American influence and example, the necessity for self-government might not have seemed so urgent. Suppose, again, that the Act of 1791 had not been passed, and that Canada, when Lord Durham visited it, had been a pure Crown Colony without any vestige of a representative institution; it does not follow that Lord Durham would at once have prescribed responsible government. Suppose, once more, that he had been deprived of his hypothesis that the French Canadian nationality must be obliterated, or that he had been sent to South Africa, as South Africa was after the late war, with the understanding that nothing was to be done to undermine the Dutch nationality, then, to judge from his Report, he would not have recommended responsible government.

It is of course a vain thing to ask what a man would have said or done many years after his death, in altered conditions and with fuller knowledge. A broad-minded man moves with the times, and Lord Durham would never have stood still ; but notwithstanding, in trying to answer the question how far the principles laid down in his Report were or are applicable to the whole sphere of settlement in the British Empire, it is right and useful to point out that his recommendations were primarily directed to the case of a particular group of provinces in a certain stage of development, and with special surroundings, and that beyond all question, he looked upon responsible government as a British prescription for a British community, and not as a recipe for non-British communities.

The third point is, that this colonial self-government which he expounded and prescribed, was, as has been already emphasized, of the most restricted character, falling very far short of colonial self-government as it exists at the present day. It must be repeated that Lord Durham, while making the reservations which he made, as being wise and reasonable in the first stages of self-government, would, in the light of later knowledge, probably have been the last man to insist that these limits were unalterable landmarks, to be upheld throughout the centuries. His Report breathes the sane and human spirit of growth and development; and, were he living now, he would doubtless rejoice in the ever broadening freedom and responsibility which has been obtained by the younger peoples of the Empire in their adult manhood. If we do not make this assumption, it is clear that his principles, coupled with his reservations, have proved to be inadequate, even for the cases to which they were intended to be applied. On the other hand, however, if we do make it, we must recognize that colonial self-government, as he prescribed it, was merely a stage in a process, the end of which is not yet in sight, and the outcome of which may or may not be one form or another of imperial unity. In other words, if we give Lord Durham credit for marking out very clearly and definitely the direction, with full intent that the road should, as it went on, perpetually broaden out, we must at the same time recognize that he had at best not found a solution, but only a way which might eventually lead to a solution.

As far as his Report shows, he intended to create a nation, but a nation which should be subordinate; whereas the result of his Report—a result which, whatever he may have intended, was absolutely inevitable—was to begin creating nations which should not be subordinate. It was an inevitable result, because it has always been true of British colonists as of Greek, that, so far as

CHAP. VII THE REPORT AND THE EMPIRE 313

they were in either case free men, they went out on the principle of being equal instead of subordinate to the citizens who were left behind. The problem, as he left it, was the connexion between two self-governing communities, one superior, and the other subordinate. The problem, as we have it, is the connexion between one older and several younger self-governing communities, which are on or are approaching the position of political equality. Judging from his Report, he seems to have contemplated that a nation could be created, endowed with national institutions, and inspired with national patriotism, but that bounds could be placed to its nationhood. Time has proved that this was a fallacy; that it was not possible in the case of overseas dominions, while the element of distance survived, and while the communities in question were growing out of infancy to the adult stage, to give self-government but assign limits to the self-government. The only limits are those which the self-governing nation may itself assign, by handing over some of its powers to a federation. Thus the critics of responsible government, as Lord Durham propounded it, had much to say for themselves. They contended that there could not be dual control; he contended that there could, that a division of authority was possible. It was not possible in the long run. The grant of responsible government was the beginning of the end of subordination, in the sense of the mother country eventually retaining any substantial power over the self-governing communities beyond the seas.

So far as such power has been retained since the time when responsible government was granted, the retention has been due not to any definite division of authority, such as Lord Durham contemplated, but to the recognition by the self-governing communities of the benefit derived from the conditions which imply control. Security against foreign invasion has been provided by the British fleet, enabling the younger peoples to grow into nations, undisturbed from the outside. The home people of the Empire has in the main paid the foreign bill of the overseas peoples, and further has largely supplied the capital required for the peaceful development of the overseas peoples. The analogy of the family holds for peoples as for individuals. The younger the children are, the more they require to be fostered and protected, and the more they are controlled. When they have been started in the world, the need for fostering and protection grows less and less, and the control diminishes *pari passu*. Lord Durham may have had this future in his mind, but it is not foreshadowed in his Report. In that Report he limited his outlook to the creation of subordinate peoples, whereas the result of his recommendation has been that equal nations have been or are being evolved.

Lord Durham's view of what has been called above the sphere of settlement in the British Empire would apparently have corresponded very nearly with the view put forward by Burke in his speech on American taxation. 'The Parliament of Great Britain sits at the head of her extensive Empire in two capacities, one as the local legislature of this island. . . . The other and, I think, her nobler capacity is what I call her Imperial character, in which, as from the throne of Heaven, she superintends all the several inferior legislatures, and guides and controls them all, without annihilating any. As all these provincial legislatures are only co-ordinate to each other, they ought all to be subordinate to her.' Lord Durham might probably have gone further than Burke in the measure of emancipation from the control of the Imperial Parliament, which he would have given to the colonies, but still they were in the end to be subordinate members of the Empire, not equal partners. It is since this time, but dating from this time, that the relation of partnership has little by little supplanted that of supremacy and subordination, leaving, and in the process strengthening, the link of common allegiance to the Crown.

It may be summed up then that a close analysis of Lord Durham's Report leads to the conclusion that, while it is to some extent a general treatise on colonial administration, the principles embodied in it are by no means of universal application; that the great Liberal, who wrote or dictated the Report, was not a preacher of self-government for the whole world, or for the whole British Empire, or for coloured races, or for non-British white races, or even for British peoples whatever may be their stage of development. Nor was he by any means a preacher of unlimited self-government. And yet it is impossible to study the Report without feeling that such a statement of its limitations does it less than justice.

It has been attempted in the foregoing pages to lay stress upon what has been termed Lord Durham's constructiveness. To all times and to all sorts and conditions of men he has preached the doctrine, that for peoples, as for individuals, the one thing worth living for is to make, not to destroy; to build up, not to pull down; to unite small disjointed elements into a single whole; to reject absolutely and always the doctrine of *Divide et Impera*, because it is a sign of weakness, not of strength; to be strong and fear not; to speak unto the peoples of the earth that they go forward. In this constructiveness, which is embodied in all parts of the Report, he has beyond any other man illustrated in writing the genius of the English race, the element which in the British Empire is common alike to the sphere of settlement and to the sphere of rule. It is as a race of makers that the English will live to all time, and it is as a prophet of a race of makers that Lord Durham lives. Of Canada he wrote (ii. 310) :

'If in the hidden decrees of that wisdom by which this world is ruled, it is written that these countries are not for ever to remain portions of the Empire, we owe it to our honour to take good care that, when they separate from us, they should not be the only countries on the American continent in which the Anglo-Saxon race shall be found unfit to govern itself.'

These words apply beyond Canada and beyond America. The spirit of them transcends the sphere of settlement, it is the living force of the whole British Empire. The words are the message of a great Englishman to his fellow countrymen, that the one thing needful is to leave behind a legacy of what is permanently sound and great. If England continues to be inspired by what Lord Durham taught so well, then as Great Britain has grown into Greater Britain, so Greater Britain will grow into Greatest Britain, to the glory of God the Creator, and to the well-being of mankind.

LORD DURHAM'S REPORT AS BEARING ON THE QUESTION OF HOME RULE FOR IRELAND

THERE is no great profit in speculating as to what view a man long dead would have taken of a political question of the present day. But colonial self-government dates from Lord Durham's Report, and reference has been and may again be made to the Report in connexion with proposals for Home Rule in Ireland. It may therefore be of use, without in any way discussing the merits either of Lord Durham's views or of Home Rule, to note very briefly how far there is any analogy between the case of Canada in Lord Durham's time, and that of Ireland to-day, and what bearing the doctrines embodied in the Report seem to have upon the Home Rule question.

It will be remembered that Lord Durham was one of the leaders, if not *the* leader, of the Radical wing of the Liberal party of his day, and also that he was a cotemporary of O'Connell, though he died before the great agitation for the Repeal of the Union. Further, the fact that in the previous twenty years there had been a large Irish immigration into Canada, and that in the recent disturbances in Canada the Irish had in the main ranged themselves with the other British loyalists on the side of the Government, in spite of aggressive Orangeism in Upper Canada, may well have kept Ireland and the Irish prominently in his mind. But notwithstanding, he does not seem to quote Ireland for the purpose of comparison or contrast with Canada, except in the passage with the marginal note, 'The French, when in a legitimate minority, would abandon vain hopes of nationality,' in which passage he says, 'The experience of the two Unions in the British Isles may teach us how effectually the strong arm of a popular legislature would compel the obedience of the refractory population' (vol. ii, p. 308). We may therefore take it that Lord Durham himself did not find much analogy between Canada, as it was in his day, and Ireland.

If we are to find any analogy, it must obviously be found in Lower Canada—the French Province, not in Upper Canada, the more or less homogeneous British Province. Lower Canada contained an overwhelming majority of Roman Catholic French Canadians, and a British Protestant minority, of strong and enterprising character, considerable in the commercial centres of Quebec and Montreal, and wholly predominant in one corner of the Province, the Eastern Townships. To this extent it rather closely resembled Ireland. The French Canadians had been led by Papineau, who was considered the O'Connell of Canada : the extremists among them talked of La Nation Canadienne, a Canadian Republic and so forth (ii. 58, &c.) ; in short, the feeling, exasperated by the recent rising, was roughly parallel to Irish feeling after one or other of the periodical disturbances in Ireland, and may be said to have combined some active and pronounced, with much more passive, disloyalty.

So far there is some similarity between the case of Lower Canada in Lord Durham's time, and Ireland both then and now. On the other hand, the points of difference are many—among them the following: (i) The time when Lord Durham went out and reported was an abnormal time, a time of crisis. There had been an armed rising, trivial, it is true, but still an open insurrection, not in Lower Canada only, but in Upper Canada also; and there had been general political discontent from want of self-government in all the British North American provinces. In Lower Canada the constitution had in consequence been entirely suspended. (ii) The scene of his mission, and the object of his recommendations, was a group of communities, not close to but distant from England. (iii) This group of communities bordered on a great self-governing community of British speech and descent—the United States. (iv) The communities in question had not at the time, and never had enjoyed so far in their history, full Parliamentary liberties, in the sense in which such liberties are understood in the United Kingdom. (v) The trouble in Lower Canada was, at any rate in Lord Durham's opinion, a trouble of animosity between a British and a non-British race, aggravated, but not caused primarily, by defects in the constitution, and not aggravated by difference of religion, religious toleration being conspicuous in Lower Canada.

HOME RULE FOR IRELAND

So much for the parallel between Lower Canada and Ireland. Now let us take the views embodied in the Report. In the Introduction to which this note is appended, it has been attempted to correct the common view of the Report, which eulogizes it—quite rightly—for recommending responsible government, but does not stop to consider the limits which Lord Durham set to responsible government, and the conditions under which alone he was prepared to concede it. Much might be said—as bearing on the Irish question—of the limits which he placed to self-government; but it will be enough to note the conditions under which, and only under which, he was prepared to grant it. It may be added that the Report is entirely misinterpreted by those who fail or refuse to see that Lord Durham was quite ready to apply what would now be called Coercion, in order to secure what he considered to be the greatest happiness of the greatest number; and that he had no intention of giving to people something that in his opinion would not be for their permanent good, simply because they asked for it.

Lord Durham, as an advanced Liberal, went out to Canada, holding that the panacea for all the evils in British North America was constitutional reform, in other words self-government. He reasoned, with irresistible force, that there was a common source of discontent in these communities, in that being composed of British citizens, or rather white British subjects, who were already accustomed to some form of representative institutions, they were not entrusted with the full management of their own local affairs, but were kept under a distant and therefore, in his opinion, a misgoverning authority; that it was specially dangerous not to give them self-government, because the self-governing United States was immediately under their eyes, and exercising a powerful attraction; and moreover, that American public opinion would be conciliated by the grant of self-government to Canada, just as American sympathy with Home Rule for Ireland is taken into account nowadays.

But when he reached Canada, and found that the evil in the Province of Quebec was more than a constitutional question, and that its root was in race, not only did he not prescribe self-government for Lower Canada as it then stood, but (i) he blamed the Imperial Government for ever having given any semblance of separate treatment to the French Canadians. 'Unhappily, the system of government pursued in Lower Canada has been based on the policy of perpetuating that very separation of the races, and encouraging these very notions of conflicting nationalities, which it ought to have been the first and chief care of Government to check and extinguish' (ii. 63); and (ii) he laid down that 'the fatal feud of origin, which is the cause of the most extensive mischief, would be aggravated at the present moment by any change, which should give the majority more power than they have hitherto possessed' (ii. 288).

What then was his prescription for Lower Canada? Not that it should be debarred from self-government, nor that the French majority should be placed under the loyal English minority in the Province—' I certainly should not like to subject the French Canadians to the rule of the identical English minority with which they have so long been contending ' (ii. 308)—but that it should be an absolutely necessary preliminary to giving self-government to the Province of Quebec, that that province should be fused—not federated —with the neighbouring province, in order that the disloyal French Canadians might be outvoted and swamped by and wholly merged in a loyal British majority, in order that the national character to be given to French Canada should be ' that of the British Empire, that of the majority of the population of British America ' (ii. 288). He did not look to self-government by itself to cure disloyalty in Lower Canada. On the contrary, he made it a *sine qua non* of giving self-government to the French Canadians that the majority should be British, which, in spite of the rising in Upper Canada, was tantamount to being loyal. Nor did he regard it as a negation of self-government that the French Canadians should always be outvoted. Further, he viewed the total incorporation of a small community in a bigger one as a gain to the small community, and where there was a doubt as to the advisability of granting self-government under existing conditions, he recommended absorption in a larger body. Thus he writes of Newfoundland, ' If it be true that there exists in this island a state of society, which renders it unadvisable that the whole of the local government should be entirely left to the inhabitants,

I believe that it would be much better to incorporate this colony with a larger community, than to attempt to continue the present experiment of governing it by a constant collision of constitutional powers ' (ii. 202).

Lord Durham, then, recommended self-government for Lower Canada, but not Home Rule ; and, if any inference can be drawn from his Report with regard to Ireland, it would seem that he not only would not have recommended Home Rule for Ireland, but would have contended that it has self-government already, and that it was a mistake ever to have given it any shred of separate treatment, such as a fixed number of members in the Parliament of the United Kingdom.

INDEX

Aberdeen, Lord, 62, 64.
Abolition of Slavery, *see* Slavery.
Abolition of Transportation, *see* Transportation.
Acts, Principal, referred to :
  (1) Imperial
  (a) Relating to Canada :
    Quebec Act of 1774, 29, 56, 58, 165, 220 and note 1, 223-4, 224 note.
    Quebec Revenue Act of 1774, 29, 40, 60, 70, 76.
    Constitutional Act of 1791, 31, 53, 78, 84, 101-2, 138, 159, 160, 162-3, 220, 221, 227-8, 233, 254, 278, 279, 291, 292, 296, 310.
    Canada Trade Act of 1822, 33, 45, 47, 55, 67, 161.
    Tenures Act of 1825, 161, 172.
    Revenue Control Act of 1831, 60, 70, 71, 76.
    Constitutional Act Suspension Act of 1838 (Government of Lower Canada), 101-3, 110, 111, 112, 168 note.
    Union Act of 1840, 221 and note, 288-9, 291, 292, 293, 294, 295, 296.
    Civil List Act of 1847, 292 and note, 293.
    Crown Revenues Act of 1852, 185, 293.
    British North America Act of 1867, 166, 204, 231, 252, 253, 284, 289, 292, 293 and note 1, 298, 301.
    Clergy Reserves Acts, 163 and note, 294, 295 and note, 296 and note.
    Passengers and Merchant Shipping Acts, 188, 191, 192, 300.
  (b) General :
    Reform Act of 1832, 18.
    Poor Law Amendment Act of 1834, 18, 198.
    South Australian Act of 1834, 156, 158.
    Municipal Corporations Act of 1835, 18, 151 and note, 214.
    Civil List Acts, 185.
    Test and Corporation Acts Repeal, 19.
  (2) Canadian
    Medical Relief of Emigrants Act of 1832, 195.
    Quarantine Act of 1832, 194.
    Sulpician Seminary Act of 1839, 168.
    Public Lands Act of 1841, 294 note.
    Civil List Act of 1846, 292, 293.
    Abolition of Feudal Rights in Lower Canada, Act of 1854, 168 note, 297.
    Seigniorial Amendment Act of 1859, 168 note.
    Clergy Reserves Acts, 165, 295, 296.
    Jesuits' Estates Acts, 166.
    Municipal Corporations Acts, 212, 298 and note, 300.
Advisory Committee, proposed by Lord Glenelg, 110-12.
America and Americans, *see* United States.
Amherst, Lord, 64, 166.
Anti-Corn Law Association, 20.
Anti-Corn Law League, 20.
Appeals, Judicial, *see* Law and Justice.
Arnold, Roman Provincial Administration quoted, 307.
Arthur, Sir George, 81, 100, 118.
Ashburton, Lord, 123.
Assembly, Houses of, 29, 31, 33, 34, 132, 277, 287, &c.
  Lower Canada, 35, 36, 38-52,

54, 56–72, 74, 77, 111, 112, 128, 139, 143, 150, 161, 183, 211, 212, 217, 233, 236.
Upper Canada, 7 and note, 54, 69, 70, 77, 79, 80, 118, 119, 143, 262, 267.
United Canada, 288–90.
New Brunswick, 82.
Newfoundland, 86–8.
Nova Scotia, 81.
Prince Edward Island, 85, 86.
Australia, 12–14, 146, 152 note, 178, 182, 193, 196, 197, 252, 264, 273, 291, 310.
Australia, South, *see* South Australia.
Australia, Western, *see* Western Australia.
Aylmer, Lord, 57, 58, 59, 64, 65, 183–5.

Baie Verte, *see* Canals.
Baldwin, Robert, 75, 79, 97, 98.
Barbados, 11.
Bathurst, Lord, 38, 41, 43 note, 49–52, 266.
Beauharnois Canal, *see* Canals.
Beauharnois Seigniory, 161.
Bidwell, Barnabas, 55.
Bidwell, Marshall Spring, 55, 69, 70, 75, 80, 81, 97.
Board of Trade, *see* Trade.
Boulton, 75, 76, 87, 88.
Britannia, the, 16.
British American Land Company, 61, 66, 67, 73, 171–2.
British Columbia, 204.
British in Canada, 24, 26, 27, 29, 31, 34, 63, 65, 66, 89, 126, 128, 129, 130, 136, 138, 148, 172, 227, 241, 248, 259, 260, 282, 284, 310, 316, *et passim*.
British North America, 11, 65, 71, 75, 84, 86, 105, 106, 107, 108, 109, 114, 115, 121, 122, 123, 128, 131, 137, 138, 146, 153, 154, 182, 185, 188, 201, 221, 244, 256, 266, 277, 279, 280, 289, 298, 303, 310, *et passim*.
Union of, 32, 121, 126, 132, 148–9, 217, 247–57, 261, 266, 289.
Brougham, Lord, 103, 123.
Brown, Thomas Storrow, 89, 91, 92, 93, 94.

Bryce, Mr., quoted, 139–40 note.
Buller, Arthur, his Report on Education in Lower Canada, 232, 233, 234–44, 247.
Buller, Charles, 3–5, 12, 21–3, 112, 117, 131, 160, 161, 175, 178, 179, 180, 189, 195, 197, 200, 210–11, 213, 222, 231 note, 235, 248, 261, 266, 267, 268, 270.
his Public Lands Inquiry and Report, 108 note, 114, 115, 121, 153, 156, 157, 168 and note, 169–70, 173, 175–82, 185–6, 189 note, 190 note, 191, 193, 195 note.
Bureaucracy, 23, 75.
Burke, Edmund, 305, 314–15.
Burton, Sir Francis, 48, 50.
By, Colonel, 203, 208.

Campbell, Sir Archibald, 82, 83.
Campbell, Sir Colin, 85.
Canada, 6, 26–30, 42, 104, 109, 118, 125, 148, 151, 156, 174, 181, 192, 199–206, 208, 227, 257, 273, 278, 287–8, 291, 296–7, 302, 310, 316, *et passim*.
Canadas, Reunion of, 44–7, 124–36, 148, 247–50, 287–9.
Canada, Lower, History of, 31–53, 55–75, 88–96, 100–3.
Canada, Upper, History of, 31–5, 37, 44, 53–5, 75–81, 96–9.
See also under other heads.
Canada Company, 169–71.
Canadian Pacific Railway, *see* Railways.
Canadien, Le, 35.
Canals, 178, 198, 199, 203–9, 264, 265.
Bay of Fundy and Baie Verte, 199–200.
Beauharnois, 206.
Chambly, 207.
Cornwall, 207.
Erie, 209, 264.
Georgian Bay, 199–200.
Lachine, 206.
Military, 203–4, 206.
Rideau, 203, 207–8.
Welland, 199, 207.

INDEX 327

Canning, 19, 52.
Canterbury, Viscount, 64.
Cape Colony, 13, 21, 146, 178, 190.
Carignan-Salières Regiment, 174.
Carleton, 28, 33, 165–6, 227, 242–3, 254 and note, 281–2.
Carlyle, 3, 131, 235.
Caroline, the, 99, 258.
Cascades, The, 206.
Casual and Territorial Revenues, *see* Crown Revenues.
Catholic emancipation, 19, 239.
Cedars, The, 206.
Chambly, 92.
Chambly Canal, *see* Canals.
Champlain, Lake, 14–15, 207.
Chartrand, 94–5, 229 and note.
Chenier, 95, 97.
Chief Justice, *see* Law and Justice.
Cholera, 194 and note 2.
Church of England, 4, 75, 78–9, 163, 164, 228, 245, 246–7, *and see* Clergy.
Church of Scotland, *see* Clergy, Presbyterian.
Civil List, 39, 40, 41, 43, 52, 58–61, 66, 70, 73, 76, 83, 105, 149, 150, 151, 183, 186, 187, 292–3.
Clergy :
(i) Anglican, 165, 239, 246.
(ii) Presbyterian, 78, 239, 247, 295.
(iii) Roman Catholic, 28, 34, 88–9, 96, 234, 239, 240, 242.
Clergy Reserves, *see* Lands.
Cobden, Richard, 2, 20.
Coburg, 213, 247.
Colbert, 174.
Colborne, Sir John, 55, 73, 75, 77–9, 89, 91, 92, 95, 96, 100, 103, 163–4, 168, 244.
Colonial Administration, *see* Colonial Office.
Colonial Advocate, the, 55.
Colonial Office, 3, 20–3, 52, 62, 124, 157, 178, 179, 188, 191, 243, 266–75.
 advantages of, 268–70, 275.
 criticisms of, 21, 266–8, 270–3.
 position of Secretary of State, 271–4.

Colonies, relations with mother country, 115, 120, 143, 149–50, 155, 285, 312–15.
Colonization Schemes, 14, 115, 155–7, 158, 179, 180, 181–2, 197, 299.
Coloured races, *see* Native Questions.
Commission, Parliamentary, on Electoral Divisions, 148–9.
Communications, 8, 14–15, 123, 179, 180, 198–210, 211, 304–5, 305 note, 308–9.
Confederated Counties, 90–1.
Constitution, British, 139, 142 note, 144.
Cornwall, 213.
Cornwall Canal, *see* Canals.
Côteau du Lac, 206.
Councils :
 (i) Special Council of Lower Canada, 102–3, 110, 168 and note, 298.
 (ii) Executive, 56, 225.
  (*a*) Lower Canada, 65, 66, 67, 70, 71, 73, 143, 144–5, 226, 231.
  (*b*) Upper Canada, 54, 79–80.
  (*c*) New Brunswick, 81, 82, 83.
  (*d*) Newfoundland, 87–8.
  (*e*) Nova Scotia, 81, 82, 84.
  (*f*) Prince Edward Island, 85, 86.
 (iii) Legislative, 29, 31, 33, 56, 151, 225, 227 and note.
  (*a*) Lower Canada, 39, 41, 43, 48, 59, 62, 65, 66, 67, 69, 71, 72, 73, 128, 161, 226, 227.
  (*b*) Upper Canada, 54, 77, 226.
  (*c*) United Canada, 288, 291–2.
  (*d*) New Brunswick, 81, 82, 83.
  (*e*) Newfoundland, 87–8.
  (*f*) Nova Scotia, 81, 82, 84.
  (*g*) Prince Edward Island, 85–6.
Courts, *see* Law and Justice.
Cousin, Victor, 237.
Craig, Sir James, 35–6, 57, 127, 167, 225.
Cromer, Lord, quoted, 135 note.

328 INDEX

Crown, the, 66, 143, 144, 145, 147, 148, 149, 151, 152, 166, 219, 227, 234, 245, 246, 275, 291, 292, 294 note.
Crown Colonies, 11, 23, 225, 266, 267, 268, 270, 273, 274, 310.
Crown Patronage, 66, 67-8, 77.
Crown Reserves, *see* Lands.
Crown Revenues, 40, 47, 52, 54, 56, 58-61, 66, 70, 73, 149, 182-8, 293.
Cunard, 16.

Dalhousie, Earl of, 42, 43, 47, 48, 49, 50, 51, 52, 56, 57, 85, 109, 133.
Davidson, John, 160, 183 note.
Davignon, 91.
Demaray, 91.
Derby, Earl of, *see* Stanley, Lord.
Detroit, 96, 99.
Dicey, Professor, quoted, 139 and note 2.
Doratt, Sir John, 194 note 2.
Dorchester, *see* Carleton.
Doric Club, 91.
Droit de Quint, 183 note, 184.
Duncombe, Dr., 97, 98.
Dunkin, 153, 167, 236.
D'Urban, Sir Benjamin, 13, 21.
DURHAM, LORD :
  his life, 1-2.
  his character and ability, 2, 6-8, 119-20, 131-2, 214, 256, 276, 316, etc.
  as a Liberal, 2, 128-30, 138, 141, 214, 215, 282, 315.
  as an Imperialist, 2, 119-23, 130, 141, 149-50, 151, 155, 180, 198, 214, 215, 217, 256, 282, 285.
  as a constructive statesman, 121-3, 216-17, 316.
  his views before his mission, 128-9.
  his views on :
    French Colonization, 24, 25.
    Nationality, 116, 129-34, 281-4, 289, 311.
    Public Lands, 153-5, 165-8, 176-80, 186-8.
    Emigration, 189 and note, 196-8, 299.

Education, 232, 234, 235, 240-3.
  Union of two Canadas, 124, 129-33, 148, 247-50, 287-8.
  Union of British North America, 132, 148-9, 210, 247-57, 261, 266, 289.
  Administration of Justice, 223-5, 229-31.
  Means of Communication, 15-16, 201, 204-5, 208-10, 304.
  Colonial Office Administration, 266, 267, 270-3, 279-80.
  Representative Institutions and Responsible Government, 125, 130, 136-42, 146-52, 252-3, 283-7, 289, 291, 303-4, 311-15.
  Municipal Government, 210-22.
  United States, 258-66.
  his Commission and Instructions, 106-10, 112, 113.
  Resignation, 211, 235.
  Death, 301.
  value of his work, 301-2, 315-17.
Dutch in New York, 264, 283.
Dutch in South Africa, 136, 283, 309, 311.

Education :
  (i) In Lower Canada, 67, 166-7, 232-44, 264, 300-1, *and see* Buller, Arthur.
  (ii) In Upper Canada, 75, 244-7, 295, 301.
Egremont, Lord, 193.
Elgin, eighth Earl of, 1, 142 note, 283, 289, 291.
Elgin, ninth Earl of, 1.
Elizabeth College, 244.
Ellice, 'Bear,' 4, 7, 45, 46, 112, 161, 297.
Ellice, the Younger, 4.
Elliot, Sir T. F., 65, 71, 189-90, 190 note, 191, 196, 273.
Emigrants' Information Office, 300.
Emigration :
  from United Kingdom to Canada, 156-8, 172, 174, 177-82, 188-98, 279, 299-300.

INDEX 329

from United Kingdom to United States, 190.
  abuses of, 189, 193-6.
  Committees and Commission on, 190-1.
  control of, 178-9, 188-92, 196-8.
  See also Lands, Quarantine, Colonization Schemes, &c.
Empire, British, 5, 7, 10, 30, 120, 121, 123, 202, 222, 254, 255, 273, 275, 277, 285, 303, 305-9, 305 note, 306 note, 311, 312, 314, 315, &c.
Erie Canal, *see* Canals.
Executive, Parliamentary, Principle of, 139 note 2, 141, 142, 291.
Executives:
  Lower Canada, 42, 44, 56, 139.
  Upper Canada, 143.
  United Canada, 149, 249.
  Relations with Legislatures, 33-4, 36, 137, 139, 142-5, 148, 290-1, *and see* Councils.
Executive Council, *see* Councils.

Family Compact, 54, 75, 164, 247.
Federal Legislature, *see* Legislature.
Federation, 132-3, 248-55, 287, 313.
Feudal Tenures, *see* Lands *and* Seigniories.
Filmore, President, 142 note.
Fils de Liberté, 91.
Finances, control of, 149, 293, &c.
  in Lower Canada, 38-44, 47, 48, 49, 51, 55-61, 65-6, 71, 73, 104-5, 182-3, 184.
  in Upper Canada, 54, 60, 76, 182.
Financial relations between Upper and Lower Canada, 44, 45, 54, 67. *See also* Civil List, Money Votes, &c.
Finlay, Hugh, 233, 234 note.
Fisheries Disputes, 257, 258.
Fitzgibbon, Colonel, 97, 98.
Fitzroy, Sir Charles, 85-6.
Foreign Relations, 149-50, 285.
Forges of St. Maurice, *see* St. Maurice.
Free Trade, 19, 20, 198, 286.
French Canadians, 24, 25, 27, 28, 31, 32, 34, 42, 46, 54, 61, 62, 63, 64, 67-8, 88, 89, 91, 95, 96, 103, 116, 118, 121, 124, 125, 128, 129, 130, 131, 151, 159, 161, 172, 175, 195, 214, 215, 225, 239, 240, 241, 243, 248, 250, 259, 260, 265, 277, 279, 280, 281-4, 309, etc.

Galt, John, 170.
George III, 41, 166.
George IV, 76.
Georgian Bay Canal, *see* Canals.
Gipps, Sir George, 65, 70, 71.
Girod, 95-6.
Glenelg, Lord, 13, 19, 20-2, 62, 64, 67, 68, 69, 73, 77, 78, 80, 83, 84, 85-6, 87, 100, 101, 158, 162 and note, 186, 231 and note, 232-3, 251 and note, 258.
  his Instructions to Lord Durham, 5, 106, 109, 112, 113, 132 and note, 147.
  his Instructions to Royal Commissioners, 65-7, 69, 71, 72.
  his Instructions to Sir F. Bond Head, 142-3.
Glengarry Highlanders, 89, 245.
Goderich, Lord, 19, 52, 53, 58, 59, 61, 68, 79, 81, 86 note, 87, 88, 164, 166, 167, 190, 226.
Gore, Colonel, 92-5.
Gosford, Earl of, 65, 67, 69, 70, 71, 72, 74, 77, 83, 88, 89, 90, 100, 162 and note, 167, 168, 185 note, 186, 232, 233 note, 235, 237.
Gourlay, Robert, 53.
Government, Imperial, *see* Imperial Government.
Greek Colonists, 312-13.
Grey, Colonel, 258.
Grey, first Earl, 1, 2, 17, 142 note.
Grey, second Earl, 191.
Grey, Sir Charles, 65, 70, 71.
Grey, Sir George, 12, 22 and note 1.
Grosse Isle, 194 and note 2.

Haldimand, General, 206.
Halifax, 16, 83, 90, 201, 204, 210.
Hamilton, 213.
Hanson, 4, 153, 164.
Harvey, Sir John, 83.
Head, Sir Francis Bond, 22, 69,

77-81, 83, 90, 96, 97, 98, 100, 142-3.
Hereditary Legislators, 227-8.
House of Commons, 7, 18, 39, 41, 60, 137, 139 note 2, 157, 158, 159, 174 note, 221, 248, 267, 274, 279, 288, 297, &c.
Committees on Emigration, 190.
Resolutions of March 1837, 72-3, 143, 144.
Select Committee of Inquiry into Civil Government of Canada in 1828, 53, 55, 56, 57, 62, 63, 75, 82, 160 note, 246.
Select Committee of Inquiry into Civil Government of Lower Canada in 1834, 62-3.
House of Commons Papers, 117.
July 1831, No. 102. Canada Crown Revenues, 40 note, 183 note.
March 1832, No. 334. Canada Waste Lands, 174 and note, 188 and note.
March 1836, No. 113. Copy of the Instructions given to the Earl of Gosford, etc., 68 note, 143 note, 162 note, 233 note.
February 1837, No. 50. Lower Canada, 185 note, 235 note, 237 note.
May 1838, No. 388. Emigration, 190 note, 191 note, 192.
February 1839, No. 2. British North America, 231, 258 note, 259.
June 1839, No. 117. Canadian Affairs, 119 note, 263 note, 276 note.
August 1839, No. 579. Nova Scotia, &c., 82 note, 84 note, 86 note, 87 note.
1840. Affairs of Canada, Part I, 299 note 1.
February 1840, No. 35. Colonial Lands Board, 294 note, 299 note.
March 1840, No. 147. Copies of Extracts of Correspondence relative to the Reunion of the Provinces of Lower and Upper Canada, 213 note, 218 note.
August 1871, C. 459. Cape of Good Hope, 146 note 2.
House of Lords, 102, 123, 151, 227 and note.
Howe, Joseph, 81, 85.
Howick, Lord, see Grey, second Earl.
Hudson Bay Company, 183 note, 256.
Hume, Joseph, 73, 76, 104.
Hungary, Language Question in, 134.
Huskisson, 19, 53, 55, 57.

Imperial Advisers, 142-5, 147.
Imperial Government, 27, 41, 44, 46, 47, 58, 59, 60, 61, 63, 68, 104, 142, 143, 144, 148, 149, 162, 166, 174, 178, 179, 184, 185, 187, 195, 207, 219, 220, 221, 223-5, 232, 233, 234, 236, 240, 243, 245, 249, 251, 252, 253, 255, 260, 271, 274, 275, 276, 278, 279, 280, 293, 295, 299, 300, 306 note, etc.
Indians, 245.
Six Nations, 175.
Inventions, Scientific, 14-17, 201, 204-5, 208, 210, 304-5 and note.
Ireland and Irish, 88, 104, 190 and note, 192, 201, 230, 305 note.
Irish in Canada, 89, 245.

Jalbert, 94.
Jamaica, 23, 142 note, 146.
Jesuit Estates, see Lands.
Joseph II, 134.

Keefer, T. C., 204 and note.
Kempt, Sir James, 57.
Kent, Duke of, 254.
King's College, Toronto, 246-7.
King's Posts, 183 and note.
King's Wharves, 183 note, 184.
Kingston, 207, 213, 220, 247.

Lachine Canal, see Canals.
Lambton, see Durham.
Land and Emigration Commissioners, 171, 179, 191, 196, 294 note, 299, 300.

INDEX

Land Registry Office, 58.
Lands :
  Clergy Reserves, 4, 37, 56, 75, 78, 152, 153, 162–5, 163 note, 169, 170, 177, 209, 228, 238, 245, 294–6.
  Companies, 61, 66, 67, 73, 169–72.
  Crown Lands, 37, 40 note, 60, 83, 114, 115, 160, 163, 169–73, 175, 182–4, 293, 299.
  in British North America, 152, 156, 158, 171, 174 and note, 177–9, 264.
  in United States, 264.
  Jesuit Estates, 5, 56, 153, 165–7, 183 and note, 232, 236, 238, 243.
  Militia Claims, 4, 153, 173–5.
  Public, 4, 108 note, 115, 120–1, 123, 149, 150, 152–88, 262, 264, 285, 293–4, 294 note.
  Tax, 176, 178, 187.
  Tenure, 56, 66, 67, 71, 152, 153, 159–62, 168 and note, 171, 174, 279 ; *see also* Seigniories.
  See also Buller, Charles.
Language, 133–6, 289, 308 note.
Laurier, Sir Wilfrid, 118, 240.
Laval, Bishop, 242.
Laval University, 242 note.
Law and Justice, 123–4, 223–31, 263, 292.
  Appeals, Judicial, 230–1, 249.
  Chief Justices, 36, 59, 225, 226.
  Civil Law, 28–9, 223–4.
  Courts of Law, 223.
  Criminal Law, 223.
  Judges, 37, 38, 56, 57, 59, 61, 66, 82, 149, 150, 225–6, 231, 292, 293.
  Juries, 223, 224, 229–30.
  Magistrates, 223, 228–9.
' Leaders and Associates,' 160.
Legislative Council, *see* Councils.
Legislatures, 33–4, 179, 219.
  Federal, 113, 251–5.
  Lower Canada, 32, 47, 51, 52, 57, 60, 64, 69, 72–4, 88, 113, 166, 172, 183, 185–7, 194, 206, 209, 224, 228, 248.
  Newfoundland, 88.
  United, 148–50, 152 and note, 187, 217, 249, 288, 291–3, 294 note, 296, 299–301.
  Upper Canada, 54, 60, 80, 113, 245, 246, 276, 295.
  Relations with Executives, *see* Executives.
  And see Assembly *and* Councils.
Lewis, Sir George Cornewall, 15, 134, 140 note, 145, 180–1, 181 note, 268–70, 286, 306 note.
Liverpool, Lord, 52, 266.
Local Government, 4, 123, 149, 152 and note, 159, 195 note, 210–22, 264, 296–9.
  in United States, 264–5.
Lods et Ventes, 184.
London (Canada), 213.
Louisiana, 131, 264, 283.
Lount, 80, 98, 99.
Loyalists, 89, 90, 91, 93, 95, 98, 159, 245, 259–61.
Loyalists, United Empire, 37, 54, 159, 174.

Macdonell, Bishop, 4, 245.
McGill, James, 244.
McGill University, 243–4.
Mackenzie, William Lyon, 55, 75, 76, 80, 81, 96–9, 214.
Mackintosh, Sir James, 7, 45.
MacNab, Colonel, 98.
Maine, 202, 256, 257.
Maitland, Sir Peregrine, 53–5, 85, 244.
Malthus, 192.
Maritime Provinces, 81, 115, 204, 249, 250, 258, 291, *and see separately* New Brunswick, &c.
Matthews, 99.
Melbourne, Lord, 14, 17, 19, 20, 62, 64, 102, 110, 123, 214, 288.
Merivale, *Lectures on Colonization*, 152 note, 157, 219 note, 298 and note 3.
Militia and Militia Laws, 51–2, 150, 212.
Militia Land Claims, *see* Land.
Ministers of Crown, *see* Imperial Advisers.
Molesworth, Sir William, 2, 12, 21, 22, 73, 101, 157 note 2, 157–8, 181, 267–8, 268 note 2, 270, 273, 274.

332 INDEX

Monarchy, hereditary, 141.
Money Votes, initiation of, 149, 292, 297.
Montreal, 15, 34, 61, 63, 67, 71, 78, 88–96, 153, 162, 167, 168, 194 note 2, 195, 203, 205, 206, 207, 212, 242 and note, 243, 282.
Montreal district, 106, 248.
Montreal, Constitutional Association of, 4, 63, 128.
Morley, Lord, quoted, 135–6 note.
Morrison, Dr., 97.
Municipalties, *see* Local Government.
Murray, General James, 28, 223.
Murray, Sir George, 55, 57, 58.

Nationality, Canada a Nation, Anglifying of Lower Canada, &c., 27, 35, 46, 61, 116, 121, 122, 125–33, 161–2, 202, 215–16, 233–4, 236, 253, 261, 266, 281–4, 286–7, 310–13.
Native Questions, 136, 146, 274–5, 309.
Navy Island, 99.
Neilson, John, 47.
Nelson, Dr. Wolfred, 74, 89, 90–4, 95, 97, 128.
Nelson, Robert, 89, 90, 128.
Neptune, the, 13.
New Brunswick, 30, 71, 72, 81–5, 90, 106, 107, 114, 204, 262, 291 note, 294 note.
  Civil List, 83.
  Crown Revenues, control of, 83.
  Deputation to England, 82–3.
  Responsible Government, 83.
New France, 24–6.
New South Wales, 12, 65.
New York, 78, 209, 258, 264, 265, 283.
New Zealand, 14, 146, 156, 291.
New Zealand Association, 14.
New Zealand Land Company, 14, 148.
Newfoundland, 65, 86–8, 106, 107, 108 and note, 113, 114, 115, 154, 171, 250, 291 and note, 294 note.
  Fisheries, 86.
  Religious troubles, 87–8.
Niagara, 96, 99, 207, 213, 263.

North-West, 200, 202, 208, 210, 256, 263.
Nova Scotia, 4, 16, 57, 81, 83–6, 90, 106, 107, 114, 204, 222, 257, 262, 265, 291 note, 294 note.
  Constitution, 84.
  Representative Institutions, 81.
  Revenue Control, 84.

O'Callaghan, Dr., 89, 94.
O'Connell, 73, 74, 104.
Ottawa, 16, 207.

Palmerston, Lord, 19.
Papineau, Louis, 38, 42, 43, 47, 49, 52, 54, 69, 70, 74, 77, 88–91, 94, 96–7, 128, 133.
  Eulogy of British rule, 41.
Parliament, Canadian, 118, 231, 290, 293.
Parliament, Imperial, *see* Imperial Government.
Parliamentary Executive, *see* Executive.
Parliamentary Reform, 17.
Parsonages, 163.
'Patriots,' 89, 97.
Patronage, Crown, *see* Crown Patronage.
Peace of Paris, 27.
Peel, Sir Robert, 12, 19, 62, 65, 99, 112.
Peninsular and Oriental Company, 16.
Petition of Rights, 62.
Pitt, William, 31.
Police Forces, 212.
Poor Law Reform, 18.
Presbyterians, *see* Clergy.
Prevost, Sir George, 36, 206.
Prince Edward Island, 85–6, 106, 107, 114.
  lands, 86.
Proclamation of 1763, 28, 29, 159, 174, 223.
Protestants, 160, 163, 164, 239, 242–3, 245–6, *and see* Clergy *and* Church of England, &c.
Public Lands, *see* Lands.
Public Works, 118, 178, 208, 209, 220, 264, 265, 298, 301.

Quarantine, 194, 195.

INDEX 333

Quarter Sessions, 223.
Quebec, 16, 30, 34, 36, 63, 65, 89, 90, 100, 183 note, 190, 194 and note 2, 195, 201, 210, 212, 214, 242 and note, 243, 282.
Quebec Act, see under Acts:
Quebec, Province, 26, 29, 31, 120, 151, 159, 220, 278, 283, 284, 298 note 2, 301.
Quebec Assembly, see Assembly, Lower Canada.
Quebec Emigrants' Society, 194.
Queen's College, 247.

Race animosity, &c., 33-7, 46, 126-31, 229, 240, 279-84.
Radenhurst, John, 170.
Railways, 8, 14-15, 178, 198-201, 210.
 Canadian Northern, 200.
 Canadian Pacific, 15, 199, 200, 205.
 Grand Trunk, 200.
 in United States, 265.
 Intercolonial, 200, 201, 204.
 La Prairie to St. John's, 14-15, 207-8.
 Stockton to Darlington, 14.
Rebellion, 24, 40, 80, 88-99, 101, 259.
 in Lower Canada, 38, 40, 88-96, 128, 258.
 in Upper Canada, 80, 96-9, 258.
 reasons for, 103-5.
Receiver-General of Canada, defalcations of, 43.
Rectories, 78, 163, 164.
Reform in England, 17-18, 42, 58, 76, 129.
Regiopolis, 247.
Reid, Stuart, 3.
Religion, 33, 87-8, 133, 239-40, 245, 279, &c. See also Clergy, &c.
Rents and Dues, 40, 183-4.
Representative Institutions, 11, 23, 34, 81, 138, 216, 217, 277, 304, 310.
Republics and Republican Institutions, 139 and note, 154, 254.
Reserves, Clergy, see Lands.
Reserves, Crown, see Lands.
Responsible Government, 5, 7, 11, 22, 77, 81, 83, 88, 123-6, 130-1, 137-52, 155, 181, 182, 187, 198, 218, 254-5, 261, 265-6, 273, 277, 289-91, 304, 310-15, &c.
 arguments for, 121-2, 137-8, &c.
 definition of, 137-8, 147-8.
 Durham's recommendations, 147-52.
 objections to, 142-6, 313.
Revenues, see Finances.
Revenues, Crown, see Crown Revenues.
Richards, John, 174, 188.
Richelieu, River, 74, 88, 89, 90, 91, 92, 93, 94, 207.
Richmond, Duke of, 39, 42, 53.
Ripon, Earl of, see Goderich.
Rideau Canal, see Canals.
Ridout, 80, 81.
Roads, 178, 198, 210, 211, 220.
 in United States, 265.
Robinson, Peter, 192.
Robinson, Sir John Beverley, 46, 54, 75.
 Life of, 126 note, 226.
Roebuck, John Arthur, 62, 71, 73, 102-3, 104, 248.
Rolph, Dr., 55, 79, 97, 98.
Roman Catholics, 88, 164, 239, 243, 245, 247, &c., and see Clergy.
Romans, 135-6 note, 222, 269, 274, 307-9.
Royal Commission (Lord Cosford's) to Lower Canada, 64-72, 74, 167-8, 185 note, 232-3, 235, 237.
Royal William, the, 16 and note.
Russell, Peter, 245, 246.
Russell, Lord John, 5, 12, 19, 72-4, 101, 102, 110, 112, 143-5, 147, 168 note, 175, 196, 213, 218, 288, 289, 290, 294 note, 297, 299.

St. Benoit, 96.
St. Charles, 90, 92, 94.
St. Denis, 90, 91, 92, 93, 94, 95.
St. Eustache, 95.
St. John's, 91, 95, 207.
St. Lawrence, 14-15, 88, 90, 91, 92, 159, 183 note, 201, 202-4, 206-9, 258, 263, 278, 283.
St. Maurice Forges, 183 note, 184.
St. Sulpice, see Sulpicians.

334 INDEX

Scotch Church, *see* Clergy, Presbyterian.
Secretary of State for the Colonies, *see* Colonial Office.
Seigniories, 28, 67, 71, 128, 152, 159, 161, 165, 167–8, 183 note, 297.
Sewell, Jonathan, 225, 254.
Sherbrooke, Sir John, 37–9, 43, 53, 172.
Simcoe, 33, 244, 246.
Sir Robert Peel, the, 258.
Slavery, abolition of, 10–11, 12, 13, 18, 22.
  in United States, 257.
Smith, Chief Justice, 254 and note, 255, 284.
Sorel, 89, 90, 92, 93, 94.
'Sons of Liberty,' *see* Fils de Liberté.
South Africa, 13, 135 and note, 136, 280, 283, 309, 311.
South Australia, 13, 14, 156, 158.
Stanley, Lord, 19, 62, 137, 171.
Steamships, 15–16, 201, 208, 305 note.
Spring Rice, 62, 63, 85, 87.
Stephen, Sir James, 10, 20–2, 273.
Strachan, Dr., 46, 54, 164–5, 246.
Stuart, James, 36, 38, 47, 49, 61, 90.
Submarine cables, 16.
Sulpicians, 67, 71, 153, 162, 165, 167–8, 242 and note.
Sydenham, Lord, *see* Thomson, Poulett.

Talon, 174.
Tasmania, 12, 100.
Taylor, Sir Henry, 20 and note, 273.
Telegraphs, 8, 15, 16.
Texas, 257, 259.
Theller, 99–100.
Thomson, Poulett, 144, 168 note, 175, 213, 218, 289–90, 294, 295–302.
Three Rivers Town Fiefs, 183 note.
Timber licences, 178, 184.
Titles of Honour, 227, 291.
Tories, 7, 14, 19, 42, 65, 247.
Toronto, 76, 78, 79, 81, 90, 96–8, 137, 165, 170, 171, 213 and note, 244.
Toronto University, *see* King's College, Toronto.
Townships, 128, 152, 160, 221, 297.
Townships, Eastern, 46, 58, 61, 89, 93, 159–60, 169, 171, 172, 248.
Trade, Board of, 300.
Transportation, 11–13, 158.
Trinity College, Toronto, 247.
Turton, 153.
Two Mountains County, 88, 95.

United Empire Loyalists, *see* Loyalists.
United States :
  (i) References to, 22, 80, 91, 93, 94, 97, 98, 99, 104, 113, 121, 122, 124, 125, 153, 154, 177, 178, 216, 252, 257–66, 278, 303, 310.
  (ii) Institutions, 54, 62, 140–1, 142 note, 215, 265.
  (iii) Causes of Prosperity, 139, 154, 265.
  (iv) Comparison with Canada, 139, 201–2, 262–6.
  (v) Frontier of, 88, 93, 96, 99, 159, 203, 256–9, 278.
Upper Canada College, 75, 245.

Van Buren, President, 257, 258.
Van Diemen's Land, *see* Tasmania.
Van Egmont, 98–9.
Vancouver, 15, 205.
Victoria, Queen, 10–19, 74, 88, 100, 185, 254, 292.
Victoria College, 247.
Vindicator, the, 89, 91.

Wakefield, Gibbon, 3–4, 14, 153, 155–8, 175, 178, 180, 181–2, 189, 197, 294.
War of American Independence, 30, 104, 174, 206, 259.
War of 1812, 34, 36, 37, 90, 97, 173, 174, 178, 203, 206, 278.
Waterways, Canadian, 205–8.
Weavers, distress among, 192–3.
Webster, Daniel, 99.
Weir, Lieutenant, 94.

INDEX

Welland Canal, *see* Canals.
Wellington, Duke of, 17, 19, 55, 61.
Wesleyans, 78, 247.
Western Australia, 12.
West Indies, 11-13, 158, 178, 277.
Wetherall, Colonel, 92, 93.
Whateley, Archbishop, 11.
Whigs, 17-20, 65, 78, 104, 111-13, 123, 129, 131, 151, 214, 219, 289.
William Henry, *see* Sorel.
William IV, 40, 65, 74, 88, 185.
Wilmot, Lemuel, 83.
Wilmot, or Wilmot Horton, 44.
Wodehouse, Sir Philip, 146.

York, *see* Toronto.
Young, William, 4, 258, 265.